COUNTER-TERRORISM
WEAPONS & EQUIPMENT

COUNTER-TERRORISM
WEAPONS & EQUIPMENT

James Marchington

The SA80 is not a single weapon, but a
weapons system which includes a LSW
(Light Support Weapon) and various
sighting options. The weapon has had a
chequered history, with early models
prone to jamming in adverse conditions.
Photo: British Army Press Service.

BRASSEY'S

First published in 2003 by Brassey's

A member of Chrysalis Books plc

Brassey's
64 Brewery Road, London N7 9NT

Distributed in the USA by:
Casemate Publishing, 2114 Darby Road, Havertown, PA 19083, USA

James Marchington has asserted his moral right to be identified as
the author of this work.

Library of Congress Cataloging in Publication Data available

British Library cataloguing in Publication Data
A catalogue record for this book is available from the British
Library

ISBN 1 85753 386 0

Edited and designed by DAG Publications Ltd
Designed by David Gibbons
Edited by John Gilbert
Layout by Anthony A. Evans
Printed in Spain

CONTENTS

INTRODUCTION

Coming literally out of the blue, the multiple attacks of 11 September 2001 shook America and the Western world. After years of relative peace and security at home, and overwhelming military dominance abroad, the American public had pushed terrorism to the back of their mind. Bombings, hijackings and kidnappings were all things that happened in unpronounceable foreign places, and had no relevance to their daily lives.

Then the unthinkable happened. Hijacked civilian airliners became devastatingly effective guided bombs, striking at potent symbols of America's financial and military

The terrorist attacks on 11 September 2001 struck a symbolic blow at the heart of America, and sparked a funda-mental change in the West's approach to terrorism. Pictured: the World Trade Center's twin towers burn, after two hijacked aircraft smashed into them. Photo: Press Association

might. As events unfolded on the morning of 11 September, people were glued to the news on television, radio and the internet with a sense of bewilderment and dread. What was unfolding? Who was behind it? And where would they strike next? In cities throughout America, Europe and beyond, people looked up nervously at the sky, as if living in a war zone. Indeed, in a sense they were.

The feeling of unease continued for weeks, fuelled by further incidents such as packages containing anthrax spores turning up in the mail. Daily life was continually disrupted by security alerts, scares and hoaxes. It was widely said that the world had changed forever, that we would never again take our safety from terrorism for granted.

Memories fade, and complacency gradually returns. But the West had learned important lessons – not least that the threat of terrorism is always present; that terrorists strike where and when least expected; and that the personal freedom to come and go as we please without oppressive restrictions also gives terrorists the freedom they need to operate unhindered.

It is easy to be wise after the event, but there were massive gaps in the West's intelligence, which allowed such an atrocity to catch America unawares. The 11 September attacks, however, were not totally unexpected. For years counter-terrorism experts had warned that western cities provided countless opportunities for terrorist attacks. The use of civil aircraft as flying bombs was just one of the possibilities that had been foreseen, along with chemical poisoning of water and food supplies, gas attacks in subways, and the detonation of a nuclear device or radioactive 'dirty' bomb in a centre of population.

Prior to 11 September, however, there had been an unspoken assumption that terrorists would not cross the line and use weapons of mass destruction against civilian populations – they would understand that some things were simply beyond the pale. The 1995 nerve gas attack on the Tokyo subway system by Aum Shinrikyo had been categorised as the actions of a few

The hand-made memorials placed at 'Ground Zero', the site of the 11 September attacks on the World Trade Centre, are a reminder of the human suffering caused by terrorism. Photo: © James Marchington.

madmen, not a true terrorist attack. Now those assumptions are gone, the rule book torn up and thrown away. It is chillingly clear that there are groups whose hatred of America and the West is so bitter that they will use any means at their disposal – including nuclear, biological and chemical – to strike at their enemy.

The public feel this, and have proved themselves willing to accept new restrictions which they see as part of the new 'war on terror'. In the wake of 11 September, security checks at airports were stepped up – causing delays that previously might have sparked a riot. New legislation has been introduced which would once have been thrown out as too draconian. Here in Britain, the public are suddenly prepared to contemplate the idea of compulsory identity cards, a measure that government had always shied away from as somehow un-British. And, it has to be said, some opportunist measures have been taken which will have little or no effect on terrorism, but have slipped through largely uncontested thanks to the new climate in which few people care to challenge anything labelled 'in the interest of security'.

The world has indeed changed since 11 September – and the forces of counter-terrorism have changed to meet the new threat.

Defining terrorism

Like 'freedom fighter', the word terrorist is much used and misused – all the more so since 11 September. Quite ordinary security and anti-crime measures are labelled 'anti-terrorist', conferring on them some added importance and urgency. And just about anyone nowadays calls their enemies 'terrorists'. So it is that a list of all those labelled as 'terrorists' at some time or another would have to include separatist movements in South America, Irish Republicans and Loyalists alike, Israel, Palestine, the Tamil Tigers, Al-Qaeda, organised crime syndicates, drug barons, and even the USA itself.

Recent legislation in Europe has sought to broaden the definition of a terrorist, to include groups such as environmental activists, anti-globalisation protesters, drugs users and common criminals. This makes it easier to use intrusive methods and apply strong penalties against such groups, which may be no bad thing, but it also devalues the word 'terrorist' and makes it harder to see the wood for the trees.

So what exactly is a terrorist? We all have a Hollywood-inspired mental picture of a desperate, evil individual with balaclava and sub-machine gun, planting a bomb or plotting some atrocity. But of course you cannot tell a terrorist from an ordinary member of the public just by sight – otherwise we would not need all that security apparatus at airports.

Neither can you distinguish a terrorist by his (or her) extreme views. There are plenty of people around the world with extreme views, but they are not all terrorists. Our definition must therefore include the ability and the will to use the weapons of terror to achieve a desired end – and a political end at that, since anything else is not terrorism but straightforward crime.

This is not just a question of semantics. The lack of an agreed definition can be a serious obstacle to international cooperation on security and counter-terrorism measures. Any effective extradition treaty, for example, requires an agreement as to what types of suspects are covered by the treaty.

There have been many attempts to produce an official definition of terrorism, none of them entirely satisfactory. In 1937 a League of Nations Convention adopted the following definition: 'All criminal acts directed against a State and intended or calculated to create a state of terror in the minds of particular persons or a group of persons or the general public.'

In 1992 the terrorism expert A. Schmid proposed a definition based on the widely accepted definition of war crimes – an act of terrorism was to be described as the 'peacetime equivalent of a war crime'.

Schmid's definition did not win widespread acceptance, and in 1999 UN Resolution 51/210 used terms similar to the League of Nations' definition of more than sixty years earlier: '… criminal acts intended or calculated to provoke a state of terror in the general public, a group of persons or particular persons for political purposes …'

The US government adopted its current definition of terrorism in 1983:

'Terrorism' means 'premeditated, politically motivated violence perpetrated against non-combatant targets by sub-national groups or clandestine agents, usually intended to influence an audience'. (For the purposes of this definition, the term 'non-combatant' includes unarmed or off-duty military personnel.)

'International terrorism' is defined as 'terrorism involving citizens or the territory of more than one country'.

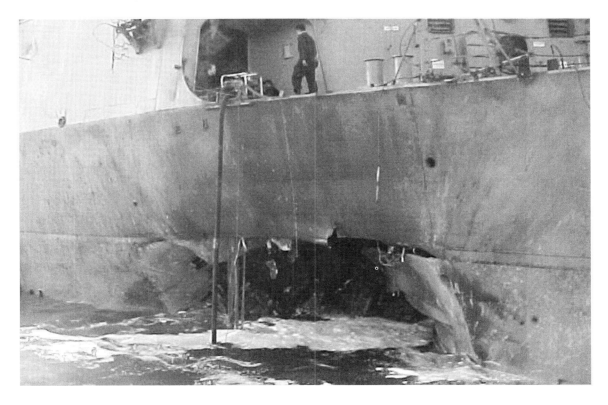

The USS *Cole* was damaged by a small boat loaded with explosives in what was dubbed a terrorist attack at Aden, Yemen, on 12 October 2000. Seventeen sailors were killed and 39 injured. Photo: US DoD.

These before and after pictures were captured by the Ikonos satellite, and show the devastation caused to the World Trade Centre by the terrorist attacks on 11 September 2001. Photo: Space Imaging.

'Terrorist group' is 'any group practising, or that has significant sub-groups that practise, international terrorism'.

The precise words may vary, but we all know terrorism when we see it. The various definitions include several common factors: i) Violence, generally, but not confined to, non-military targets; ii) Planned action, generally as part of a campaign, with a specific political purpose; iii) The intention to create a state of terror in the minds of a specific audience, either to influence them directly or to put pressure on the state; and iv) Terrorism is something carried out by organised groups, rather than by individuals or entire states.

So a bombing campaign by one state against another would not qualify as 'terrorism' under this definition, even though it might be intended to create terror in the general population and thereby lead to the overthrow of the head of state. Such a campaign, however, would no doubt be decried as 'terrorism' by the country under attack.

Likewise, a campaign of bombings by an individual would usually be classed as criminal acts rather than true terrorism. A notable exception to this rule was the campaign of bombings in the US carried out by Theodore Kaczynski between May 1978 and April 1995. Kaczynski became known as the 'Unabomber' as he taunted the authorities and promoted his anti-technology agenda. This was a carefully planned series of acts calculated to induce terror in the population and further the Unabomber's extreme political aims; indeed, he succeeded in having his political diatribe published in the *New York Times* and the *Washington Post*, with the threat of further attacks if his manifesto was not made public. Ironically, this success led to his capture, when his distinctive writing style was recognised.

The terrorist threat

Since 11 September 2001 there has, inevitably, been a strong focus on terrorism of extremist Islamic origin, particularly by Al-Qaeda and associated groups. A massive military effort has been made to seek out and destroy Al-Qaeda leaders and supporters throughout Afghanistan, while behind the scenes an even greater effort is under way to trace their network of connections across the world, and gain intelligence that will make it possible to prevent further attacks, if not to smash the network altogether. For example, on 8 May 2002, US security officers arrested Abdullah al-Muhajir at O'Hare International Airport in Chicago. He was later charged with being an 'enemy combatant', implicated in a plot to detonate a 'dirty bomb' in the heart of Washington DC. An American national, he had been followed by intelligence operators of several different nations, including Pakistan and the UK, as he travelled to and from meetings with known Al-Qaeda terrorists.

With all this effort understandably directed against Al-Qaeda, it is important not to forget that there are many other active terrorist groups around the world – some practising 'international terrorism' as defined above, others active on a more local level, although no less dangerous in their own way.

A trawl through newspapers and online news services revealed, on a day picked entirely at random (actually Monday 17 June 2002), reports of the following terrorist-related activity:

Israel: Palestinian suicide bomber blows himself up, no one else injured.
Philippines: Unknown gunmen fire on US troops; Philippine army clashes with Muslim rebels.
Pakistan: US Embassy reopens after car bomb attack killed twelve a few days before.
Lebanon: Hezbollah builds up forces along the southern border with Israel.
USA: Congress expresses support for CIA covert operations to topple Saddam Hussein's regime in Iraq; clean-up of mail sorting office contaminated by anthrax is nearing completion.
Basilan: MORO Islamic Liberation Front denies it helped bandits escape to Zamboanga.
Malaysia: Wife of terror suspect complains about her treatment during two-month arrest.
Kashmir: Twenty-one killed in separate incidents with separatists; two rifle grenades fired at building where Chief Minister Farooq Abdullah was chairing an official ceremony.
China: Chinese government says Islamic extremists have, in recent years, assassinated local officials and religious leaders, poisoned livestock and blown up buses.

Scotland: Police chief criticises Nelson Mandela's visit to the man convicted of the Lockerbie bombing.

Northern Ireland: Investigation finds that security forces colluded with loyalist paramilitaries to assassinate Catholics.

Guatemala: Death threats and attacks against government critics spark fears of a return to the terror of the civil war.

Colombia: Gun battles in Medellin indicate the civil war is now spreading to the major cities.

Egypt: USA hands over a man implicated in the assassination of President Anwar Sadat.

Burundi: Rebels kill thirteen in roadside ambush.

Greece: Firebombs damage three government vehicles.

Nepal: Government sources claim fifty Maoist guerrillas were killed in a firefight around a remote army post.

Uganda: Soldiers have rescued ninety people abducted by rebel forces.

Sudan: At the request of the USA, a suspected member of Al-Qaeda is detained for interrogation.

The day in question was not atypical; on any other day there would be a similar number of similar acts being carried out around the world. Bearing in mind the increased security and general sense of unease that a single such incident leaves in its wake, it soon becomes clear that a large number of the world's population are living in fear of terrorism at any given time.

Terrorists' objectives

Terrorism is not random, thoughtless violence. Quite the opposite. Terrorist activity may seem random to the victims, in the sense that one cannot predict where and when it will happen, and the victims are often members of the public who, through sheer bad luck, just happen to be in the area at the time. But the terrorist carefully plans and orchestrates his campaign to achieve specific objectives. Just as a public relations 'spin doctor' will time a press event to gain the best media coverage, so a terrorist bomb may be timed to catch the Sunday papers or the evening news, or to exert pressure at a time when sensitive negotiations are under way.

Bruce Hoffman, in his excellent book *Inside Terrorism* (Victor Gallancz, 1998), explains that a typical terrorist campaign moves through different phases as the group and its motives gain wider recognition:

1. Attention – The terrorists grab attention through media coverage of dramatic, violent acts.

2. Acknowledgement – They gain acknowledgement, perhaps even sympathy and support, for their cause.

An aerial view of the destruction caused by a civilian aircraft flown into the Pentagon by terrorists on 11 September 2001. Photo: US DoD.

3. Recognition – The terrorist group is recognised as the spokesman of the people they claim to represent.
4. Authority – They gain the influence to make changes in government or society.
5. Governance – The terrorist group consolidate their power, effectively becoming the government.

Early in the process, it is very much in the terrorists' interest to stage sensational acts of violence. The bigger the bomb, and the more innocent victims killed and injured, the greater the media impact.

The terrorist always has the upper hand over the security forces. The terrorist decides where and when he will strike, while the security forces must constantly be on the alert. As more than one terrorist group has said: 'We only have to be lucky once; you have to be lucky all the time.'

Intelligence is the most powerful weapon available to the security forces. Physical security measures – checkpoints, patrols, internment, etc – are of limited use, and may even encourage the population to support the terrorists.

As it gains respectability and influence, a terrorist group typically renounces violence somewhere between steps 3 and 5 – at this stage bombings and shootings would be counter-productive.

As with the IRA, however, this is the point where hardliners may break away and form splinter groups that refuse to 'negotiate with the enemy' and wish to continue the campaign of violence. If the original terrorist group is to form a credible government, they find themselves in the ironic position of having to deal with their former colleagues' terrorism.

Does terrorism work?

Governments like to argue that terrorism does not work. This is clearly untrue. History shows that a number of groups have used terrorism to gain power, generally following the process outlined above.

Classic examples are the FLN in Algeria, who succeeded in gaining independence for Algeria from France; the Greek Cypriot group EOKA; the Palestine Liberation Organisation; and more recently the IRA.

Even 'pressure groups' such as the Animal Liberation Front have achieved the first few steps in the process, currently hovering between steps 3 and 4 above. Although they have no ambition to run the country, they have reached a position where they dictate the agenda and influence legislation favourable to their ends.

Changing threats

The nature of terrorist threats changed dramatically with the end of the Cold War. Most obviously, the West no longer had to fear terrorist attacks from Soviet-sponsored groups. But every silver lining has a cloud. With the collapse of the old Soviet regime their arsenal of nuclear and other Weapons of Mass Destruction was broken up and is steadily appearing on the black market. Both the weapons themselves, and the scientists with the knowledge of how to make them, are available to the highest bidder. Much effort has gone into keeping track of both weapons and individuals, and removing them from the open market wherever possible.

Firefighters tackle the blaze at the Pentagon caused by the terrorist attack on 11 September 2001. Photos: US DoD.

For a long time terrorists had drawn the line at using nuclear, biological and chemical weapons. This was partly due to the expense and technical know-how necessary to deploy them, making them the province of state-sponsored groups rather than smaller groups with more limited resources – and any state tempted to assist the use of WMD would know that, if caught, they would face massive retribution.

Then in 1995 the Aum Shinrikyo sect released nerve gas into the crowded subway system in Tokyo. The threshold had been crossed; the only way for a terrorist group to gain the maximum media coverage was to raise the stakes one step further. The 11 September attacks took terrorism to a new level – a military-style strike on America's homeland, using civilian airliners as guided bombs. Indeed, this almost went beyond the pure definition of terrorism; if it had been carried out by a state it would be a straightforward act of war. There appeared to be no intention to exert pressure on the US for a political purpose, simply to cause the maximum harm and demoralisation.

One area that has tended to decline is that of nationalist/separatist groups, although specific areas still pose a threat. The IRA, for instance, now claims to be committed to the peace process – yet a few hardliners, under the banner of 'Continuity IRA', refuse to compromise and are determined to continue with violent methods. There are frequently suspicions that even those promoting peace are, at the very least, keeping open the option of returning to violence if it should suit their purpose. Other groups, such as the Basque separatist group ETA, remain active and show no sign of giving up their violent methods.

Islamic extremism is but one example of the old problem of state-sponsored terrorism – where a 'pariah' state or group of states actively fosters terrorist activity, not simply turning a blind eye but, for example, providing military training to terrorists, making available training facilities and operational resources, and even providing weapons and explosives. Countries such as Libya, Iran, Iraq, Afghanistan, North Korea, Cuba, Sudan and Syria all stand accused of supporting or harbouring terror-

ists; on the West's side, US government agencies have been accused of terrorist-like activity in South America, and British security forces are known to have cooperated with loyalist paramilitaries in Northern Ireland. In the field of terrorism, things are rarely black and white, more often different shades of grey.

To complicate the issue, it is rare to find a 'pure' terrorist group with high ideals and no ulterior motives. Such groups attract people for various reasons, and there will always be those within a group who are out to increase their own personal fortune or power base, while ostensibly serving the 'higher' political aims of the group. Many terrorist groups are closely linked with organised crime and the drugs trade, not least because these provide a source of revenue to fund the group's activities.

Organised crime and drugs trafficking are not terrorism by any normal definition of the word, but often involve terrorist-like activity and are often combated by the same state departments, using the same methods and equipment. In Britain, for example, the Police, MI5, MI6 and Special Forces like the SAS are all required to fight terrorism, drugs and other organised crime, and deploy the individuals and equipment best suited to each task on its merits. The role of MI6, for instance, is defined in the Intelligence Services Act 1994: '... obtain and provide information relating to the actions or intentions of persons outside the British Islands ... with particular reference to defence and foreign policies ... the economic well-being of the UK ... or in support of the prevention or detection of serious crime.'

The overall picture is that terrorist threats are always changing, but there is no prospect of terrorism becoming extinct – and the West must constantly be on its guard against terrorist attack.

Terrorist groups

The United States Department of State, in its publication 'Patterns of Global Terrorism 2001' (released on 21 May 2002) listed thirty-three 'Designated Foreign Terrorist Organisations' and twenty-eight 'Other Terrorist Organisations'. The combined list is as follows:

Abu Nidal Organization (ANO)	Armed Islamic Group (GIA)
Abu Sayyaf Group (ASG)	Army for the Liberation of
Al-Aqsa Martyrs Brigade	Rwanda (ALIR)
Al-Gama'a al-Islamiyya (Islamic	Asbat al-Ansar
Group, IG)	Aum Supreme Truth (Aum
Al-Ittihad al-Islami (AIAI)	Shinrikyo)
Al Jama'a al-Islamiyyah al-	Basque Fatherland and Liberty
Muqatilah bi-Libya	(ETA)
Al-Jihad (Egyptian Islamic Jihad)	Cambodian Freedom Fighters
Al-Qaeda	(CFF)
Alex Boncayao Brigade (ABB)	Continuity Irish Republican Army
Allied Democratic Forces (ADF)	(CIRA)
Anti-Imperialist Territorial Nuclei	First of October Antifascist
(NTA)	Resistance Group (GRAPO)

HAMAS (Islamic Resistance
    Movement)
Harakat ul-Jihad-I-Islami (HUJI)
Harakat ul-Jihad-I-
    Islami/Bangladesh (HUJI-B)
Harakat ul-Mujahidin (HUM)
    (Movement of Holy Warriors)
Hizballah (Party of God)
Irish Republican Army (IRA)
Islamic Army of Aden (IAA)
Islamic Movement of Uzbekistan
    (IMU)
Jaish-e-Mohammed (JEM) (Army
    of Mohammed)
Japanese Red Army (JRA)
Jemaah Islamiya (JI)
Kahane Chai (Kach)
Kumpulan Mujahidin Malaysia
    (KMM)
Kurdistan Workers' Party (PKK)
Lashkar-e-Tayyiba (LT) (Army of
    the Righteous)
Liberation Tigers of Tamil Eelam
    (LTTE)
Lord's Resistance Army (LRA)
Loyalist Volunteer Force (LVF)
Mujahedin-e Khalq Organization
    (MEK of MKO)
National Liberation Army
    (ELN)–Colombia
New People's Army (NPA)
Orange Volunteers (OV)
People Against Gangsterism and

Drugs (PAGAD)
Palestine Islamic Jihad (PIJ)
Palestine Liberation Front (PLF)
Popular Front for the Liberation
    of Palestine (PFLP)
Popular Front for the Liberation
    of Palestine–General
    Command (PFLP-GC)
Real IRA (RIRA)
Red Hand Defenders (RHD)
Revolutionary Armed Forces of
    Colombia (FARC)
Revolutionary Nuclei
Revolutionary Organization 17
    November (17 November)
Revolutionary People's Libera-
    tion Party/Front (DHKP/C)
Revolutionary Proletarian Initia-
    tive Nuclei (NIPR)
Revolutionary United Front (RUF)
Salafist Group for Call and
    Combat (GSPC)
Sendero Luminoso (Shining
    Path, or SL)
The Tunisian Combatant Group
    (TCG)
Tupac Amaru Revolutionary
    Movement (MRTA)
Turkish Hizballah
Ulster Defense Association/Ulster
    Freedom Fighters (UDA/UVF)
United Self-Defense Forces/
    Group of Colombia (AUC)

Clearly the problem of terrorism is not going to go away. Indeed, there is every sign that it will not only be around for many years to come, but will multiply and become harder to combat as terrorists become ever more sophisticated and make more effective use of the powerful tools that new technology provides.

Recent developments

The previous edition of this book, written by Michael Dewar, was published in the mid-1990s. Looking back at that book today, it is immediately clear how much – and how little – has changed in the intervening years.

Perhaps the most striking of recent huge advances have been in computing and electronics. Eight years ago, there was little specialist electronic anti-terrorist kit. What then existed was bulky and clunky by modern standards. Today's anti-terrorist forces can call on a huge range of highly sophisticated electronic kit – communications equipment, bugging and surveillance devices, GPS. No doubt with the pace of development in electronics and technology this current crop of equipment will in turn look clumsy and unsophisticated in just a few years' time, but it is certainly opening up new avenues in the field of anti-terrorism, as elsewhere.

The 'miniature' equipment, such as surveillance cameras and microphones, of the 1990s looks positively archaic alongside today's miniature marvels – a camera no bigger than a 10p piece, a microphone hardly bigger than a pinhead. Thermal imaging and night vision equipment has come on in leaps and bounds during this time, too. The previous book shows a small number of first- and second-generation image intensifiers, but the current equipment has effectively turned night into day for security forces – and all but the best are available on the civilian market and therefore available to terrorists as well, even those without state sponsorship.

Behind this specialist equipment lies another layer of technology that, although less visible, has seen enormous change and development in the past few years. Smaller, faster computers and storage media, more powerful software, sophisticated networking solutions, the internet and the general spread of computers in offices and homes have changed the face of anti-terrorism work.

For instance, information can now be carried around on minuscule storage media, and protected by strong encryption. While I was writing this book, I carried the files around on a Compact Flash card little bigger than a postage stamp. With the aid of a simple USB adapter, I could read and work on the files in various locations, and even on a palmtop computer while travelling on the train. There was no reason to encrypt the files, but if I had chosen to I could have scrambled them so that they were unreadable to anyone without the passphrase.

This clearly poses an entirely new set of problems for security services. The renegade MI6 agent, Richard Tomlinson, described in his book, *The Big Breach* (Narodny Variant Publishers, Moscow, 2000), how he prepared his manuscript on a Psion palmtop computer, encrypted the text and stored it on a Compact Flash card. When police burst into his hotel room he was able, with a little sleight of hand, to hide the card and retain his manuscript despite a search. When MI6 eventually got copies of his files, they were unable to break the encryption and read the text. Whether or not you support Tomlinson's stand on MI6's actions, the same technique would enable a terrorist group to hide plans for an attack, lists of targets and the like with ease.

Today's terrorists (and criminals and drug barons) are likely to use the internet, mobile phones, digital cameras and all the other paraphernalia of modern life. Powerful encryption software tools are freely available on the internet, with civil liberties and privacy groups distributing advice on their effective use. The jury is still out over whether the security services are able to crack the most widely used encryption software, PGP (Pretty Good Privacy) – and naturally enough they are not telling. No doubt in years to come the story will be told, as with the wartime story of Enigma.

Steganography tools make it possible to hide plain or encrypted text within another type of file, such as a jpeg picture or an mp3 sound file. Such innocent-looking files can be e-mailed or copied to a web server without attracting unwelcome attention, where they can be accessed by terrorists with no need for direct contact between groups or cells.

The benefits of technology are not all in the terrorists' favour, of course. The security services have developed an impressive array of equipment and techniques for tracing and tracking users of computers, mobile phones and the internet. Many people imagine that they can remain anonymous on the internet, not realising that their every click leaves a digital trail that can be followed just as a dog follows a scent on the ground.

The author was able to download this satellite image of Downing Street in London freely from the internet. Such images could be useful to terrorists in planning an attack. Photo: Author's collection.

With the resources available to the state security services such as MI5 or the Metropolitan Police's Intelligence unit, SO11, it is a simple matter to intercept and locate the origin of a mobile phone call or an e-mail in just a few seconds.

A notable exception to the trend of increasing technology was Osama bin Laden, who was noted for his dislike of modern technology, preferring to rely on traditional, low-tech methods such as human messengers. It is said that his attitude was strengthened after US surveillance aircraft managed to target him via his personal satellite phone. Other groups have developed their own ways of combating the problem – the IRA, for instance, kept a 'pool' of mobile phones which were swapped around frequently so that the security services could never be sure who was carrying the mobile phone they were tracking.

If terrorists are using modern technology, then anti-terrorist forces must stay at least one step ahead. This results in the use of technology like Echelon and Carnivore to sift through millions of e-mails and faxes each day, using massive processing power to search for pre-programmed key words and phrases. It means using sophisticated decryption software, password 'cracking' tools, Trojan horse programmes, internet packet sniffers, Tempest technology (to read the words displayed on a computer monitor nearby) and much more.

Only a few years ago, the tools available to modern security services were the stuff of dreams and science fiction. Today it is possible to connect a network of CCTV cameras to a computer that will scan every face pictured, and compare it against a database of known suspects. If a match is found, a human operator will be alerted, while the system continues to track the suspect's movements, all the while recording the moving images for use as evidence later. Facilities such as GCHQ and Menwith

Hill can scan massive amounts of internet traffic for suspicious messages. Sophisticated monitoring and direction-finding equipment will quickly track down the source of any unauthorised radio broadcast. Cameras mounted in helicopters, fixed-wing aircraft, unmanned aircraft and satellites can photograph activity on the earth's surface from every conceivable angle, night and day, and transmit high-quality images back to a command centre in real time.

All this is the stuff of Hollywood – or George Orwell's *1984* if you take the opposite view – and yet counter-terrorist work is still ninety-nine per cent sheer hard slog.

Modern CCTV systems are a valuable weapon in the fight against terrorism; these are just a few of dozens of cameras monitoring people passing through Victoria railway station in London. Photo: © James Marchington.

The fancy, high-tech tools are all very well, but as the 11 September attacks demonstrated only too well, nothing can beat good old-fashioned 'humint' – human intelligence gained from agents on the ground who know their stuff. Even high-tech listening and surveillance devices need to be placed within close range of their target by operators who can get in, do the job, and get out again undetected. And when the time comes to rescue hostages held by a desperate group of terrorists, no technology has yet been found that can replace a team of highly trained CRW specialists armed with stun-grenades and 9mm sub-machine guns.

So alongside the modern electronic marvels, this book also contains much simple kit that is still in use for the very good reason that it works. More than twenty years after the famous Iranian Embassy Siege, the Heckler & Koch MP5 sub-machine gun is still the weapon of choice, for example, among anti-terrorist forces around the world, for the very good reason that it does the job reliably, with the minimum of fuss. Elaborate camera systems are wonderful in the right place, but there are times when a simple mirror on a stick does everything you need – simply, cheaply and with no batteries to run down or mains supply to worry about.

It is said that when the Americans sent men into space, they realised they would need to write in zero gravity. They spent several years and millions of dollars developing the ultimate ballpoint pen, with a pressurised refill filled with specially developed ink, that would write at any angle, in air, under water or in a vacuum, regardless of gravity – a miracle of modern engineering. The Russians, of course, faced the same problem. They bought a pencil.

The story carries an important point. Technology has a habit of becoming an end in itself. It is vital that we do not allow ourselves to be so impressed by fancy modern electronics that we forget what we set out to achieve in the first place. The terrorists are well aware of this, and are quite capable of staging a spectacular attack against the state with little more than a pocket knife, or a box of matches and a can of petrol. Counter-terrorist forces would do well to remember the old maxim: 'If it's stupid and it works, it ain't stupid'.

One final thought before we move on to examine the weapons and equipment used by counter-terrorist forces. We often describe the battle against terrorism as 'defending freedom'. In the UK, our freedoms were hard-won and are precious to us. But to fight terrorism effectively, we may have to sacrifice some of those freedoms – allowing the state to intrude more into our personal lives, renouncing our age-old right to be presumed innocent until proved guilty, and so on.

There is a compromise to be struck here. If the price of defeating terrorism is to give up our freedom, then we have not won the battle, we have lost.

1 SURVEILLANCE

Surveillance and monitoring are the bread and butter of counter-terrorism work. Many tedious hours, days, weeks and months may be spent watching members of a terrorist cell going about their business in order to gather sufficient evidence for a conviction, to learn about planned operations and to track the cell's links with leaders and other terrorist groups. It is slow, painstaking work, but there is no substitute if the security forces are going to crack the group and prevent their planned attacks.

This is one area where modern technology has brought enormous benefits to the counter-terrorist operative. Modern security forces have a huge arsenal of surveillance, bugging and tracking devices at their disposal. In this chapter we will review the range of commercially available products, including sophisticated night vision devices, CCTV and eavesdropping systems. It should be remembered, however, that each service has its technical experts who are constantly adapting commercially available equipment and developing their own devices to meet the particular needs of their operators in the field.

Examples of this 'home brewed' kit rarely come to the attention of the public, but there was a notable exception in December 1999 when the IRA announced they had discovered a bug in the car used by Gerry Adams to travel to and from 'peace process' negotiations. Much to the embarrassment of the British security services, the device was paraded in front of the press, and photographs of it appeared in the newspapers. The device consisted of an adapted mobile phone, microphone and antenna, and was intended to broadcast any conversation that took place in the vehicle. It would also have given an accurate fix on the position of the vehicle at any given time.

The device would, of course, have had to be installed by a technical expert at some point, perhaps when the vehicle was left with a garage for servicing – it was hidden within the vehicle's bodywork, with the microphone placed in the centre of the roof, and would not have been discovered without a determined search.

Modern high-tech surveillance devices certainly allow security services to do things not possible in the past, but they do not replace skilled operators. It is still necessary to carry out a CTR, to position surveillance equipment, gain access to computers, and the like. Indeed, the modern counter-terrorist operator is expected to be an expert in many different, highly technical fields.

The proliferation of security cameras installed by businesses can help the security services to track criminals and terrorists. These pictures, taken by a camera in a bank ATM, were released as part of a 'wanted' notice by the US Government.

Britain's security services have had the advantage, if that is the right word, of many years' experience in Northern Ireland. The battle against IRA terrorists has provided ample opportunities to develop and refine new techniques and equipment, and gain experience in their practical use in real conditions against a real enemy – just as the USA's campaign against Al-Qaeda and the Taleban in Afghanistan has made possible the battle-testing of new weapons and equipment such as thermobaric bombs and miniature UAVs (of which more later).

Cameras, telescopes, binoculars, etc

Much basic surveillance kit consists of equipment available on the civilian market for everyday use. In order to obtain photographic evidence, operators use a variety of still and video cameras, both digital and traditional film types, which were primarily designed for serious hobbyists or professional photographers working in other fields. Similarly, regular binoculars and spotting scopes are standard kit in the field.

It is not proposed to deal with these here, since they are not specifically anti-terrorist kit any more than a regular cellphone or laptop computer – even though all these items are in daily use by anti-terrorist units. Suffice to say that anti-terrorist agencies are continually evaluating any new equipment that comes on to the market, and are quick to adopt any – such as 'image-stabilised' binoculars – that offer real advantages in the field rather than mere marketing hype.

The British Army has many years' experience of dealing with terrorism in Northern Ireland, and the threat of attacks on the British mainland. Photo: British Army Press Service.

NIGHT VISION: IMAGE INTENSIFIERS

Night vision devices have become standard equipment for any anti-terrorist operation. Image intensifiers (II) are true 'night vision' devices, in that they 'turn night into day', enabling the operator to see in conditions of almost complete darkness.

A true Image Intensification device (as opposed to a Thermal Imager, discussed below) uses light in the visible and infra-red parts of the spectrum. It is a passive system that amplifies the ambient light from man-made and natural sources including the moon and stars – which gave it the nickname 'Starlight Scope' in US military service during the 1962–75 Vietnam War.

As a passive device, Image Intensification does not send a signal, so there are no emissions that an enemy could detect and deduce that he is under surveillance (unlike radar, for instance). Having said that, it is possible to improve the close-range performance of night vision devices by adding infra-red illumination. This light is not visible to the naked eye but can be seen clearly through an Image Intensification device. It is particularly useful in places where there is no natural light – not even the tiny amount needed for a modern image intensification device to function – places such as inside buildings, ships and aircraft.

The end of the Cold War released a huge range of low-cost Russian-made Image Intensification equipment on to the civilian market, including binoculars and hand-held systems with IR illumination. First Generation (Gen I) systems such as the T3C2 can now be bought for as little as £100. This has led to the use of Image Intensification equipment by everyday criminals as well as terrorists. Image Intensification can be extremely useful in planning and carrying out a criminal or terrorist attack. One way to combat this threat is to ensure that vulnerable buildings and installations are screened from view by fences, walls or vegetation.

A Russian-made First Generation night vision device, typical of the equipment that is now available for a few hundred pounds on the civilian market. Photo: © James Marchington.

Image Intensification devices have been improved greatly in recent years. The first devices, now known as First Generation or Gen I, produced a murky green image with dancing specks all over. They were badly affected by 'flaring' around light sources, and would be blinded or 'bloomed-out' for several minutes by a sudden bright light such as a car's headlights appearing unexpectedly. 'Blooming-out' fogs the screen by producing a temporary after-image. These Gen I devices were hardly better than using a decent pair of binoculars, which can be remarkably effective at night once your eyes have grown accustomed to the dark after half an hour or so.

Performance and reliability have been enhanced through three generations of Image Intensification equipment. Second Generation (Gen II) Image Intensification equipment has improved light intensification up to 20,000 times, compared to 1,000 times in Gen I equipment. Filtration is incorporated so that Gen II kit does not 'bloom-out' if the user points it at a light source such as car headlights.

Third Generation (Gen III) is a further improvement on Gen II, with better filters helping to give a clearer image in difficult conditions, but the enhancement is relatively small for the increase in cost, making it unattractive to all but government agencies.

Image Intensification technology has now moved on a stage further. In 1999 Litton Industries (now Northrop Grumman), one of the US military's major suppliers of night vision and surveillance equipment, delivered the first production quantities of Fourth Generation (Gen IV) Image Intensifier tubes to the US Army Night Vision and Electronic Sensors Directorate (NVESD). Gen IV tubes take Image Intensification performance levels a stage further by taking advantage of new technology, and by rethinking traditional tube design concepts.

The key difference in Gen IV Image Intensifier tubes is that there is no ion barrier film. In conventional Gen III tubes this barrier prevents damage to the photocathode coating by shielding it from ions back-scattered from the microchannel plate (MCP). Northrop Grumman describe this as a significant breakthrough. Gen IV tubes used in night vision goggles have demonstrated substantial increases in target detection range and resolution, particularly at extremely low light levels.

Northrop Grumman's Gen IV MX-10130E/UV tube will be used in the US Special Operations Command's (USSOCOM) Improved Night/Day Fire Control & Observation Device (INOD) weapon sight, which at the time of writing is undergoing Initial Production Testing.

Image Intensification devices are available in various formats, including monocular viewers, weapons sights and Passive Night Goggles (PNGs). The goggles are particularly suited to driving vehicles or flying aircraft, especially helicopters. PNGs were first used operationally by British helicopter crews in the Falklands War of 1982, to insert Special Forces by night on to the islands. They have since become standard kit for pilots and drivers on the modern battlefield, and are widely used by Special Forces and anti-terrorist operators.

There is a splendid story, perhaps apocryphal, of a UK Special Forces Flight pilot practising with PNGs prior to being deployed to the Gulf War; he chose to drive a high-performance sports car around the M25 motorway in the early hours of the morning. The police were somewhat baffled when the blacked-out vehicle flashed past at a speed approaching 200mph! True or not, the story demonstrates that with PNGs it is possible to drive or fly at night as though it were daytime – giving a significant advantage over an enemy who is less well equipped.

Northrop Grumman Electro-Optical Systems
Northrop Grumman (formerly Litton Electro-Optical Systems) produce Image Intensification systems for the US Army, Navy, Marine Corps, Special Operations, and many

international customers. Products supplied to the US armed forces include AN/PVS-7D Infantry Night Vision Goggles, AN/PVS-14 Monocular Night Vision Systems, and AN/AVS-6 Aviator Night Vision Systems.

Northrop Grumman AN/PVS-7B/D
This goggle is a Second Generation design, with improved performance and ergonomic features. The AN/PVS-7D, adopted by the US Army, incorporates an advanced image tube with very high resolution.

Passive night vision goggles effectively turn night into day, making it possible to drive a vehicle or operate a weapon in conditions of near-total darkness. The goggles shown are in service with the British Army. Photo: © James Marchington.

Northrop Grumman AN/PVS-7A/C
The AN/PVS-7A is a rugged, lightweight, compact, single-tube goggle for hand-held, helmet or face-mask mounting for the dismounted soldier. It was the first design of this type and offered excellent performance at an attractive cost. It has x1 magnification for short- to medium-range surveillance, combat, security, law enforcement, search and rescue, etc. x4 and x6 magnification versions are also available. The AN/PVS-7C is a modified design that is submersible to 20m (66ft). Weighing only 0.68kg, it operates from two 1.5v AA alkaline batteries or a single lithium battery, and contains an IR Light Emitting Diode.

Northrop Grumman AN/AVS-6
AN/AVS-6 are Rotary and Fixed Wing Aviators' Goggles. The high performance, high resolution twin Gen III tube design extends pilots' operational capability into the night. It is helmet mounted with simple adjustments, fast breakaway and system redundancy for safety. Compatible with most aviator helmets, the AN/AVS-6 features 25mm eye relief, low fatigue design, flip-up stowage, superior light sensitivity and fast flash response.

Northrop Grumman AN/PVS-15
This Gen III twin-tube goggle is a ruggedised navy qualified system that offers dual-channel depth perception. It can be hand held or helmet mounted, and has improved 'flash response' to maintain sharp image detail even through flares or lights. A 25mm eye relief allows use with masks or goggles.

Northrop Grumman AN/AVS-9 (M949)
While incorporating the same proven operational features as AN/AVS-6, M949 is claimed to be the highest resolution, longest range x1 magnification night viewing system available today. It uses Northrop Grumman's Gen IV Image Intensification technology, including Filmless MCP, Auto-Gated Power Supply and patent-pending 'Halo-Free' design. The M949 with Gen IV tubes is restricted from export.

PW Allen Nite Watch

While the Northrop Grumman range described above is typical of the type of night vision kit issued to land forces in combat, the PW Allen Nite Watch is the type more typically used for surveillance by police and internal security forces. The Nite Watch is remarkably light and compact, weighing only 330g (including lens and batteries), making it pocket sized and easily concealed. The modular construction of Nite Watch Plus enables it to be swiftly added to most types of SLR, Video and CCTV cameras with a range of adaptors.

When used in low light level conditions, the Nite Watch Plus typically provides over 7,000 hours of life, making it more cost-effective than many cheaper alternatives. Typical light intensification is over 20,000 times, compared with a Gen I system with a maximum light intensification of less than 1,000 times.

Nite Watch Plus is available in two basic mechanically different forms. The original Nite Watch form incorporates three miniature lithium batteries; the newer option incorporates two AAA batteries in a 'side-pack' version. The Nite Watch System is subject to UK Government Export Licensing Regulations, and cannot be exported from the UK without a licence.

Features

Weighs only 330g including lens and batteries
Modular construction
Covert system
Shockproof
Interchangeable lenses
Push-button or rotary switch

Available with Gen II plus, Super Gen II or Gen III tube technologies
Over 7,000 hours continuous use
Water resistant (ruggedised units only)

Specifications

Intensifier Type	Second or Third Generation 18mm channel plate wafer tube
Resolution	Typically 32 1p/mm
Supply Voltage	2.5 to 3.5v
Supply Current	Typically 18 mA
Battery Life	Typically 30 hours continuous use from three lithium cells type DL1/3N or 2AAA depending on type
Weight	Typically 330g (11.64 oz) including lens and batteries
Size	46mm (1.8in) diameter x 120 mm (4.7in) long including f/1.4 25mm lens
Objective Lens	Standard C-mount f/1.4 25mm
System Field of View	34° with 25mm lens (42° for side-pack version) 11° with 75 mm lens (15° for side-pack version)
System Magnification	x1 with 25mm lens x3 with 75mm lens

PW Allen NVSK 1/00 Night Vision Surveillance Kit

The Nite Watch system forms the basis of PW Allen's NVSK 1/00 Comprehensive Night Vision Surveillance Kit, described as 'a fully comprehensive surveillance kit for night-time observation, intelligence and evidence gathering'. This kit provides all the equipment required to view and record activities by day or night; all the equipment in the kit has been field-proven by security forces in the UK and overseas.

The kit consists of the following items, packed in a rugged case with anti-shock foam inserts:

Gen III Nite Watch Monocular Sight	Sony Mini Digital Video Camera
SLR Camera Adaptor	Canon EOS IV SLR Camera
SLR Interface Mount	Rangefinder
Mini Digital Video Camera Adaptor	IR Illuminator
Mini Digital Video Camera Interface Mount	Waterproof Case
75mm f/1.3 Objective Lens	Cleaning Kit
75mm f/1.8 Objective Zoom Lens	Instruction Manual
	Spare Batteries 6x AAA

Leica Geosystems

Leica Geosystems of Switzerland produce a range of sturdy, proven night vision products, including pocket monoculars, night vision goggles and night binoculars. Export of Leica's night vision products is subject to Swiss export regulations.

Leica BIM25 Night Pocketscope

The Leica BIM25 is a general-purpose, monocular night vision device in a watertight, nitrogen-filled housing. It provides an actual size image (x1 magnification). There is a choice of image intensifier tube – Gen II, Gen II super or Gen III. It is suited to security and reconnaissance applications, and can also be fitted to a SLR or video camera by means of an adaptor, in order to record evidence for later use.

Leica BIM35 Night Pocketscope

Leica's BIM35 monocular is identical to the BIM25, except that a larger objective lens provides 3x magnification. This makes it more suitable for observing a target at a distance from a static position such as an OP.

Leica BIG25 Night Vision Goggles

Leica BIG25 are night vision goggles suitable for a wide range of tasks such as CTR, vehicle driving, navigating and operating various types of equipment in night conditions. The goggles have a single objective tube containing a Gen II or III image intensifier. The intensified image is passed to binocular viewing lenses. The goggles can be hand-held, or worn attached to the head by means of an optional harness – leaving both hands free for driving, etc.

Leica BIG35 Night Binoculars

The BIG35 binoculars are similar to the BIG25, but with a x3 magnification object lens. The much larger lens makes it impractical to wear the binoculars with a head harness. The large lens barrel is rubber-covered, giving a good grip, and the binoculars are designed to be used for extended periods without eye-strain. They have rubber eye-cups for comfort, and to prevent light spillage which could give away the user's position.

Leica Night Vision Equipment – Specifications				
	BIM25	BIM35	BIG25	BIG35
Magnification	x1	x3	x1	x3
Field of View	>40°	>12.5°	>40°	>12.5°
Focus	0.25m-inf	10m-inf	0.25m-inf	10m-inf
Weight	0.43kg	1.16kg	0.55kg	1.19kg

Simrad Optronics

Simrad of Norway offer an array of Image Intensifier night sights for security services and armed forces. As well as image intensifying monoculars, goggles and binoculars, Simrad produce the KN series, which can be clipped on to existing day scopes or sighting systems without modification. This has the advantage that the existing set-up of a weapon sight, etc remains unchanged, and the sight's performance is retained twenty-four hours a day. The KN system uses Gen II or III image intensifier tubes depending on the customer's requirements.

Simrad KN250 and KN200 Image Intensifiers

The Simrad KN200 and KN250 image intensifiers are add-on units providing a night time capability to optical day sights. The night vision image is viewed through the eyepiece of the day sight. This allows the user to retain the same eye position, aiming reticle and magnification for both day and night shooting. The KN series have adjustable focus and variable gain control, and can be supplied waterproofed to 20 metres. A separate laser illuminator and pointer are available.

Simrad KN 200 – Specifications	
Field of View	10°
Weight (incl. batteries)	1.56kg
Magnification	x1
Dimensions (w x h x l)	127 x 192 x 220mm
Focusing range	25m to infinity
Operating Temperature	−40°C to 50°C
Storing Temperature	−40°C to 65°C
Battery	2 x 1.5v AA cells
Battery life	>80h at 20°C

Simrad KN 250 – Technical Specifications

Field of View	12°
Weight (incl. batteries)	1kg
Magnification	x1
Dimensions (w x h x l)	107 x 142 x 187mm
Focusing	25m to infinity
Operating Temperature	−40°C to 50°C
Storing Temperature	−40°C to 65°C
Battery	2 x 1.5v AA cells
Battery life	>80h at 20°C

Simrad GN Night Vision Goggles

Simrad GN Night Vision Goggles are extremely compact and lightweight binocular night vision goggles, with a flip-up mechanism so they can be worn ready to flip into position at short notice. They have proved popular with a wide range of users, including mainstream infantry units, Special Forces, police, customs and immigration control. At the time of writing, Simrad indicate that they expect shortly to announce an improved goggle that is even lighter and more compact.

Features	**Typical applications**
Gen II or Gen III tubes	Vehicle driving/commanding
Range focus	Patrolling
Eyepiece focus	Surveillance
IR illuminator	Weapon handling
Lightweight, ergonomic	Parachuting
Head mount or helmet mount	Reconnaissance
Flip-up mechanism	Logistical operations
Waterproof to 10m	Search and rescue
NATO Codified	Map reading

Specifications

Magnification	x1
Weight (incl. batteries)	390g
Field of View	40°
Size (w x h x l)	155 x 73 x 58mm
Focusing Range	0.2m to infinity
Weight – head mount	230g
Batteries	2 x 1.5v AA cells
Battery life	>80h at 20°
IR source on	>40h at 20°
IR source	LED

Simrad KDN250 Day/Night Vision Binoculars

Simrad's KDN250 is a highly useful surveillance tool – a pair of observation binoculars that provide a high quality image twenty-four hours a day. The binoculars essentially have a two-channel system, with separate night and day optics.

Features
x3.5 magnification
Lightweight (1.5kg)
Binocular viewing
Completely passive
Waterproof to 20m
NATO codification
Compatible with 2nd or 3rd generation 18mm image tubes
Dovetail quick-release mechanism fitted to night channel
Adjustable interocular distance
Focusing wheel on the night channel

Specifications	
Magnification	x3.5
Weight (incl batteries)	1.55kg
Field of view	12°
Dimensions	158mm x
(w x h x l)	140mm x
	229mm
Focusing range	25m to infinity
Operating temperature	–40°C to 52°C
Storing temperature	–40°C to 67°C
Battery	2 x 1.5v AA
	cells
Battery life	>80h at 20°C

Pilkington Kite Night Vision Systems

The Pilkington Kite Observation Sight, or KOS, and MAXIKOS or Maxi Kite Observation Sight, are the observation variants of the British Army Kite Individual Weapon Sight and MaxiKite Crew-Served Weapon Sight. Having no need to be mounted on a weapon, or used for aiming, the relevant mounting system and aiming marks are omitted, but the working parts and silhouette are identical.

KOS provides x 4 magnification and an 8.5° field of view, weighing only 1kg. MAXIKOS is slightly heavier, at 1.3kg, and gives a magnification of x 6, with a 5.5° field of view.

Both Kite systems are available in binocular variants, as BinoKite and MaxiBinoKite. These offer similar performance to the monocular Kite and MaxiKite, but are more comfortable to use for prolonged periods of surveillance. All the Kite observation variants can be hand-held or tripod-mounted, and are powered by standard 1.5V AA batteries.

Specifications	Kite	MaxiKite	BinoKite	BinoMaxiKite
Magnification	x4	x6	x4.5	x6.7
Field of View	8.5°	5.5°	8.8°	5.2°
Weight	1kg	1.3kg	1.1kg	1.5kg
Power Supply	x2 1.5v AA	x2 1.5v AA	x2 1.5v AA	x2 1.5v AA

THERMAL IMAGING

The Spyglass HHTI (Hand Held Thermal Imager) is in service with the British Army. Photo: Author's collection.

Criminals and terrorists have for some years had access to Image Intensification. However, unless they were sponsored by state organisations they were until recently unlikely to have Thermal Imaging (TI) equipment. Despite state attempts to restrict the availability of TI technology, TI cameras are now being sold to the civilian market for use in areas such as commercial security and anti-poaching patrols. It is inevitable, therefore, that they will fall into the hands of undesirable elements.

Thermal Imaging presents a picture showing the different heat patterns produced by men, machines and other objects, whether natural or man-made. It is enormously useful to anti-terrorist units for a wide range of surveillance operations, tracking of suspects and the like, as well as for search and rescue operations. Many modern units use a colour display to show the range of temperatures, so warm objects may show up red-orange against a blue-green background.

Thermal Imaging allows operators to see through visual camouflage and smoke, so a person or vehicle screened by a net or vegetation would show up warm through the cover. Thermal Imaging is extremely useful in search and rescue operations, since operators can find survivors in dense cover or smoky rooms. They can also locate small heat sources, such as a life-raft in the open sea, or a live body in an expanse of snowy hillside.

Unlike Image Intensifiers, Thermal Imaging equipment detects heat sources, such as a warm engine or human body, and can 'see' through visual camouflage and smoke. Photo: Author's collection.

Thermal Imaging was first used by the British Army operationally in the Falklands in 1982, where the heat 'signature' of sheep roaming across the moorland caused some confusion for operators! Thermal Imaging can be used by day as well as by night, without special filters. As with Image Intensification, Thermal Imaging equipment has been made much smaller than the early bulky systems; modern Thermal Imaging equipment is no more bulky than a video camcorder. It is also a great deal more effective than the early models: modern TI equipment can detect a difference of less than half a degree Centigrade at several hundred yards, making it possible, for example, to see a vehicle's track by the tyres' slight warming effect on concrete or tarmac some minutes after it has passed.

Thermal Imaging is enormously useful, but it does have its limitations. It does not perform well, for instance, in rain or sandstorms. The picture it produces at medium and short ranges has a clearly defined, recognisable shape, but at longer ranges the operator sees just a warm 'blob'. In the Gulf War of 1991, this contributed to some of the 'blue on blue' or friendly fire casualties.

TI equipment is generally bulkier and heavier than Image Intensification kit, which has restricted its use somewhat. There are, however, much lighter and more compact systems coming into use, which will make TI a great deal more versatile and open up new possibilities in the fight against terrorism.

Thermal Imaging was literally a life-saver during conflicts such as the Gulf War and, more recently, in Afghanistan. With no ambient light on a cloudy night in the desert,

Image Intensification equipment is useless. Only HHTI (hand-held thermal imaging) equipment allowed soldiers to locate enemy positions in conditions of total darkness.

PW Allen 600-305 Thermal Imager
The 600-305 Surveillance Thermal Imager, known as BlackCat, is a simple-to-use night vision camera for Police, Coastguard, Border Guards, Customs and Security Guards. It is easily fitted with a range of lenses from 50mm to 150mm depending on the requirement, and can be used hand-held or tripod-mounted.

Specifications

Spectral range	7–14 micron
Sensor type	Uncooled FPA, ferroelectric
Resolution	320 x 240 pixels
Sensitivity	<0.1ºC
Interchangeable lenses	50mm f1, 75mm f0.8, 100mm f1, 150mm f1, 50–150mm zoom (Germanium)
Video output	Yes
Data display	Provides time and date
EMC	EEC regulation 89/336
Sealing	IP55
Operation temperature	–20°C to 50°C
Weight (excl. lens)	2.2kg
Dimensions (excl. lens)	Length 310mm, Width 115mm, Height 156mm
Internal battery life	4 hrs

Optional Image Transmission System

Antenna impedance	50 Ohms
Transmitter frequency	1,394MHz
TX power output	500mW (max)
Oscillator	PLL (Phase Locked Loop)
Channel bandwidth	10MHz
Video input/output	1v p-p
Video output	NTSC. E1A 525 lines 60Hz
Modulation method	Frequency modulation (FM)
Current consumption	800mA additional
Indoor range	Typically 50 to 100m
Outdoor range	More than 100m
Base station monitor	6 inch
Operation temperature	–25°C to 60°C

Base station can be operated on mains 110/240v or for two hours minimum on the built-in Ni-MH rechargeable battery
The base station is housed in a Pelican case 460 x 320 x 180mm

Thales Optronics

Thales Optronics Ltd (previously Thomson-TRT) is the UK-based optronics division of Thales, one of the world's largest electronics groups. The company has been at the forefront of thermal imaging since the early 1970s. Working closely with the UK Ministry of Defence, they have developed a unique capability in the design, development and manufacture of optical and electro-optical sensors for a wide range of applications including navigation, situational awareness, surveillance, target acquisition and infra-red search and tracking.

Thales Optronics is a leading supplier of electro-optical systems and equipment to the UK MoD, including thermal imaging telescopes and lenses, sensor image enhancement systems, the Battle Group Thermal Imaging system (chosen for the Warrior and CVR(T) vehicles) and STAIRS C thermal imaging modules.

The Pilkington Lite Thermal Imager is a hand-held device that provides an image through fog and smoke, even in pitch darkness, making it a valuable surveillance tool. Photo: Pilkington.

Radamec 1000L

RADAMEC System 1000L is a lightweight electro-optical surveillance system for ground-based applications, designed to operate in harsh military environments anywhere in the world. The system provides covert detection and observation of all types of targets in poor visibility, in the dark or bad weather, and at distances well beyond the limits of normal human vision.

Using proven modules from Radamec's well-established range of military electro-optical systems – over one hundred of which have been sold to customers worldwide, including the UK MoD – System 1000L offers a mature, proven, reliable and cost-effective solution to land-based surveillance requirements. System 1000L comprises two major assemblies: an electro-optical director, complete with electro-optical sensors, and an operator's control and display unit.

Features	
Border and Coastal Patrol	Positive Identification
Key Facility Protection	Twenty-four-hour Operation
Battlefield Reconnaissance	Lightweight and Portable
Artillery Spotting	Range of Configurations
Passive Detection	

Below and opposite page shows the Microbus MP5 mobile computer system fitted in a vehicle operated by the UK Atomic Energy Authority Constabulary. The computer itself is fitted in the boot, and relays data to a touch-sensitive monitor on the dashboard. It integrates several systems in the vehicle, including data communications, video cameras, GPS, and Talon automatic number plate recognition software. Photos: Microbus.

Electro Optical Director

Located remotely from the operator, this unit comprises a dual axis servo director head carrying the electro-optical sensors that act as the eyes of the system. The director features smooth slow-speed performance for tracking of long-range moving targets and high-speed acceleration for rapid transfer between targets.

The primary sensors mounted on the director comprise a TV camera for daylight use and a thermal imager for use at night or during poor visibility. These high-performance sensors are fully self-contained and provide both good sensitivity for long-range target detection and high resolution for threat recognition.

Operator's Control Console: Control of the director is accomplished from a compact control unit. This unit contains the controls for the director and sensors and their associated electronics. It also houses two TV monitors that display the sensor images. The console elements can be supplied as separate units where space is restricted.

Vehicle tracking systems

In 1994 Racal launched a system that opened up a whole host of possibilities for counter-terrorist work – a system that could spot a vehicle number plate among the clutter of a CCTV image, recognise the combination of letters and numbers, and pass that information to a computer program for matching against a database of known or 'suspect' vehicles.

Unlike a human operator, the system can read vehicle number plates twenty-four hours a day in a wide range of environmental conditions, and cope with traffic flow speeds that a human operator could never keep up with in real time. Applications range from access control to urban security and traffic monitoring.

The Racal system, called Talon, was the result of an agreement with Cambridge Neurodynamics Ltd, an engineering company that had undertaken extensive research in the field of digital signal processing and pattern recognition. Talon was a significant step forward, based on a new generation of pattern-recognition techniques that make use of neural-network technology.

The neural-network approach offered much greater potential for pattern recognition than conventional template-matching techniques. A neural network is not programmed in the traditional sense, but instead 'learns' by trial and error. Rather than having definitive templates for individual character shapes, the network builds a statistical model that adapts to the features making each individual character distinctive. Consequently, neural

networks are more resilient to 'noise' than conventional recognition techniques, so that performance is not compromised when licence plates are skewed and the numbers are partially obscured, dirty or distorted.

The Racal Talon system is modular and can be configured for various applications. Development has produced simple, single-camera systems for parking access control, to multi-camera systems for urban security, traffic control and automatic toll collection.

Comprehensive systems comprising Talon, video and data communications links, control programs and database interrogation can be tailored for individual

customer requirements. The ease in providing custom systems means many different and varying applications can be addressed, from the identification of vehicles violating traffic regulations to international border surveillance and road traffic surveys.

The Microbus Talon-ready MP5 mobile computer takes Racal Messenger's Talon Automatic Number Plate Recognition System on the road. This in-vehicle computer has a touchscreen in the front of the vehicle, which can display video input switchable from one or more video cameras, so that separate units such as in-car video and mobile data systems can be operated from a single touchscreen. This terminal provides a single viewing point for the escalating number of systems police vehicles have to carry.

The Talon mobile terminal is adapted to the demands of use in a vehicle. This includes protection against shock, vibration and temperature extremes. It is designed to maintain links to radio networks in difficult reception areas.

The main MP5 unit containing the PC platform is ultra-compact. It mounts in the back of the vehicle, and includes an Intel low-power mobile Pentium processor, PCI SoundBlaster compatible sound, PCI 10/100Mbs Ethernet, video output both to the touchscreen and a monitor, PAL/NTSC video input, 8-channel optically isolated digital inputs and outputs, six serial and one parallel ports, a 3GB or larger hard disk, and the usual PC functions. Built-in options include GPS, and a radio or GSM communications modem. The system runs Microsoft Windows NT software, with extra application software. The Talon hardware fits in the main unit and allows input from up to eight video cameras.

At the 2002 ACPO Conference and Exhibition at the NEC in Birmingham, Microbus Mobile Data showed their new in-vehicle computer, the M-PC, installed in a United Kingdom Atomic Energy Authority Constabulary (UKAEAC) vehicle. The UKAEAC was set up under the Atomic Energy Authority Act 1954 with a statutory remit to protect nuclear materials and sites. The Constabulary is authorised to deploy armed police officers to protect nuclear material.

The Microbus Mobile Data computer installed in this armoured vehicle supports GPS-based mapping and Automatic Number Plate Recognition (ANPR) software, and interfaces with the Constabulary's advanced wireless data network. It also has the ability to support the vehicle's emergency functions such as radios, lights and sirens via the high-brightness rugged touchscreen.

BIOMETRICS

Facial recognition

Automatic number plate recognition technology has been available and in use for some time, but it is only quite recently that the science of biometrics has advanced sufficiently that a computer-based system can identify an individual face with anything like the reliability of the human brain. This area has been the subject of much research and development recently, however, partly fuelled by the new climate following 11 September 2001.

Two of the leading companies in this field, Visionics Corp. and Raytheon, announced that in May 2002 they successfully tested a facial recognition system at Boston Logan Airport in the USA. The system was powered by Visionics' FaceIt Argus System, and achieved a 'high level' of successful matches. Similar systems had already been in use for some time: in November 1998 the London Borough of Newham connected over 200 CCTV cameras to a control room running Visionics' FaceIt system, and at other airports around the USA the system had already made several positive 'watch list' identifications.

The potential is enormous for biometrics generally, and facial recognition in particular. There are many commercial applications, such as the identification of customers using bank ATMs. In the field of anti-terrorism, it would be possible to have entire towns, or every border post, covered by cameras linked to a facial recognition system, comparing every face against a database of known 'players'. Much of the hardware is already in place in the UK, where air and sea ports, town centres and

railway stations are already comprehensively covered by CCTV.

Typical CCTV systems rely on human operators to analyse countless images transmitted to security monitors. Inevitably, there are times when they are distracted, or need to take a break; when tired, operators' performance will be reduced. A software-based system, however, is always watching, with no decline in performance as the day wears on.

Early attempts at facial recognition were based on matching faces to a set of master templates called eigenfaces.

A small number of operators can keep watch over a large area using a network of sophisticated CCTV cameras linked to facial recognition software. Photo: Visionics Corp.

CCTV camera systems are widely installed throughout the UK, and can be linked to facial recognition software programmed to watch for known terrorists. Photo: © James Marchington.

Combining coefficients from the various eigenfaces produces a unique identity for every individual's face, rather like defining a colour in terms of percentages of the primary colours.

Visionics discovered that the eigenface approach failed to compensate for real-world variations in lighting, pose, expression, facial hair and other variables. They have developed a system based on a different approach, known as Local Feature Analysis (LFA). This analyses each face in terms of identifiable 'landmarks' on the face, closely related to the underlying bone structure. LFA maps out the spatial relationships between the landmarks into a complex mathematical formula, called a faceprint. This faceprint is unique to each individual, and can be matched and compared to others with remarkable accuracy. Because its make-up is based on the actual shape of the face, it is very resistant to changes in lighting, skin tone, spectacles, ageing, facial expression, hairstyle and pose.

The capabilities of the FaceIt software engine are listed as:

LFA (Local Feature Analysis) analyses each face in terms of 'landmarks' and produces a 'faceprint' that is unaffected by lighting conditions, spectacles, hairstyle and facial expression. Photo: Visionics Corp.

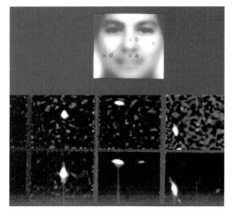

Visionics' facial recognition software can 'read' a face from a CCTV picture or still image, and compare it with known faces from a database at the rate of one million per second. Photo: Visionics Corp.

- ■ Detects single or multiple faces, even in complex scenes
- ■ Provides either Authentication (one-to-one matching) or Identification (one-to-many matching, e.g. against a database of known individuals)
- ■ Evaluates quality of image for face recognition and, if needed, prompts for improved image
- ■ Crops faces from background
- ■ Generates digital code or internal template, unique to an individual
- ■ Monitoring: follows the presence and position of an individual in the field of view
- ■ Surveillance: can find human faces anywhere in the field of view and at any distance, continuously tracking them and matching the face against a 'watch list'
- ■ Totally hands-off, continuous and real-time
- ■ Compresses facial images down to 84 bytes in size

Visionics FaceIt software engine
Specifications

Platforms supported	Windows 95/98/ME/NT/2000/XP
Input	Any source of visual signals including photographs, live or recorded video and digital video files
Speed Head Finding	200 milliseconds
One-to-one matching	< 1 second
One-to-many matching	60 million per minute from memory, 15 million per minute from hard disk
Faceprint size	84 bytes
Database size	Software supports unlimited number of records
Motion	Detects moving or static faces
Pose	Face finding with both eyes visible (up to 45 degrees from frontal)
	Recognition unaffected up to 15 degrees from frontal, matching ability slightly reduced between 15 and 35 degrees. Matching ability decreases sharply beyond 35 degrees
Race and Gender	System unaffected by race and gender
Spectacles	Designed to match faces with or without spectacles, so long as eyes are visible
Image size	Can detect faces as small as 20 x 30 pixels, or less than 1 per cent of total image area. Optimal recognition achieved at head size of 80 x 120 pixels
False accept rate	< 1 per cent
False reject rate	< 1 per cent

Fingerprint scanning systems

Facial recognition is perhaps the most headline-grabbing of the new developments in biometrics, but steady progress is being made in other areas. There are various fingerprint scanners available, for instance, that may be used to verify identity, restrict and audit a user's access – either physical access to a cockpit, secure building, or the like, or access to computer resources such as sensitive database records.

One example of this is the Identix Fingerscan V20 UA. This consists of a unit mounted at the access point, with a keypad, display screen and fingerprint reader. The unit can also be set up to recognise 'smart' access cards and badges. It can be installed as a standalone system to protect a single doorway, or any number of units can be networked to cover a large facility. Each unit is capable of storing up to 32,000 fingerprint 'templates' and can be programmed to allow specific users access only at certain times. All transactions can be recorded, so that an employee's attendance and movements can be monitored.

Fingerprints can be scanned and matched electronically, making it possible to use fingerprint technology to control access to restricted areas or data. Photo: Visionics Corp.

Identix Fingerscan V20 UA

Specifications	
Dimensions	171.45mm x 165.1mm x 88.9mm
Enrolment time	<5 seconds
Verification time	<1 second
Template size	512 bytes
Finger rotation	+/– 18º
Power	12v DC, 1.5A
Weight	2lbs
Communications	RS485, Wiegand, RS2332; optional Ethernet or modem
Baud rate	9,600 to 57,000 bps
Template storage	512 or optional 5,000 or 32,000.
Card reader input	Wiegand, proximity, magnetic stripe, smart card, barcode
Operating temperature	–10º C to 50º C

Communications monitoring

Any modern organisation, terrorists included, relies on modern telecommunications systems to share information, and pass orders and instructions between members of the team. The security services have a huge arsenal of communications monitoring systems at their disposal to sift through the background clutter and monitor the communications of suspicious groups and individuals. In the case of more sophisticated groups, this may involve decrypting encoded messages, or locating messages hidden in innocent-looking picture or sound files by steganography.

Much of the equipment and methods used are highly secret. It would not be appropriate here to disclose details of systems used, for instance, at the UK security services' monitoring station at GCHQ in Cheltenham, or the US equivalent at Menwith Hill. Certain information about communications monitoring has been released into the public domain, however, and no harm is done by reviewing it here.

Key findings published in 'Interception Capabilities 2000', a report prepared by the journalist Duncan Campbell and submitted to the Director General for Research of the European Parliament, were:

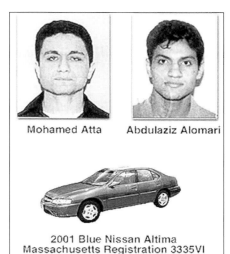

Mohamed Atta   Abdulaziz Alomari

2001 Blue Nissan Altima
Massachusetts Registration 3335VI

- Comprehensive systems exist to access, intercept and process every important modern form of communications, with few exceptions.
- Contrary to reports in the press, effective 'word spotting' search systems automatically to select telephone calls of intelligence interest are not yet available, despite thirty years of research. However, speaker recognition systems – in effect, 'voiceprints' – have been developed and are deployed to recognise the speech of targeted individuals making international telephone calls.
- Recent diplomatic initiatives by the United States government seeking European agreement to the 'key escrow' system of cryptography masked intelligence collection requirements, and formed part of a long-term program which has undermined and continues to undermine the communications privacy of non-US nationals, including European governments, companies and citizens.
- There is wide-ranging evidence indicating that major governments are routinely utilising communications intelligence to provide commercial advantage to companies and trade.

Modern TB communications make it possible for security services to transmit pictures of suspects in seconds, as with this US Government 'wanted' notice. Conversely they may also be used by terrorist groups to share information and transmit instructions.

Echelon

Echelon is a system that enables the security services of the United States, United Kingdom, Canada, Australia and New Zealand (NSA, GCHQ, DSD, GCSB and CSE) to search automatically through millions of intercepted messages for pre-programmed keywords or fax, telex and e-mail addresses. It consists of a global network of listening stations, including GCHQ and Menwith Hill in the UK. Computers sift through every word of every message in the frequencies and channels selected. The contents of each message are compared with a list of key words and phrases known as a dictionary. Each of the parties to the agreement, known as the UKUSA agreement, can add their own choice of keywords to the dictionaries used at the various stations around the world, and have results fed back to them.

Carnivore

There has been much alarmist nonsense written about the US 'sniffer' program known as Carnivore. In fact the capabilities of Carnivore were clearly defined in a statement by Donald M. Kerr, Assistant Director, Laboratory Division, Federal Bureau of Investigation, to a subcommittee of the US House of Representatives Committee on the Judiciary:

> In response to a critical need for tools to implement complex court orders, the FBI developed a number of capabilities including the software program called 'Carnivore'. Carnivore is a very specialized network analyzer or 'sniffer' which runs as an application program on a normal personal computer under the Microsoft Windows operating system. It works by 'sniffing' the proper portions of network packets and copying and storing only those packets which match a finely defined filter set programmed in conformity with the court order. This filter set can be extremely complex, and this provides the FBI with an ability to collect transmissions which comply with pen register court orders, trap & trace court orders, Title III interception orders, etc.
>
> It is important to distinguish now what is meant by 'sniffing'. The problem of discriminating between users' messages on the Internet is a complex one. However, this is exactly what Carnivore does. It does NOT search through the contents of every message and collect those that contain certain key words like 'bomb' or 'drugs'. It selects messages based on criteria expressly set out in the court order, for example, messages transmitted to or from a particular account or to or from a particular user. If the device is placed at some point on the network where it cannot discriminate messages as set out in the court order, it simply lets all such messages pass by unrecorded.
>
> Carnivore is a small-scale device intended for use only when and where it is needed. In fact, each Carnivore device is maintained at the FBI Laboratory in Quantico until it is actually needed in an active case. It is then deployed to satisfy the needs of a single case or court order, and afterwards, upon expiration of the order, the device is removed and returned to Quantico.
>
> The second issue is one of network interference. Carnivore is safe to operate on IP networks. It is connected as a passive collection device and does not have any ability to transmit anything on to the network. In fact, we go to great

A US Government diagram illustrates the principles of Carnivore: the 'sniffer' program monitors traffic on an IP (Internet Protocol) network, and collects data packets relating to a particular investigation.

lengths to ensure that our system is satisfactorily isolated from the network to which it is attached. Also, Carnivore is only attached to the network after consultation with, and with the agreement of, technical personnel from the ISP.

This, in fact, raises the third issue – that of ISP co-operation. To date, Carnivore has, to my knowledge, never been installed on to an ISP's network without assistance from the ISP's technical personnel.

Tempest

Tempest is another acronym that is widely misunderstood: it is often employed to describe technology by which a computer monitor can be viewed at a distance – using sophisticated electronics that can receive emissions from a monitor and convert them into a readable picture. In fact 'Tempest' is a specification for computer equipment to prevent just such monitoring.

As long ago as 1994, the US Joint Security Commission issued a report to the Secretary of Defense and the Director of Central Intelligence called 'Redefining Security'. It is worthwhile quoting the entire section that deals with Tempest:

Tempest (an acronym for Transient Electromagnetic Pulse Emanation Standard) is both a specification for equipment and a term used to describe the process for preventing compromising emanations. The fact that electronic equipment such as computers, printers, and electronic typewriters give off electromagnetic emanations has long been a concern of the US Government. An attacker using off-the-shelf equipment can monitor and retrieve classified or sensitive information as it is being processed without the user being aware that a loss is occurring. To counter this vulnerability, the US Government has long required that electronic equipment used for classified processing be shielded or designed to reduce or eliminate transient emanations. An alternative is to shield the area in which the information is processed so as to contain electromagnetic emanations or to specify control of certain distances or zones beyond which the emanations cannot be detected. The first solution is extremely expensive, with Tempest computers normally costing double the usual price. Protecting and shielding the area can also be expensive. While some agencies have applied Tempest standards rigorously, others have sought waivers or have used various levels of interpretation in applying the standard. In some cases, a redundant combination of two or three types of multi-layered protection was installed with no thought given either to cost or actual threat.

Communications monitoring receivers

Much of the equipment used to monitor terrorist communications is fixed, connected to the network being monitored – the public telephone system, or the internet. When a terrorist group is using mobile radio transceivers, a different approach is required. Sophisticated radio receiving equipment is used, either in fixed positions or mounted in vehicles, or a combination of both.

Typically the security services will use equipment such as the Racal RA3720 range of receivers, which offer monitoring and direction finding (DF) across the full range of HF, VHF and UHF bands of the radio spectrum. These receivers can be mounted in a vehicle, and used in conjunction with a directional antenna. Using three or more such vehicles makes it possible to obtain an accurate fix on any given transmission by means of triangulation.

The RA3720 receiver offers fast, comprehensive scanning capability, enabling the operator to acquire a new signal quickly. It is able to monitor and measure low-level signals in the presence of higher level emissions from nearby transmitters. The receivers incorporate integral panoramic displays with

Sophisticated vehicle-mounted radio monitoring equipment can be used with a direction-finding antenna to locate the source of a target's radio transmissions. Photos: Thales.

sweep widths that are adjustable up to 9.6MHz from the centre of a tuned frequency. RS232 and fast Ethernet interfaces allow remote control of the equipment, as well as data recording for later analysis of signal information.

Bugging and countermeasures

There is a huge amount of 'bugging' equipment available commercially, much of it sold to jealous wives/husbands, paranoid bosses and crooked businessmen looking to

Charles Bovill, who died in 2001 at the age of 90, teaching a class in electronic countermeasures. Bovill worked for SOE during World War II, and in later life developed a wide range of surveillance and anti-surveillance devices. Photos: © James Marchington

steal a march on their competitors (no doubt there are a few who fall into all three categories). These devices are interesting insofar as they provide a clue to the type of components available today, and are quite likely in use by certain criminal and terrorist organisations. However, it is probably fair to say that no self-respecting state security agency would use commercially available bugging equipment – not least because their targets can easily obtain and deconstruct the equipment and devise ways of defeating it.

Typical of such items are microphone/transmitters hidden in various innocent-looking items of office equipment – pens, calculators and the like. Alternatively the 'bug' may be small enough to be concealed inside a pot plant, under a table, behind a ceiling tile and so forth.

Battery life is one of the major problems with such items, so an ingenious solution is to build the bug into something that is normally plugged into the mains,

There is a wide variety of semi-professional 'bugging' equipment available on the open market, often with devices hidden in innocent-looking equipment such as mains adaptors, calculators and the like. Even a simple baby monitor can be adapted and used for surveillance.

drawing enough current from the supply to power the transmitter; one popular item is hidden inside a mains plug adaptor, while another replaces a regular mains socket fascia plate and is indistinguishable from the outside.

With video chips becoming smaller and cheaper every year, similar devices are now available with video capability. High Street electronics stores nowadays sell a video camera that fits in a match-box, and amateur James Bonds everywhere have tried their hand at fitting them into clocks, books, soft toys and a host of other likely and

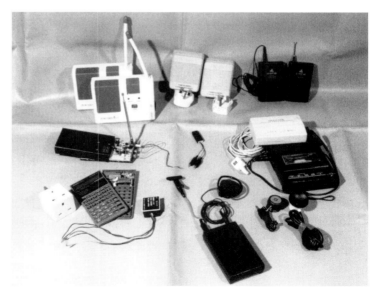

unlikely objects. A quick review of webcams on the internet will show that there are few places where you cannot place a camera nowadays!

Also available to the semi-professional are a wide range of telephone 'tapping' devices, either working on the induction loop principle or simply connecting across the pair of copper wires leading to the exchange. In fact, such items are so simple that they could quickly be constructed from easily available materials by anyone with a basic knowledge of electronics.

For the nervous businessman or unfaithful husband, also available commercially are a range of 'bugging detectors' and 'frequency jammers'. These might prove successful against an amateur bugging attempt, but might equally well lead to a dangerously false sense of security. Being widely available, they are of course well known to professional anti-terrorist operators, who have devised ways of defeating them.

The sort of amateur and semi-professional bugs described here transmit on predictable frequencies (advertised in the marketing companies' literature) and are quite easily discovered with simple detection equipment. A hard-wired device would present slightly more of a problem, but would be quickly found with the right equipment, such as an NLJD (Non-Linear Junction Detector). For the terrorist, the bugs he should worry about are the ones he cannot find!

The kind of semi-professional equipment available on the market has its place, but in inexperienced hands can give a false sense of security. Photo: © James Marchington.

AIRBORNE COUNTER-TERRORISM OPERATIONS

The modern terrorist is likely to find himself glancing nervously up at the sky from time to time. He is unlikely to see anything, but he knows there are eyes up there that can watch his every move, even listen to his conversations, and relay every detail back to the security services in real time.

Since the end of the Cold War, an impressive array of spy planes and satellites have been re-tasked to the fight against drugs, organised crime and terrorism. But development did not stop at the end of the Cold War. Work continues apace, and in addition to the familiar satellites, fixed-wing aircraft and helicopters, we now have a variety of unmanned craft that can be flown into hostile or inaccessible spots to record evidence and carry out reconnaissance – some of them looking uncannily like the UFOs of twentieth-century science fiction.

The trend is for these craft to become smaller, and hence less easily noticed by the target. One day this will lead to surveillance craft no bigger than insects, which could be flown unobtrusively into highly sensitive areas such as a terrorist training camp.

That is something for the future, but even today it is entirely possible that a terrorist meeting might be watched by a spy satellite orbiting in space, AWACS aircraft several miles up in the atmosphere, a FLIR-equipped helicopter on the horizon, and a Predator Unmanned Aerial Vehicle (UAV) – not to mention various ground-based bugs and sensors, and human operators in an OP.

Quite apart from the intelligence that all this surveillance can provide, knowing that the state security services have this capability acts as a deterrent, and places severe limitations on the terrorists' ability to operate effectively.

The US and other NATO forces are finding UAVs (Unmanned Aerial Vehicles) valuable in the fight against terrorism. Photo: US DoD.

Helicopters

Helicopters have long been used as an observation and surveillance platform for anti-terrorist work. One high-profile example was the murders of Corporals David Howes and Derek Wood in Penny Lane in Andersonstown in west Belfast on 19 March 1988. The two soldiers were in civilian dress when they mistakenly drove their silver Volkswagen into the funeral cortège of IRA terrorist Kevin Brady in Andersonstown Road. The atmosphere was highly charged; Brady himself had been killed a few days earlier in a lone loyalist's attack at the funeral of three IRA members who had been shot by the SAS in Gibraltar.

The UH-1N 'Huey' is designated a light-lift utility helicopter, and can carry up to 13 people or the equivalent weight of equipment. Helicopters like the Huey are widely used in counter-terrorist operations. Photo: US Air Force.

An army helicopter monitoring Brady's funeral filmed as the two soldiers were dragged from their vehicle, stripped, beaten, then taken in a black taxi to Penny Lane where they were shot dead. The army released some of the helicopter footage to the media, and it was shown on TV news – highlighting the ability of helicopters to obtain good-quality footage of places and events where it would not be possible to place cameras and operators on the ground.

The equipment has been improved over the years, and helicopters equipped with high-tech, gyro-stabilised, night-and-day surveillance equipment have become invaluable to police and anti-terrorist forces. They are used widely for tracking fugitives, both in vehicles and on foot, and have become a familiar sight over any demonstration or disturbance. During the May Day 2002 demonstrations in London, for example, four or five helicopters were circling slowly over the affected parts of central London for much of the day.

One notable exception to the use of helicopters for this type of work was the funeral of the Queen Mother in London in 2002. An air exclusion zone was established, and the Metropolitan Police did not fly helicopters over the area for fear of disrupting the solemnity of the occasion; instead coverage was provided by RAF aircraft flying much higher overhead.

It should be noted that the full range of military helicopters may be used in support of anti-terrorist operations. In Northern Ireland, for example, helicopters have been employed to insert patrols in difficult areas, and to deliver quick-reaction forces in the shortest possible time. Attack helicopters such as the Apache may be used to support an attack on a terrorist base, or in clearance operations. And the helicopter is a favourite method of inserting a SWAT or CRW team close to their objective with the minimum of warning – teams practise abseiling, fast-roping and jumping from helicopters on to ships, buildings and the like as part of hostage-rescue training.

Eurocopter AS 355N Twin Ecureuil ('Squirrel')

The Metropolitan Police's use of helicopters is typical of many modern police forces. Their machines are operated by the force's Air Support Unit (CO53). The resource is shared with Surrey Police and is officially titled the South East Region Police Air Support Unit. The unit operates three Eurocopter AS 355N 'Twin Squirrel' helicopters, with at least two aircraft on standby at any given time. This means that a helicopter can be in position anywhere in their area of coverage within a maximum of twelve minutes.

The view from a US Air Force MH-53 Pave Low helicopter: the full range of military helicopters is available for anti-terrorist operations when needed. Photo: US Air Force.

The unit's primary role is to support the policing of major events where public order or security could be an issue, but the craft are also used for various operations where overhead surveillance and tracking are an advantage – to pursue a fugitive, search for a missing person, etc.

The AS 355N is operated by many other police and security forces in the UK and elsewhere, inlcuding the Garda Síochána in the Republic of Ireland, the Dyfed-Powys Police in Wales, and the East Midlands and Lancashire Constabularies in England.

Power is provided by two Turbomeca Arrius 1A turboshafts, which provide high power with relatively low vibration (helping to reduce the noise experienced on the ground). The cabin is spacious and uncluttered, with good visibility, allowing specialist equipment to be installed.

A typical installation would include a thermal imaging camera and TV camera housed in a gyro-stabilised pod under the machine's nose. There will also be searchlights, PA system, moving map navigation, and a wealth of communications equipment – including encrypted radio links and microwave downlink to feed images to a control room in real time.

Specifications

Maximum take-off weight	2,540kg (2,600kg with cargo sling)
Take-off power	420kW
Cruise speed	235km/h (127 knots)
Range	720km (388 nautical miles)
Fuel capacity	577kg
Fuel consumption	180kg/h
Endurance	5 hrs max at 100km/h
Capacity	1 pilot, 4–6 passengers depending on tactical equipment fitted

Robinson R44 Police Helicopter

The Robinson R44 Police Helicopter is the police variant of Robinson's best-selling R44 Raven, an extremely successful small helicopter that is noted for its reliability and low operating costs; other variants include a Newscopter for TV news broadcasting.

The R44 Police comes ready-equipped with communications and imaging equipment, including an infra-red camera system. Hydraulic flight controls eliminate stick shake and control forces, improving control and reducing pilot fatigue. The cockpit provides panoramic views for pilot and passengers.

The aircraft has a cruise speed of 130mph, with a fuel consumption of 12–16 gallons per hour. It operates for 100 hours between inspections, and 12 years or 2,200 hours between overhauls.

McDonnell Douglas 500E

Another helicopter favoured by police and counter-terrorist forces is the McDonnell Douglas 500E. It is operated, for instance, by the Mesa Police Department Aviation

Section in the US. The Mesa Police helicopter averages ten flight hours per day, seven days per week, and answers an average of forty-eight calls each day. If the helicopter is in the air, the average response time to a scene is thirty-six seconds. Since the Aviation Section began using the helicopter, they have assisted in recovering over $4,600,000 in stolen property and in locating nearly 1,500 missing persons, most of them lost children.

Fixed wing aircraft

Helicopters are well suited to certain types of police and security work, such as crowd control or a fast response to a pursuit. However, fixed-wing aircraft have considerable advantages in other types of work – their higher operating altitude and greater range make them better suited, for example, to monitoring suspected drug- or arms-running vessels at sea.

Britten-Norman Defender 4000

Britten-Norman's Defender 4000 has become a popular choice with police and security forces worldwide, and is now used for law enforcement in more than twenty countries. It is used, for example, by the Greater Manchester Police, and by the Garda Síochána.

A high-wing monoplane with a rectangular fuselage section, the Defender 4000 is based on the well-proven Islander series. It is a robust and simple design which is simple to operate and maintain, and has the advantage of relatively low operating costs. Power comes from two Rolls-Royce Allison 25-B17F turbine engines, which are noted for their quiet operation.

The aircraft has an extended fuselage, which can accommodate a maximum of sixteen people, or be fitted with a range of surveillance and communications equipment. The nose cone will accommodate a 360-degree rotating antenna. Typically the equipment installed includes daylight and thermal cameras, digital radios and moving map navigation technology.

Specifications	
Maximum take-off weight	8,500lbs (3,855kg)
Maximum payload	1,598lbs (724kg)
Ceiling	25,000ft
Operational height	12,000–14,000ft
Cruise speed	176 knots (326km/h) max
Range	1,006 nautical miles
Endurance	>5 hours

E3-A Sentry

The E3-A Sentry is the main AWACS (All-Weather Surveillance and Control System) aircraft used by US and NATO forces. It is based around a modified commercial Boeing 707/320 airframe, with a rotating radar dome containing a radar that can identify and track vehicles and low-flying aircraft at a range of more than 320km.

The E3 Sentry AWACS aircraft was upgraded in 2001 to improve its anti-jamming capabilities and make use of the GPS navigation system. Photo: US Air Force.

The E-3 fleet was upgraded in 2001 to provide four major enhancements:

- Electronic Support Measures for passive detection, an electronic surveillance capability to detect and identify air and surface-based emitters.
- Joint Tactical Information Distribution System to provide secure, anti-jam communication for information distribution, position location and identification capabilities.
- An increase in the memory capability in the computer to accommodate JTIDS, EMS and future enhancements.
- Global Positioning System, a satellite-based positioning capability to provide precise global navigation.

Other major subsystems in the E-3 are navigation, communications and data processing. Consoles display computer-processed data in graphic and tabular format on video screens. Console operators perform surveillance, identification, weapons control, battle management and communications functions.

The radar and computer subsystems on the E-3 Sentry can gather and present broad and detailed battlefield information. Data is collected as events occur. This includes position and tracking information on enemy aircraft and ships, and location and status of friendly aircraft and naval vessels. The information can be sent to major command and control centres in rear areas or aboard ships. In time of crisis, this data can be forwarded to the President and Secretary of Defense in the United States.

In support of air-to-ground operations, the Sentry can provide direct information needed for interdiction, reconnaissance, airlift and close-air support for friendly ground forces. It can also provide information for commanders of air operations to gain and maintain control of the air battle.

It is a jam-resistant system that has performed missions while experiencing heavy electronic countermeasures. The flight path can quickly be changed according to mission and survival requirements. The E-3 can fly a mission profile for more than eight hours without refuelling. Its range and on-station time can be increased through in-flight refuelling and the use of an on-board crew rest area.

E3 aircraft are used as a surveillance asset in support of counter-drug and counter-terrorist missions.

Specifications	
Primary Function	Airborne surveillance, command, control and communications
Builder	Boeing Aerospace Co.
Power Plant	Four Pratt and Whitney TF33-PW-100A turbo-fan engines
Thrust	21,000 pounds (9,450 kilograms) each engine
Length	145 feet, 6 inches (44 metres)
Wingspan	130 feet, 10 inches (39.7 metres)
Height	41 feet, 4 inches (12.5 metres)
Radome	30 feet in diameter (9.1 metres), 6 feet thick (1.8 metres), mounted 11 feet (3.33 metres) above fuselage
Speed	Optimum cruise 360 mph (Mach 0.48)
Ceiling	Above 29,000 feet (8,788 metres)
Maximum Take-off Weight	347,000 pounds (156,150 kilograms)
Endurance	>8 hours (unrefuelled)
Unit Cost	$123.4 million
Crew	Flight crew of 4 plus mission crew of 13–19 specialists (depending on mission)
Date Deployed	March 1977
US Inventory	33 in service

U-2

First deployed back in 1955, the U-2 continues to provide continuous day and night, high-altitude, all-weather surveillance and reconnaissance in direct support of US and allied ground and air forces. It provides critical intelligence through all phases of conflict, from peacetime surveillance through low-intensity conflict to large-scale hostil-

The E3 Sentry is used by US and NATO forces for surveillance, command and control. It is based on a modified Boeing 707/320 airframe, and has a rotating radome measuring 30 feet in diameter. Photo: US Air Force.

The ageing U-2 continues to prove its worth as a high-altitude surveillance craft. Current models are derived from the original, 1955 version, but carry modern sensors. Photo: US Air Force.

ities. Intelligence gathered by U-2s was vital, for instance, to US and allied operations in the Gulf War and Afghanistan.

The U-2S is a single-seat, single-engine, high-altitude, surveillance and reconnaissance aircraft. Long, narrow, straight wings give the U-2 glider-like characteristics and allow it to lift heavy sensor payloads to unmatched high altitudes quickly, and keep them there for a long time.

The U-2 is capable of collecting multi-sensor photographic, electro-optic, infra-red and radar imagery, as well as collecting signals intelligence data. It can downlink data in near real-time to anywhere in the world.

The aircraft is notoriously difficult to fly due to its unusually challenging take-off and landing characteristics. Because of its high-altitude mission, the pilot must wear a full pressure suit. The aircraft has a General Electric F-118-101 engine that is fuel efficient and lightweight, negating the need for air refuelling on long missions.

The somewhat ageing fleet is currently undergoing an update that includes complete rewiring to reduce its electronic noise signature and allow a quieter platform for the newest generation of sensors. The sensors themselves are constantly being upgraded. The cockpit is being redesigned to replace the 1960s vintage round dial gauges with multifunction displays and complete 'glass cockpit' technology.

Current models are derived from the original version that made its first flight in August 1955. It was the U-2 that photographed the Soviet military installing missiles in Cuba on 14 October 1962, sparking the 'Cuban Missile Crisis'. It provided critical intelligence data during all phases of operations Desert Storm and Allied Force. The U-2 provides daily peacetime indications and warning intelligence collection from its current operating locations around the world.

Specifications	
Primary Function	High-altitude reconnaissance
Contractor	Lockheed Martin Aeronautics
Power Plant	One General Electric F-118-101 engine
Thrust	17,000 pounds
Length	63 feet (19.2 metres)
Height	16 feet (4.8 metres)
Wingspan	105 feet (32 metres)
Speed	475+ miles per hour (Mach 0.58)
Maximum Take-off Weight	40,000 pounds (18,000 kilograms)
Range	7,000 miles (6,090+ nautical miles)
Ceiling	Above 70,000 feet (21,212+ metres)
Crew	One (two in trainer models)
Date Deployed	U-2, August 1955; U-2R, 1967; U-2S, October 1994
Cost	Classified
US Inventory	37 in service

Aircraft-mounted cameras and imaging systems

In surveillance and counter-terrorist operations, an aircraft is little more than an airborne, mobile platform for the cameras and other sensors that provide the images needed. The effectiveness of aircraft in this role depends on the capabilities of the imaging systems they carry.

Modern cameras are capable of producing extraordinarily detailed images by day or night, through smoke and haze, at long range. They are mounted in stabilised turrets that allow the cameras to produce good results despite the inevitable vibration and movement of the aircraft. The resulting images are transmitted by radio link directly to the command centre in real time, providing accurate intelligence for commanders as well as recording evidence for later analysis and use in court proceedings.

Such equipment is invaluable in supporting a wide range of missions, including counter-drug operations, intelligence and evidence gathering, suspect tracking, crowd control and public safety.

FLIR Systems UltraForce II

FLIR Systems, based in the US and Sweden, designs high-performance stabilised camera systems to meet surveillance needs, day or night and on a variety of different platforms. The company's UltraForce II is a good example. It incorporates a four-axis stabilised composite turret that delivers exceptionally stable imagery.

The system features the next generation long-wave infra-red imager and a x54 zoom, 3-CCD broadcast quality colour TV camera. This flexible day/night, long-range imaging capability allows surveillance at greater altitude and at longer stand-off ranges than previously possible. An optional laser rangefinder and a host of other ancillary devices are available to extend the mission performance of UltraForce II.

FLIR Systems Star SAFIRE II

Continuing the evolution of the SAFIRE family, Star SAFIRE II sets new standards for range performance, stability and image quality. Incorporating the latest InSb focal plane array technology, Star SAFIRE II enables users to adopt stand-off distances 50 per cent greater than before, thereby increasing mission safety and stealth.

With increased magnification comes increased demands for stability, so FLIR has also developed new stabilisation techniques to address these needs. This is accomplished through the use of an advanced five-axis active stabilisation system to provide precise motion correction.

FLIR Systems UltraMedia LE

The UltraMedia LE is a long-range airborne stabilised surveillance system featuring an ultra-low-light camera. It combines a state-of-the-art low-light broadcast camera with FLIR's five-axis precision-stabilised turret, making a powerful surveillance system that can gather clear images under a wide range of lighting conditions.

The UltraMedia LE's 1,104mm zoom lens increases magnification by 46 per cent over the previous generation of systems. This translates into increased stand-off range, a greater ability to maintain stealth during surveillance missions, and higher-quality video evidence. UltraMedia LE's low-light capability enables it to pull images out of the darkness – from thousands of feet in the air.

Aerial Films GyroCam DNV

Aerial Films is another leading manufacturer of gyro-stabilised camera systems, offering airborne packages geared towards high-altitude surveillance applications for high-speed fixed wing aircraft. Aerial Films' GyroCam DNV camera system provides a high standard of long-lens performance, day or night. This surveillance system is a derivative of their popular GyroCam 36X, which has been widely used by major television stations across the United States and abroad.

Some of Aerial Films' GyroCam customers include the Tampa Police, the DEA, Pennsylvania State Police, Amtrak Police, Argentinian Federal Police, WNBC in New York and other broadcasters and law enforcement agencies around the world.

The GyroCam DNV surveillance package provides law enforcement with a multi-mission camera system that is operational in bright light, low light or no-light conditions. In conjunction with the GyroCam DNV system, Aerial Films has developed special long-range live technology which allows video images and sound to be sent live and in full colour from an aircraft to anywhere in the world. The GyroCam packages can also include a variety of videotape recorders, satellite GPS information and encryption units.

To showcase the GyroCam surveillance package, Aerial Films uses its own Gulfstream I demonstration aircraft equipped with a GyroCam DNV system and an array of transmission, monitoring and recording equipment. Aerial Films' team of in-house fabricators and engineers has designed and mounted GyroCams and the associated equipment to a variety of helicopters and fixed wing aircraft.

The GyroCam surveillance package is suited to surveillance, drug interdiction, maritime patrol, aerial mapping, as well as search and rescue.

RPVs/UAVs

The last twenty years have seen tremendous development in remote-controlled aircraft, equipped with an array of sensors, which can be flown over hostile territory without risking the life of a human pilot. These are known as Remotely Piloted Vehi-

An X-45A UCAV (Unmanned Aerial Combat Vehicle) at the NASA Dryden Research Center at Edwards Air Force Base, California. The aircraft completed its first flight 22 May 2002. Unmanned aircraft like this are set to transform the nature of warfare. Photos: US Air Force.

cles (RPVs) or Unmanned Aerial Vehicles (UAVs). They were used extensively in conflicts such as Kosovo and Afghanistan, where detailed intelligence was needed, yet few troops were available on the ground, and a slow, low-flying helicopter would run an unacceptably high risk of being hit by ground fire.

USAF RQ-1 Predator

The RQ-1 Predator is a medium-altitude, long-endurance unmanned aerial vehicle system for reconnaissance, surveillance and target acquisition. A fully operational system consists of four aircraft (with sensors), a Ground Control Station (GCS), a Predator Primary Satellite Link (PPSL), and fifty-five personnel for continuous twenty-four-hour operations.

The basic crew for the Predator is one pilot and two sensor operators. They fly the aircraft from inside the GCS via a C-Band line-of-sight data link or a Ku-Band satellite data link for beyond line-of-sight flight.

The aircraft is equipped with a colour nose camera (generally used by the aerial vehicle operator for flight control), a day variable aperture TV camera, a variable aperture infra-red camera (for low light/night), and a Tactical Endurance Synthetic Aperture Radar (TESAR) for looking through smoke, clouds, or haze. The cameras produce full motion video and the SAR still-frame radar images. The three sensors are carried on the same airframe but cannot be operated simultaneously.

Predators are also capable of being used in the offensive role, carrying the Multispectral Targeting System, laser designator and two laser-guided Hellfire anti-tank missiles. A Predator thus equipped destroyed a 4x4 vehicle thought to be used by a Taleban leader in Afghanistan in 2001.

Each Predator aircraft can be disassembled into six main components and loaded into a container nicknamed 'the coffin'. This enables all system components and support equipment to be rapidly deployed worldwide, usually being carried in a C-130 Hercules.

Below and on the opposite page, the Predator UAV can be used in the offensive role, armed with a targeting system and two Hellfire anti-tank missiles. Photos: US Air Force.

Specifications

Primary Function	Airborne surveillance reconnaissance and target acquisition
Contractor	General Atomics Aeronautical Systems Incorporated
Power Plant	Rotax 914 four-cylinder engine producing 101 horsepower
Length	27 feet (8.22 metres)
Height	6.9 feet (2.1 metres)
Weight	1,130 pounds (512 kilograms) empty, maximum take-off weight 2,250 pounds (1,020 kilograms)
Wingspan	48.7 feet (14.8 metres)
Speed	Cruise speed around 84 mph (70 knots), up to 135 mph
Range	> 400 nautical miles (454 miles)
Ceiling	> 25,000 feet (7,620 metres)
Fuel Capacity	665 pounds (100 gallons)
Payload	450 pounds (204 kilograms)
System Cost	$40 million
Inventory	48 in service with US forces

USAF Global Hawk

Global Hawk, launched in February 1998, is a high-altitude, long-endurance, unmanned air vehicle designed to operate with a range of 13,500 nautical miles, at altitudes up to 65,000 feet and with an endurance of forty hours. During a typical reconnaissance mission, the aircraft can fly 3,000 miles to an area of interest, remain on station for twenty-four hours, survey an area the size of the state of Illinois (40,000 square nautical miles), and then return 3,000 miles to its operating base. Sensors on

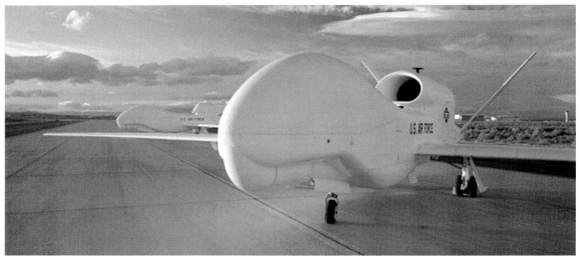

The unmanned Global Hawk can fly 3,000 miles to a target area, spend 24 hours relaying images in near real-time, and then return 3,000 miles to base. Photos: US Air Force.

board the aircraft can provide near-real-time imagery of the area of interest to the battlefield commander via worldwide satellite communication links and the system's ground segment.

USAF DarkStar

The DarkStar system is designed for aerial reconnaissance in highly defended areas by using low observable characteristics. It can operate at a range of 500 nautical miles from the launch site and will be able to loiter over the target area for eight hours at an altitude of more than 45,000 feet, carrying either an electro-optical or synthetic aperture radar payload.

DarkStar did not get off to an auspicious start. The first vehicle crashed during its second flight, on 22 April 1996. The craft underwent radical modifications to its structure and control software, and re-emerged as Tier III Minus DarkStar.

The new craft was trialled successfully at the NASA Dryden Flight Research Center, Edwards Air Force Base, California, in June 1998. It flew for forty-four minutes, achieving a height of 5,000 feet and successfully executing a fully autonomous flight from take-off to landing using the GPS.

The US Air Force's Tier III Minus DarkStar is a 'stealth' UAV, which can spend up to eight hours at 45,000 feet above a target area, observing with electro-optics or synthetic aperture radar. Photo: US Air Force.

Phoenix (UK)

Britain's first excursion into the field of UAVs was not a huge success. Phoenix was ten years in development, and came into service six years late, at a cost of £300m. It was available in time for the conflict in Kosovo, but did not acquit itself well. It was unable to provide the real-time images that the US and UK forces required, and twelve of the craft were lost, at a cost of £200,000 each. One was captured intact and went on display in a museum in Yugoslavia. The programme was officially abandoned in 2002.

Phoenix was made almost entirely of composite materials, including Kevlar, glass fibre, carbon reinforced plastics and Nomex honeycomb. It was powered by a 25hp two-stroke, flat-twin engine. It had a wingspan of 5.5m, launch weight of 177kg, oper-

Phoenix was not very successful in Kosovo; twelve craft were lost, and one ended up on display in a Yugoslav museum. The programme was abandoned in 2002. Photo: BAe Systems.

ating radius of 50km and a maximum altitude of 2,700m (9,000ft). The surveillance equipment, which had a day-night capability, was data-linked to a ground station to transmit the intelligence gathered directly to a command post.

Watchkeeper (UK)

With the demise of Phoenix, the UK MoD announced a £500m procurement programme for its successor, Watchkeeper, to provide tactical reconnaissance and surveillance capability for the next thirty years. Thales Defence has put together a team based at its Crawley site in the UK to develop Watchkeeper. The Thales team includes Thales Sensors, Elbit Systems, QinetiQ, Aerosystems International, Thales Defence Information Systems and Thales Optronics. They have chosen the Elbit Systems/Silver Arrow Hermes 180 and 450 as the basis for the Watchkeeper air vehicles.

AROD, MSSMP and beyond

The US military Spawar Center in San Diego has been working on remotely flown craft since the early 1980s. Their early craft was named AROD (Airborne Remotely Operated Device) and went through several variants. Powered by a 26hp petrol engine driving a single propeller, it was controlled with a joystick by an operator on the ground. The device trailed a fibre-optic cable which carried the flight control information and relayed back images from the two on-board cameras. AROD proved not to be sufficiently stable in flight, however, and the need to trail a cable limited its range and usefulness, so the program was dropped in the late 1980s.

One of AROD's successors, MSSP (Multipurpose Security and Surveillance Mission Platform) gives an idea of how such devices may look in the future. The MSSP program was begun in 1992, and was designed to provide a rapidly-deployable, extended-range surveillance capability for a wide range of missions, including support to counter-drug and border patrol operations as well as a range of military roles such as fire control and assessment of areas suspected of being contaminated with biological or chemical agents.

MSSP is based on Sikorsky's Cypher, a vertical take-off and landing vehicle with a single, large, enclosed rotor. The sensor package includes a visible light video camera, infra-red video camera and laser range finder. Combined with GPS positioning technology, this can pinpoint the location of a target to within a few centimetres.

The MSSP craft carries electronics to process the information received by its sensors. It is capable of reacting to events, following a pre-programmed response and alerting the operator, as well as sending images back to the operating station by radio.

MSSP was demonstrated in a MOUT (Military Operations in Urban Terrain) scenario 1997 at Fort Benning in Georgia. The vehicle flew down city streets, looking through upper- and lower-storey windows, providing look-out support ahead of advancing troops. It also was able to drop sensors in inaccessible spots, and carried a laser rangefinder/target designator. It could fly to a suitable vantage point, land and continue to relay back pictures and data.

In other words, the vehicle proved it could search for and find a target, relay a picture and precise location back to the command centre, and then 'illuminate' the target for an aerial strike by a 'smart' bomb – all without the need for a single human being to put his boots on enemy soil.

Such devices are not yet in widespread use, but development work continues, often in secret. As they become smaller and more powerful, we can expect to see them becoming a regular feature of counter-terrorist operations.

Satellite imaging

The United States currently operates two major satellite imaging systems – Keyhole and Vega. A new program, known as 8X, is under way and will provide better coverage of the entire surface of the globe.

Although originally conceived to keep watch on the Soviet Union and other Cold War enemies, the 'spy satellite' network has proved to be enormously useful in the war against terrorism, as well as in operations against drugs and organised crime.

In the past, satellites were of limited value in these roles because of the relatively poor-quality imagery they produced, and the fact that they only passed over the required location at intervals of twenty-four hours or more. Both these problems have

Some high-quality satellite imaging is available commercially: this picture of the Pentagon was captured by the Ikonos satellite, which can provide 1-metre resolution images. Photo: Space Imaging.

A US Multispectral Thermal Imaging satellite was launched in March 2000, and may be used to monitor arms proliferation. This MTI image shows a highway intersection in Albuquerque, New Mexico. Photo: Sandia.

been addressed, however, and satellite imagery is now a vital part of anti-terrorist operations. As the US continues to upgrade its satellite network, this trend will continue.

Keyhole

The latest version of the Keyhole series is the KH-13, which is about 4.5 metres in diameter, and over 15 metres long. It operates with a perigee of about 150 miles and an apogee of about 600 miles. The latest version carries more fuel than the original model – between 10,000 and 15,000lbs – which permits a longer lifetime of up to eight years. The satellite can adjust its orbit to provide coverage of areas of particular interest, and can manoeuvre to avoid anti-satellite interceptors.

KH-13 carries infra-red and thermal infra-red imaging equipment, enabling it to produce images during darkness. The satellites carry the Improved CRYSTAL Metric System (ICMS), which places markings on its returned images that allow accurate matching of images with mapping and GPS data. The satellite has sophisticated electronics to digitally enhance images before relaying them in real time to ground stations via Milstar relay satellites. Its image resolution is approaching 10 centimetres.

The later models have advanced infra-red capability which can 'see through' camouflage, and even detect buried structures. Using the thermal data to detect temperature differences between objects, analysts can determine such things as which factories are operational and whether tank engines have been running recently.

Each Keyhole satellite passes over a given point at the same time each day, making it easier to detect changes taking place in the target area by comparing one day's photos against another. This does, however, have the disadvantage that a well-informed target can hide for the few minutes each day when the satellite is overhead. This tactic was reportedly used by Serb forces in Kosovo, and by Osama bin Laden's terrorist camps in Afghanistan.

8X

The first 8X satellite was launched in May 1999. It was the first of a series of twenty-four multi-function satellites that will eventually cover the globe, passing over any given spot on the planet every fifteen minutes.

The 8X satellite has superior optics to Keyhole, and typically follows an elongated, elliptical path, known as a 'Molniya' orbit, where its speed slows down dramatically at the apogee. Its high-quality sensors compensate for the longer ranges.

Titan IVB is used to carry US military satellites into space. It can lift a payload of up to 47,700 lbs (21,682kg) into a low earth orbit. Photo: US Air Force.

Vega

The first Vega satellite was launched on 2 December 1988 from the space shuttle orbiter *Atlantis*. A second followed in March 1991, and a third in October 1997. The satellites have operated in orbits of approximately 400 miles and at inclinations of 57–68 degrees respectively.

Unlike the electro-optical system of the Keyhole series, Vega satellites carry an imaging radar. This closes what had been a major gap in US capabilities by providing imagery even when targets are covered by clouds.

Vega has a resolution of 3–5 feet, which is reportedly sufficient to allow discrimination between tanks and armoured personnel carriers.

COMMUNICATIONS, COMMAND AND CONTROL

Fast, effective, secure communications are vital to every anti-terrorist operation. Clearly the members of a team must communicate with one another during the operation, but the role of communications goes much further than this. Commanders and their political masters must be kept informed, and their decisions passed back to those who will implement them. Agencies need to communicate internationally so as to coordinate their efforts and cooperate, so that they can effectively combat terrorist groups that are increasingly operating across international borders.

Throughout the chain, the communications systems used need to be robust enough to overcome the practical difficulties of distance and difficult terrain (including urban environments which are notoriously troublesome for radio communication), and resist attempts to intercept or jam the signals.

Modern communications systems are expected to handle much more than simple voice communication. The ability to send data, still images and video enables the security services to work much more effectively – for example, distributing a photograph of a suspected terrorist to border control points, or transmitting an image of a suspected IED to an EOD expert who has encountered a similar device before.

Anti-terrorist operations involve a range of different agencies, including a state's army, navy and air force, Special Forces, police, immigration, air traffic control and a host of others. It is a huge challenge to provide a communications system that

Anti-terrorist operations may involve several different agencies, including the armed forces and police. Integrating communications between them can pose difficulties. Photo: Thales.

enables all these different groups to work together effectively, make the most of the capabilities of modern communications, and not become outdated within a short time.

It is worth noting that military and police communications systems are fundamentally different. A police system is built on the premise that officers are working in 'friendly' territory, where communications equipment such as repeaters and antennae can be installed at fixed points. Military systems, on the other hand, must be capable of operation in 'hostile' territory. An army cannot assume there will be any infrastructure available to them; every piece of equipment they use must be rugged and highly mobile so that the communications system can keep up with the ebb and flow of battle. It must also continue to operate effectively in the face of hostile action – including a host of electronic warfare measures that may be taken by an enemy trying to jam their command and control system.

This fundamental difference in the requirements of police and military users explains their very different type of equipment and operating procedures. It can also lead to complications in joint operations involving multiple agencies. During the Foot and Mouth Disease outbreak in the UK in 2001, we frequently saw the army commander, Brigadier Alex Birtwhistle, talking to an army radio operator while taking a call on his personal mobile phone, as he liaised between army units in the field, police and local authorities, and the government in Westminster. A joint services anti-terrorist operation faces the same challenges.

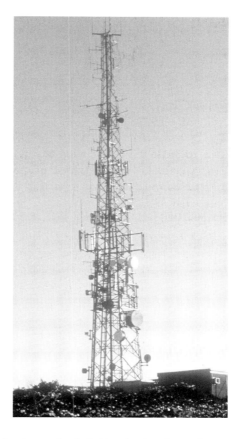

Modern anti-terrorist communications use a broad range of frequencies in the radiomagnetic spectrum, ranging from 2MHz to microwaves of 1,500MHz and above. Photo: © James Marchington.

Terrestrial Trunked Radio

Modern police forces are increasingly moving towards digital trunked radio systems, which provide highly versatile and effective communications between individual officers, vehicle patrols, control centres and senior commanders.

Police in the UK are in the process of transferring to a new trunked radio system known as Airwave. Airwave is the name given to the Terrestrial Trunked Radio

The RA4800 field telephone system can be deployed quickly and will interface with radios and public telephone systems. Photo: Thales.

(TETRA) national public safety radio communications project being managed by PITO (the Police Information Technology Organisation). TETRA offers fast call set-up, excellent group communication support with remote or local call centres, direct operation between handsets, data handling for maps and documents, and excellent security features.

Previously the police forces around the UK were using a variety of systems. The Metropolitan Police Service, for instance, were using an analogue

Right: Terrestrial Trunked Radio systems represent the future of police radio systems. They allow transmission of data such as text messaging and images as well as voice communication, and can interface with other systems such as the public telephone network. Photo: Motorola.

Top right: Unlike the old analogue systems, modern digital police radio systems are not vulnerable to eavesdropping with simple scanners available in High Street electronics stores. Photos: Motorola.

Right and far right: A variety of terminals can connect to a trunked radio network, allowing data communication as well as voice calls. Photo: Motorola.

trunked radio system known as Metradio, which was introduced from 1996. Many of the systems in use were vulnerable to eavesdropping. Anyone with a simple scanner costing a hundred pounds or so could tune in to the police frequencies and listen to their communications. Hobbyists published frequency lists on the internet, so it was a simple matter for a criminal or terrorist to look up the frequencies used by police and security services covering his intended area of operation. The new digital trunked radio systems address this and many other operational problems that have dogged security forces for many years.

The contract for Airwave was announced in March 2000; the £2.5bn contract, paid for by the Home Office, was awarded to BT. The service is a fully managed, digital

One of the important features of a digital trunked radio system is the emergency call facility. An officer in trouble can put out an instant alert; his message may contain GPS data to identify his precise location. Photo: Motorola.

private mobile radio service, based on the TETRA open standard which has been developed over a number of years by members of the European Telecommunications Standards Institute (ETSI) to meet the future needs of emergency services through-out Europe and beyond. The service will provide a range of features including:

- Mobile radio coverage on all motorways, A and B roads.
- Hand-held radio coverage to meet individual force requirements.
- Voice calls through the network, including point-to-point, broadcast and group calls.
- Data transmissions including Short Message Service, Status Messaging and Packet-Mode (IP) data.
- The ability to connect Airwave with other systems including the national Public Switched Telephone Network, Private Telephone Networks, Inter net Protocol (IP) data, call recording systems and communications and control equipment.
- Roaming and inter-working between users within a single organisation, or different organisations using the Airwave service, between control rooms of the same or different organisations, across any geographic area covered by the Airwave service.
- Emergency call facility for officer safety.
- Encryption to protect voice and data messages from eavesdroppers.

Airwave was piloted by Lancashire Constabulary. The pilot system was accepted into operational service on 6 September 2001, triggering the national roll-out – starting with Greater Manchester police (GMP), who hoped to be using the Airwave Service in time for the Commonwealth Games in 2002. It is planned to complete the roll-out to all fifty-three police forces in England, Scotland and Wales within five years.

TETRA handsets are smaller, lighter and more sophisticated than their analogue predecessors, giving officers better communications that are more reliable and secure. Photo: Motorola.

Suffolk Police announced in early 2002 that they had gone 'live' on Airwave, becoming the first police force in the country to use the new generation, smaller and more technologically advanced radio handsets provided by Motorola through SIS (Securicor Information Systems).

Colin Jackson, Suffolk Police's Airwave project manager, was quoted at the time highlighting the advantages of the new system:

The radio is the operational police officer's lifeline. The existing radio network in Suffolk is more than 20 years old. The network had huge holes in it, where officers would have no communication, or – because of something called 'East Coast Interference' – our officers often had more chance of talking to trawler fishermen in the North Sea or taxi drivers in Holland than with their colleagues just a few miles down the road.

And, to make matters worse, for just a few pounds local criminals could buy a scanner and listen to the police network, so they were always warned of any police activity and could avoid arrest or ditch incriminating evidence. Airwave will provide a reliable, secure communication network across the entire county. It comes with the added benefits of allowing officers to make telephone calls out and generally being more accessible to their colleagues and the community.

This type of digital trunked radio system represents the future of police and security services communications, and will be the preferred choice for anti-terrorist operations of the future.

MILITARY COMMUNICATIONS

Military communications systems are designed for battlefield conditions and use a wide range of hardware, including hand-held tactical sets, man-pack radios and vehicle-mounted sets. Photo: Thales.

As explained earlier, military communications systems are based around the needs of the battlefield. The military uses the full radio spectrum, from short-wave in the area of 2MHz through to microwave frequencies of 10GHz and even beyond, with battlefield communications generally in the HF, VHF and UHF frequencies. A huge range of equipment is employed, including small handheld tactical sets, man-pack radios and vehicle-mounted sets.

Clansman

The equipment used by the British Army is typical of the radio equipment used by many forces worldwide. They currently use the Clansman family of tactical radios, which comprises several different sets operating on HF, VHF and UHF frequencies (between 1.6MHz and 470MHz). This equipment came into general service around the time of the Falklands Conflict in the 1980s. At the time it offered significant advantages, notably:

The Thales RA108 headset, one of a range of headsets designed for use by infantry and special forces. Photo: Thales.

■   The audio gear and battery charging equipment can be interchanged between radio sets. This simplifies spares support.
■   Common operating controls and procedures. This reduces the training time for operators.
■   Simple maintenance features which reduce time spent in training and repairs.
■   Interoperability between different radios.
■   Several radios can be used in close proximity, even in the same vehicle, without interfering with each other.
■   Capable of worldwide deployment in rugged conditions.

Among many of the soldiers who used the newly introduced Clansman equipment during the Falklands campaign in 1982, there was considerable enthusiasm. Gone were the problems of 'netting-in' and the constant sound of static in the operator's ears. The PRC-349 section radio was reliable and with its throat microphone allowed section commanders to communicate easily while handling a weapon, notebook or map. The PRC-351 man-pack platoon radio was lighter, at 8.2kg, and more reliable than its predecessor. This led to platoon and company commanders carrying radios, which meant that command and control became faster and more reliable.

Clansman has several deficiencies, particularly its vulnerability to electronic attack. The problem of Electronic Counter Measures (ECM) was identified from experience in the Falklands and work in Project Targe in 1983. A number of improvements have been made to Clansman over the years, in particular the introduction of a Tactical Data Encryption System (TDES) known as Kipling. This has brought a major change in the way information is exchanged in the forward battle area – from voice to data transmission. There has also been widespread use of Clansman Secure Speech Harness (CSSH), which allows Clansman to operate in a secure mode.

Regardless of this, Clansman is not and never will be a twenty-first-century tactical radio system. Due to problems with implementing CSSH across the full range of Clansman equipment, operators still have to use BATCO (a form of manual encryption using sheets issued at intervals) or TDES, which limits their operational effectiveness. It is significant that, during the Gulf War, when 7 and 4 Armoured Brigades started their short but intense drive across southern Iraq, they dispensed with BATCO since its use slowed operations and had the potential for confusion.

The Clansman system also does not use the electromagnetic spectrum effectively. There is considerable congestion in the VHF part of the spectrum, between 30 MHz and 300 MHz, used by Combat Net Radio. This is compounded by the limited frequency range of individual VHF sets. That in turn limits flexibility in frequency management, especially in response to interception and jamming. Clansman has a limited capacity for transmitting and handling data and cannot support the future data distribution requirements of CIS on the battlefield.

Clansman equipment can be integrated with Ptarmigan, the British Army's mobile, secure battlefield communications system. Ptarmigan is computer-controlled and consists of a network of electronic exchanges or Trunk Switches that are connected by satellite and multichannel radio relay (TRIFFID) links, providing voice, data, telegraph and fax communications. Ptarmigan also offers mobile telephone or Single Channel Radio Access (SCRA), which gives isolated or mobile users an entry point into the system.

Bowman

Having identified the problems with the Clansman system, and set out the requirements for a Future Combat Radio, the British MoD set up the Bowman project. Bowman was intended to provide a whole range of benefits accruing from the latest technology in radio communications, including:

- Making effective use of a congested and hostile EMS (Electro Magnetic Spectrum).
- Incorporating effective ECM techniques.
- Fully secure.
- Provide flexible modes of communications (data and voice).
- Interoperable with allies' equipment.
- Survivable in conventional and NBC environments.
- Flexible, reliable, simple to operate, easy to maintain and robust.

The Bowman project was beset with problems, as costs spiralled and the original specification was overtaken by changing requirements and new technology. The project was put back out to tender, and eventually awarded to CDC (part of General

Dynamics) in a £1.7bn deal – some nineteen years after the need for a new combat radio had originally been raised. Some 20,000 military vehicles will be equipped and 100,000 personnel will be trained on Bowman by October 2007.

Bowman will provide a secure digital voice and data communication system for the UK armed forces, and will be based on Internet protocol. It will include land-based command and control systems, and will provide the infrastructure to support all digitisation applications over the next 30 years. It will allow voice communications on secure radios over the air and through gateway interfaces to systems using agreed NATO, European and commercial standards and protocols.

Britain is not the only country to find that its military communications systems are lagging behind the needs of its users. During peacekeeping operations in Bosnia in 2002, US soldiers took to purchasing commercial FRS (Family Radio Service) units, such as the Motorola Talkabout and Uniden Eco, for squad-level communications.

Thales PR4G Fastnet combat net radios provide secure voice and data communication, using encryption and fast frequency hopping. Free channel search helps combat enemy attempts at jamming. Photo: Thales.

The RA3185 Modular Cobra headset is designed for modern rapid reaction forces. The system includes various components that are interchangeable in seconds, so the equipment can be quickly reconfigured as needed. Photo: Thales.

These units were smaller, more powerful and more reliable than the issued equipment – such as the AN/PRC-127, AN/PRC-119 and F3S – despite being originally designed for families to keep in touch when hiking or at the shopping mall. Similarly, British soldiers on exercise have often discovered that their personal mobile phone provides an effective way to call up fire support when the combat net is busy – although this would not be an option in a real battle.

Thales AN/PRC-148 Tactical Hand-Held Radio
The Thales AN/PRC-148 is a good example of a modern tactical hand-held radio (THHR). It has been selected by the US Marine Corps under their THHR program.

Weighing less than 2lbs, it is a powerful and capable radio that interfaces well with other radios in a system.

Output power is selectable between 100mW and 5W, and the radio will operate on frequencies between 30 and 512MHz, using AM or FM, with frequency steps of 5 and 6.25kHz. It can handle voice and data communications, with optional SINCGARS SIP, HAVEQUICK II, ANDVT, and Retransmit. It has 100 pre-set memory channels, which can be user-programmed using the front panel, programmed via a PC computer link, or 'cloned' from one radio to another.

Controls include an On/Off/Volume/Whisper/Zeroize knob, sixteen-position channel select knob, large tactile PTT (Push-To-Talk) switch, squelch override push-button, backlit seven-button keypad (NVG Compatible) and two software config-urable option keys. There is a 32x80 pixel backlit LCD display showing channel name/frequency, group name, clear/secure mode, key location, battery capacity and transmit power.

The radio offers a variety of standard connectors, allowing it to interface with other equipment such as GPS receivers, antennae, microphones, etc. It offers security to US COMSEC Type 1.

Specifications	
Length	8.44ins (21.44cm)
Width	2.63ins (6.68cm)
Depth	1.52ins (3.86cm)
Weight	30.6oz (867.5g)
Finish	Matt black, non-reflective
Operating Temperature	–31° to 60° C
Immersion	20m (AN/PRC-148(V)1(C) version)
Batteries	Rechargeable Lithium-Ion 3,000 mAH
	>8 hours life at 5W*
	Commercial Lithium cells
	10 hours life at 5W*
	*Standard Duty Cycle (8:1:1)
Accessories available	Vehicle adaptor
	Radio holster
	Radio system carrying bag
	AC powered single battery charger
	AC/DC powered 6-way battery charger
	Specialised audio accessories
	GPS, cloning and data cables
	PC programmer
	Special power adaptor interface

Covert and special purpose radio accessories

In addition to the general need for communications between fixed and mobile units, command posts, etc, anti-terrorist operations often require various types of special

A headset enables the user to maintain radio communication while leaving both hands free to aim and fire a weapon. Photo: Thales.

equipment. Surveillance operations sometimes require operatives to work under-cover – maintaining communications with other team members while appearing to be going about their ordinary daily business unencumbered by radio equipment. Assault teams in hostage rescue and similar operations have their own, very specific require-ments. Special equipment has been developed for these uses, and is constantly being refined in response to the needs of CRW and SWAT teams.

Davies CT400 communications system

Davies Industrial Communications Ltd was established in 1972 for the design and manufacture of communications equipment. In the late 1980s Davies successfully completed development and trials for a new generation of Special Forces' ancillaries known as the CT100 System. Today, Davies is recognised as the world's primary supplier of Special Forces' audio ancillaries with their latest range, the CT400 System.

CT400 was developed to enhance the quality of communication within Special Forces teams by offering individual users a large range of options specifically to meet their requirements.

Davies Waterproof Special Forces Communications Systems

Davies produces a number of diverse waterproof communications systems that are currently in service with SF teams throughout the world. These systems allow the submersion of most two-way radios to 25 feet (8 metres), whether they were originally manufactured to be waterproof or not. They are particularly suited to waterborne Special Forces operations, and harsh environments such as jungle.

Davies FAST Communications Harness

An important part of the CT400 system is the communications harness, which attaches to the user's body and links the various parts needed to operate the radio while engaged in an operation. The Davies FAST range of Communications Harnesses all incorporate a junction box, a PTT switch, a microphone and an earphone.

Some of the FAST systems are designed to be used in conjunction with a respirator, and incorporate a Respirator Microphone Adaptor. This fits on to the external speech port of a respirator such as the SF10, and does not compromise the integrity of the respirator.

FAST Systems that incorporate a Wired Earphone can be used with a wide range of accessories including Ear Hangers, Acoustic Tubes and Electronic Ear Defenders.

Davies Tacmic CT

The TACMIC CT is a Speaker Microphone and Communications Harness in one. There are five models within the TACMIC CT range, each of which features a speaker, microphone, side mounted heavy duty PTT switch, 3.5mm earphone socket, remote PTT socket and ancillaries socket.

The ancillaries socket allows the connection of a large range of communications headsets, inductors, or other types of microphone such as a throat microphone or body microphone.

Certain TACMIC CT models are fitted with an internal inductor for use during covert applications and/or sequential tone signalling. This allows the user to repeatedly press his PTT switch and transmit tone signals instead of speech. The number of presses will translate to a pre-defined team code.

Davies Lash

The Davies LASH is a throat microphone and earphone in one, and is widely used in the USA. A non-occluding acoustic tube/earmould is fitted to the earphone to direct all received sounds to the user's ear.

Davies Covert Systems

Davies's range of body-worn covert communications equipment uses the latest microcomputer technology to offer advanced features and extend operational capability. Certain systems are fitted with sequential tone signalling. The Covert 500 range comprises four systems, each of which incorporates the following:

> ■ A junction box with built-in tone board (three out of four systems feature sequential tone signalling)
> ■ A PTT/sequential tone signalling switch (where applicable)
> ■ A micro-loop inductive loop with internal microphone or a Collarset I inductive coil with built-in microphone
> ■ An inductive ear piece

Phonak Communications Phonito

Davies Industrial Communications Ltd distributes Phonito, manufactured by Phonak Communications AG. Phonito is a wireless earpiece that fits comfortably and discreetly in the ear and incorporates a volume control, loudness-limiting circuit (to protect the user from high sound levels) and a squelch circuit, which silences the receiver totally when there are no speech signals present.

Phonito has been designed to have very low battery consumption. An average battery lifetime is 100 hours and an end-of-life battery circuit produces a warning signal to inform the user when the battery needs changing.

Phonak Communications MicroEAR

Phonak also produce the MicroEar, claimed to be the smallest radio receiver in the world. MicroEar is supplied pre-tuned to the user's selected frequency (VHF narrow band FM between 138 and 240MHz). It has a battery life of fifteen to thirty hours, volume control, background noise filter and automatic frequency control, and offers good reception within distances up to a mile, depending on transmitter and radio conditions.

Thales Acoustics RA500 covert audio accessories

Thales Acoustics produce a range of covert radio accessories for use in surveillance work and the like. The system is based around the RA502 Inductive Earpiece, a wireless earphone that receives radio signals from a combined induction coil and microphone that is installed under the user's collar or shirt. The third part of the system is a PTT switch which is held in the user's hand, typically with the cable hidden in the sleeve. The induction coil/microphone and PTT switch are connected to the radio transceiver via a connector block.

The system is designed to connect to most available transceivers. The transceiver itself is worn concealed in a holster under the clothing. The system allows an operator to appear unencumbered with radio equipment, yet remain in constant communication with other team members. If he cannot talk into the microphone without compromising himself, pressing the PTT switch a pre-arranged number of times will make it possible to communicate in a simple code of 'one press means yes, two means no', etc.

The Thales RA500 series of radio accessories enable a covert operator to remain in contact with other team members, and can be concealed under normal clothing. Photo: Thales.

Elbit SC3 Sniper Control System

The Elbit SC3 Sniper Control System is designed for situations where a number of snipers are deployed to cover an incident – typically this might be a hostage scenario, where a group of terrorists is holding hostages in a building, train, bus or aircraft.

The system has a camera on each sniper's telescopic sight, which relays the sight pictures to a central point, using either a fixed cable or radio link. The camera fits on to the telescopic sight in thirty seconds, with no effect on the rifle's zero. The camera is connected to an image processor/transmitter contained in a ruggedised box, which will transmit the image in real time for a distance of up to 5km in open country, or about 850m in built-up areas.

The sight pictures are displayed on 4-inch monitors at the control point, together with a 'ready' indication operated by each sniper. This provides the commander with a constantly up-to-date picture of the situation, and the ability to coordinate the fire of a sniper group in a way that would be impossible with the alternative method of radio checks with each sniper in turn.

Command post

Displays	4in CRT with brightness and contrast controls
Electrical supply	12/24v DC, or from mains power with adaptor.

Sniper modules (SP-10)

Weight	400g
Dimensions	100 x 55 x 45mm
Transmitted power	8W
Carrier frequency	800–950MHz FM
Power supply	Lithium batteries, life approx 8hrs continuous

Satellites like Inmarsat and Skynet provide truly global communications for security forces using the new generation of smaller, lighter SATCOM ground terminals. Photos: BAe Systems.

SATELLITE COMMUNICATIONS

SKYNET 4B SATCOM system

Satellite Communications (SATCOM) systems enable the exchange of secure voice and data, to and from nearly anywhere in the world. Operations in the Falklands and Namibia proved the value of satellite communications, and during the Gulf War and in Afghanistan there was extensive use of SATCOM ground terminals. Now that manufacturers have produced truly man-packable SATCOM terminals, satellite communications are a realistic option – and a very useful one – for remote Special Forces patrols, OPs and the like.

SCAMP

The Collins Single Channel Anti-jam Man-portable (SCAMP) AN/PSC-11 terminal uses the Milstar system to provide worldwide secure, jam resistant, covert voice, data and imagery communications.

Raytheon AN/PSC-5

AN/PSC-5 has capabilities for UHF/VHF, LOS and SATCOM/DAMA. With all these features, it reduces the operator's burden, while increasing his communications capability. Although this system was originally created as a man-pack, its versatile design means that it can be used in other applications such as airborne, vehicular, shipboard and fixed station.

Man-pack terminals have made satellite communications a viable option for small patrols and OPs. Photo: US Army.

Electronic Countermeasures and 'Jamming'

'Jamming' of enemy signals, and protecting one's own side from such 'electronic countermeasures' (ECM) have become a standard feature of modern warfare. In counter-terrorist work the requirements are somewhat different. One would not normally set out to 'jam' the terrorists' communications, simply to intercept them for intelligence.

There are exceptions to this, however. One is the jamming of bombers' remote control devices. This became a game of technological leap-frog in Northern Ireland in the latter part of the twentieth century, with terrorists adapting a wide range of commercially available equipment for the purpose. It included infra-red garage door openers, police radar speed detectors and camera flash synch devices, as well as the more obvious command wires and model radio control systems. In each case the security services, once aware of a new technique, had to develop ways to block or mask the signal, or somehow render the receiving circuit inoperative. There are also anecdotes of bombs being detonated prematurely, while still in the terrorists' hands, by security services transmitting on the appropriate frequency.

Electronic 'jamming' is also used in a hostage situation, where the security services want to take control over the terrorists' communications. A suitable device set up close to an occupied building, aircraft, etc will prevent mobile phones, 'walkie-talkie' transceivers and the like being used by the terrorists (or hostages) to communicate with the outside world. This forces them to accept the police negotiator as their route for requests of any kind, rather than leaving them the option of, for instance, using a mobile phone to call a TV or radio station to publicise their demands.

Some such devices are described in Chapter Six.

4

ACCESS CONTROL AND PERIMETER PROTECTION

At 4 a.m. on 31 July 2002, Otis Ferry, the nineteen-year-old son of the singer Bryan Ferry, approached British Prime Minister Tony Blair's home in Sedgefield, Co Durham. A supporter of fox-hunting, he was planning to stick pro-hunting posters to the walls in protest at plans to ban the sport. As he approached the gate, however, he was challenged by two armed policemen, arrested and taken to a nearby police station.

Ferry was later quoted as saying: 'When I heard the CCTV cameras rotating towards me, I thought I had better go, but when I turned round there were two armed policemen there. One of them was carrying a machine gun.'

To the newspapers, the incident was notable because of Ferry's celebrity connections. For the security services, however, it had a different significance. A high-profile target had been threatened. The threat had been detected at a safe distance, and met with a proportionate response. The target, the Prime Minister's house, remained uncompromised – as it would if, instead of a protester, it had been an IRA bomber approaching the house that night.

There are many such targets in any country in addition to the homes and offices of political leaders and other high-profile figures. Examples include military installations of all types, power stations, telephone exchanges, public water supplies, air and sea ports, railway stations and many more. Any major venue or event can become a target when it is in the news, simply because terrorists can potentially gain exposure for their cause by attacking it – as in the case of the Olympic Games in Munich in 1972 when the Palestinian Black September Group seized Israeli athletes hostage, leading to the deaths of eleven Israelis, five terrorists and a policeman (according to at least one account, most of the terrorists who escaped were later tracked down and assassinated by Israeli agents).

As well as protecting potential targets of terrorism, there is a need to monitor and control borders – in order to combat arms and narcotics smuggling, illegal immigration and the like. In areas of known terrorist activity – such as parts of Northern Ireland – it is necessary to monitor zones for movement of individuals who may be engaged in terrorism.

This monitoring and protection must be carried out wherever it is needed, whether in a remote rural area or in a busy city centre. Often it is important that the surveillance itself remains undetected. If the purpose is to catch criminals and terrorists in the act, then clearly they must not be aware that an area is under surveillance, or they will revise their plans accordingly. If the surveillance remains undetected, however, the security forces can move to deal efficiently with a threat, minimising the risk to themselves as well as to the public, and improving their chances of apprehending the intruder.

Traditionally this kind of area and perimeter protection was provided by a range of seismic and infra-red sensors – similar in operation to those of a domestic 'burglar alarm' system – connected to a central controller which would continually monitor the state of each sensor and sound an alarm when one of them was triggered.

Today, the traditional sensor types have been augmented with more sophisticated equipment, including video cameras, image intensifiers and microwave radar movement detectors. These can be linked to a computer that analyses the inputs from multiple sensors of different types, using sophis- ticated software algorithms to assess the overall picture, and separate out a pattern of activity that indicates a genuine intrusion from the random movements of wildlife. This gives a greatly improved level of protection, while reducing the number of 'false alarms' which can lead to operators losing faith in the system and failing to react properly when a real intrusion occurs. The computer running the system can overlay sensor information on digital mapping, to provide an intu- itive picture of the ground covered, and indicate the location of any intruder.

Using a network of sensors, includ- ing long lengths of piezo-electric cable,

connected to surveillance cameras, it is possible to place an 'electronic wall' along a border or around a perimeter, so that no human or vehicle can pass without being detected, classified and recorded. It is a powerful weapon in the fight against terror- ism.

Physical measures such as razor wire are just one part of a perimeter protection system, which may include invisible sensors to warn of an intrusion. Photo: © James Marchington.

Thales Classic 2000 System

The Thales Classic (Covert Local Area Sensor System for Intruder Classification) 2000 System has been sold to forty countries and is in service with twelve NATO countries. It is used by military, paramilitary, police, border control agencies and commercial organisations worldwide.

Classic was originally developed by Racal, and has been refined and updated over the years. It offers a compact, easily deployed and highly flexible system that can be adapted to suit a wide range of tasks in different environments, from dense jungle to built-up urban areas.

A soldier emplacing a Classic sensor to warn of enemy activity. The system is highly flexible and can be adapted to suit a wide variety of tasks in different environments. Photo: Racal.

Compared with previous-generation ground sensor systems, Classic 2000 is half the weight and size, and is less costly. It has been designed so that the software can be upgraded to take advantage of future developments, or to customise the system for a particular user's requirements.

Classic can detect and classify personnel, wheeled and tracked vehicles over the area covered by the sensors. The data collected may be sent to a distant monitor in a short, covert radio message – either direct or via a relay.

The basic Classic 2000 system consists of an RA4310 Monitor unit, a TA4312 or TA4314 Sensor and an RTA4311 Relay unit. The sensor detects an intruder, and transmits a signal to the monitor, which then sends an alert – either to a VHF radio receiver or via the SMS service to a GSM mobile telephone. The system can be extended by adding further sensors – a single monitor can receive intrusion data from up to ninety-nine sensors.

All sensors, relays and monitors in the Classic 2000 system are programmable. The programming software runs on a Windows PC, and the required configuration is downloaded to the monitor. The monitor is then used to transfer the information to the sensors and relay units. Sensors and relays can also, if required, be programmed directly from the PC.

RA4310 Monitor

The Monitor unit measures 177 x 95 x 62mm, weighs 1kg and is powered by six AA batteries. It has a keypad and LCD display on the front, and a helical 'rubber duck' type antenna. It operates on a frequency range of 148 to 155MHz, with a channel spacing of 25kHz.

Each monitor unit can receive intrusion data from up to ninety-nine sensors, and contains a database of information about its sensors and relays, stored in non-volatile memory. The database is downloaded from a standard PC running the Classic 2000 programming software, and includes details such as equipment type (sensor/relay/etc), confidence alarm interval, action on tamper, channel number and transmit frequency. The monitor's main function is to receive and display intrusion information to the operator, but it can also transfer programming information to the sensors and relays under its control.

TA4312 Seismic/PIR Sensor

The TA4312 Seismic/PIR sensor is essentially the control box that is attached to various types of sensor devices (tripwires, pressure pads, pressure sensitive piezo-electric cable, etc). It contains software that analyses the signals from these devices, to detect an intrusion and classify it as personnel, wheeled vehicle or tracked vehicle. The TA4312 unit then transmits this information to the controlling monitor unit via a radio signal.

The TA4312 contains all the algorithms necessary for the geophone, PIR (short, medium or long-range version), piezo-electric cable, and a range of contact closure devices (tripwires, pressure pads etc). The algorithms are held in software which can be upgraded to take account of future developments.

Frequency range and channel spacing of the TA4312 are, naturally enough, the same as the monitor unit. Its RF output power is a nominal 0.5W, and it is powered by a battery pack loaded with eight AA batteries, either manganese alkaline or lithium ion type. The unit measures 120 x 120 x 52mm, including the battery pack, and weighs 0.85kg. It has a covert whip antenna.

TA4314 Magnetic/PIR Sensor

The TA4314 Magnetic/PIR sensor unit is very similar in size and shape to the TA4312, and is substantially the same in operation. Like the TA4312, it will operate with the PIR sensors and contact closure devices. The difference, however, is that the TA4314 has a built-in magnetic sensor. This will detect the proximity of a large mass of iron or steel – typically a vehicle – and send an alert to its controlling monitor unit accord-ingly. It can therefore be used to detect the presence or passage of vehicles along roads and tracks and at suitable choke points – gateways, bridges and the like.

MA4320 Geophone

The MA4320 Geophone is designed to be buried in the ground and attached by cable to the TA4312 sensor unit. It has a spike to assist driving it into soft ground, and there is a pull-loop so that it can be retrieved without digging.

The software in the TA4312 analyses the signals from the geophone, and can classify the intruder as personnel, wheeled or tracked vehicle. The sensor allows the operator to adjust the seismic gain of the geophone (equivalent to the volume adjustment on a microphone), and there is an adaptive threshold feature that minimises nuisance alarms due to background noise such as rain.

The performance of the geophone depends on the nature of the ground in which it is buried, and the care taken in its placement. Hard-packed, moist ground gives better detection ranges than loose-packed, dry ground. In ideal conditions, detection ranges of up to 100m can be achieved.

4559 12 Piezo-Electric Cable

Piezo-electric cable for the Classic 2000 system is available in lengths of 25 to 1,000 metres. Like the geophone, it is connected to a TA4312 sensor, and detects vibrations transmitted through the ground. These vibrations are analysed in the sensor unit and classified as personnel, wheeled or tracked vehicles.

The significant difference between this and the geophone is that the piezo-electric cable provides detection and classification along its length, rather than at a single point. This makes it suitable for covering a wider front, such as a border, where traffic is not necessarily channelled along a road or track. A sufficient length of cable could provide complete perimeter protection for a vulnerable installation. In good conditions, the piezo-electric cable can provide a detection range of up to 50 metres.

Passive Infra-Red Transducers

There are three PIR (Passive Infra-Red) transducers designed for use with the Classic 2000 system. These are the MA4323 Short-Range PIR, MA4321 Medium-Range PIR and MA4322 Long-Range PIR. Their maximum detection ranges for a single human target are 12m, 50m and 100m respectively.

Like the other sensors for use with Classic 2000, the PIR transducers are connected to a sensor unit (TA4312 or TA4314) by a cable. The three different PIRs are interchangeable, and use the same interface cable. The sensor unit contains the software to analyse the input from the device, and send an alert to the monitor unit as necessary.

The PIRs are described as sophisticated dual-beam pyrometers, with high accuracy optics. They have twin detection zones, so in combination with the sensor unit software they can provide directional information about the target. The software is particularly effective at eliminating nuisance alarms, without affecting the detection rate for a genuine intrusion.

Thales MIS (Miniature Intrusion Sensor)

The Thales MIS (Miniature Intrusion Sensor) is described as the next generation of passive ground sensors. Like Classic 2000, it offers a range of different sensor types, and can classify an intrusion as personnel, vehicle, etc. The MIS system is highly flexible, and the individual units are designed to be small, light, and simple to emplace and operate. The system can also be integrated with other conventional surveillance systems.

At the 'sharp end' is a small sensor unit with a spike containing a built-in geophone. This unit measures 138mm from the top to the tip of the spike. When the spike is pushed into the ground, only the top of the unit protrudes; this is shaped like an inverted truncated cone, measuring 65mm from top to base, and 63mm in diameter. It weighs just 0.25kg and is powered by a single AA battery. Typical battery life (at four alarms per hour) is fifty days, and a 'battery low' alert is transmitted when the battery power falls below a predetermined level.

The unit is 'plug and play'. Inserting the battery activates the sensor, at which point it performs a self-test and transmits its status. It transmits a 'confidence' signal every twenty-four hours, and will send a 'tamper' alarm if it is removed from the ground. There is no need to adjust the seismic gain, as the unit automatically adapts to the background environment.

The MIS will reliably detect personnel at ranges of 20 to 60m, whether they are crawling, walking or running. The software has been designed to ignore unwanted targets such as cats, dogs, deer and other animals. It will also classify vehicles, and is particularly good at detecting slow-moving vehicles which might be missed by other ground surveillance equipment.

The unit transmits in the UHF band at around 433MHz. Transmit power is a nominal 100mW, giving a typical line-of-sight range of around 500m.

In addition to the built-in geophone, there is a range of external transducers that can be connected to the MIS unit. These include piezo-electric cable, PIR heads and a magnetic transducer that can detect a vehicle at ranges of 15–50m depending on the vehicle's size and speed.

Up to 999 sensors communicate with a personal monitor, which alerts the user to an intrusion with a synthesised speech alarm using a small covert earpiece. The sensors will also communicate with a gateway communications hub, which can pass on an alert via existing channels, including combat net radio, satcom, a mobile phone network or trunked radio.

Koor 6000 laser system

The Koor 6000 is an example of a 'laser fence' perimeter protection system which can be set up around an area or installation that needs to be secured against intrusion. It consists of a series of posts that are erected around the area to be protected, each of which can both emit and receive a number of laser beams. The posts are arranged so that the beams from one post are received by the next.

The beams are invisible to the naked eye, but anything crossing the space between the posts will interrupt the beams, causing a signal to be sent to the control unit. Laser beams are unaffected by weather and climatic conditions, making this system particularly useful for outdoor use in areas where a PIR-based system, for example, might give an excessive number of false alarms.

As with most intruder systems, the control unit may be set to respond in a number of ways, depending on what is appropriate for the area being protected. It can sound an audible alarm to warn off the intruder, alert an operator, activate a CCTV system, and send a signal to a remote monitoring station via radio or telephone.

Laser systems such as this obviously do not present any obstacle to an intruder – unlike, for example, a physical barrier or fence. This can be an advantage in certain situations: a laser system can be arranged covertly so that an intruder is unaware that any protection is in force, and does not know that he has been detected. This gives a reception party time to seal off any escape routes before the intruder is alerted to the danger, improving the chances of apprehending him. Alternatively, it means that the intruder can be watched, and his movements monitored and recorded for use as evidence later.

Sentry 2000

Sentry 2000, produced by RDS Electronics of Huntingdon in Cambridgeshire, is a portable PIR-type protection system that can be set up quickly wherever it is needed. It is ideal for protecting parked aircraft or vehicles, for instance – and can be carried in the boot of a vehicle to be set up as needed. This makes it particularly suitable for VIP protection, where a terrorist might gain access to an unprotected vehicle and attach a bomb or other device without the protection team's knowledge.

The Sentry 2000 unit consists of a self-contained post with a wide base, which stands up with no need for any sort of fixing. It contains a PIR detector, processor, battery and radio transmitter. The unit is simply placed near the object to be protected, and switched on. Anyone approaching the device will be detected by the PIR sensor, and an alarm signal is transmitted to a receiver carried by the operator. The unit can also communicate an alarm via telephone.

There are several different models of Sentry 2000, intended for different types of use. The normal model is brightly coloured and marked to act as a deterrent. Other models are camouflaged for covert use, or offer a differently shaped detection pattern for use on gateways, tracks, etc.

Remsdaq Sabre Perimeter Systems

We have seen systems that detect an intruder by passive infra-red, seismic vibrations, lasers and magnetic field detection. The Sabre Perimeter System, from Remsdaq in the UK, uses a different technology: fibre optics. Sabre products are field-proven and extensively used in government, military and industrial applications worldwide. They are suitable for a wide range of security applications including:

- Fence, wall, gate and roof protection
- Covert protection of sterile areas and open ground
- Storage and freight container security
- Underwater protection of vessels, etc
- Guarding sewage outfalls and culverts
- Ventilation and air-conditioning duct protection

The system is based on the principle of laser light being transmitted along a fibre-optic cable. A laser at one end of a cable shines along the fibres, and a receptor at the other end measures the light received. The light transmission characteristics of the cable are easily altered by flexing. A suitable cable can be attached to a fence or similar construction, and any attempt to breach the fence or circumvent it by climbing or digging will be detected.

The Sabre SabreFonic sensor cable is specifically designed to detect any attempt to cut or climb a perimeter fence or security gate. It is easily attached to a fence or gate and is sensitive to a wide range of vibrations, flexing, compression and cutting. The cable is suitable for use on a wide range of fence fabrics, and no special conduit is required to attach the sensor to the fence. The fibre-optic system is inherently safe, as it carries no current and is a passive system with no emissions. It is therefore suitable for hazardous locations where there is a risk of fire or explosion.

Remsdaq produce a family of products based on the same technology, to protect different types of installation. SabreLine, for instance, is a buried sensor designed to provide covert protection of sterile areas or open ground. Once installed, SabreLine is completely invisible and cannot be detected using metal detectors.

SabreTape is a steel tape that can be

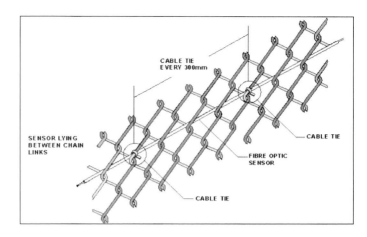

Remsdaq's SabreFonic sensor cable can be incorporated into most types of fence or gate, and uses fibre-optics to detect any attempt to climb or breach the perimeter. Picture: Remsdaq.

SabreLine is buried in the ground and detects any attempt to cross the protected area. Picture: Remsdaq.

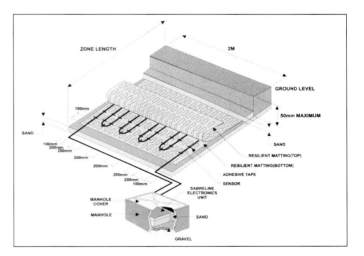

installed as a complete fence system or as a series of collapsible outriggers added to an existing fence. It is available in a barbed or a non-aggressive finish and is also suitable for protection of gates, walls or the sides of buildings.

Optimesh and Aquamesh employ a woven optical fibre net or mesh that acts as a continuity sensor. Both products are normally tailor-made for the individual application and give highly effective security protection. Optimesh can be deployed in the fabric of a building wall, ceiling or floor but is also highly suited to use in stores, partitions and freight container shells. Aquamesh is a specially developed version of the mesh sensor designed for underwater security applications but can also be deployed for protection of sewage outfalls and culverts.

The Sabre processor module is the 'brains' of the system. It constantly monitors the light transmission characteristics of the cable, combining digital signal processing and environmental compensation algorithms to provide the highest levels of detection and discrimination whilst ensuring a minimum of nuisance alarms due to natural causes. It will reliably classify events such as cutting and climbing of the protected fence.

MSTAR Radar Surveillance System

MSTAR is an example of the new generation of ground surveillance radar which can be used to watch borders, areas of likely terrorist activity, and approaches to sensi-

MSTAR ground surveillance radar can be broken down into three man-portable loads, and can spot a man at a range of 20km. Photo: Racal.

tive installations. A pulse doppler type radar operating in the J band (10-20GHz), it is an LPI (Low Probability of Intercept) radar, meaning that it is very difficult for the target to detect.

Although often vehicle mounted (on the Warrior Artillery Observation Vehicle, for instance), MSTAR can be broken down into three man-portable loads where necessary, and can also be used in semi-permanent installations such as observation towers overlooking vulnerable borders or rural areas favoured by terrorists.

MSTAR can detect personnel, vehicles of all types and low-flying aircraft such as helicopters – accurately classifying the various types of contacts. The results are displayed on an electro-luminescent screen, which can superimpose a map grid at 1:50,000 scale so that contacts can be quickly transferred to a map.

The system provides twenty-four-hour all-weather surveillance, with a range of more than 20km. It gathers intelligence covertly; the target is not alerted to the fact that he has been spotted, until confronted by the reaction force. MSTAR can also be integrated with Classic 2000 and similar systems to create an impenetrable 'electronic wall' extending for great distances.

Portapungi

After the high-tech perimeter protection and surveillance systems earlier in this chapter, the devices for stopping vehicles look positively medieval.

The Portapungi, for example, is a simple system of massive steel prongs set over a pit in the ground. The prongs are hinged on a steel shaft, and are normally locked in the flat position, forming a roadway over which a vehicle can pass safely. If a vehicle appears to be a threat, however, the Portapungi can be activated instantly simply by throwing a switch. This triggers a hydraulic mechanism that immediately lifts the prongs to face the oncoming vehicle at an angle of about 45 degrees. If the vehicle attempts to drive on, it will become impaled on the prongs, which usually remove the front axle and become deeply embedded in the underbody, bringing the vehicle to a sudden stop.

Clossur Stoperse

The Clossur Stoperse is another device for stopping vehicles breaking into protected areas – it is particularly suitable where it may be necessary to prevent a vehicle bomb being driven into an entrance.

It consists of two pits dug into the roadway, each with a metal grille hinged so as to form a platform that vehicles can drive over. When the roadway is closed, or when a threat is detected, the grilles are quickly pivoted to an angle of about 45 degrees facing the oncoming vehicle, revealing a row of steel spikes.

If the vehicle fails to stop, the spikes will shred the front tyres and catch on the underside of the vehicle, often raising the vehicle off the ground as they swing round in an arc before depositing the vehicle heavily back on the ground with its rear wheels in the pits. The system can stop even a heavy truck in its tracks, potentially averting a suicide-type vehicle bombing of a sensitive location.

5 BOMB AND NBC DETECTION

The bomb or IED (Improvised Explosive Device) has long been a favourite weapon of terrorists. From a terrorist's point of view, a bomb has many advantages over other tactics. Even at times of high security alert, there are many more potential targets than the security services could ever watch twenty-four hours a day. A bomb can be emplaced at a time and place convenient to the terrorist, perhaps at night when an area is less closely watched and darkness helps to cover his movements. The bomber can then make his getaway before the security services are alerted to the threat. Even a bomb that fails to detonate is guaranteed to cause widespread disruption, occupy security service resources and obtain considerable media coverage.

As a terrorist tactic, IEDs provide the maximum gain for minimum risk. It is a very versatile tactic, too; the permutations are endless. Bombs may be large or small, blast or incendiary. They may contain improvised projectiles to cause injury and death to those in the vicinity of an explosion.

A bomb may be posted to the target individual or organisation in a letter or packet. It may be dropped into a litter bin, or hidden in a car to be parked by a target building. It can even be strapped around the waist of a 'suicide bomber' for delivery into the heart of a busy market or street. There are many possible trigger mechanisms that can be employed, from a simple booby-trap or timer to a command-wire or remote control device.

Bombs may contain any number of sophisticated anti-handling devices to complicate the work of the EOD (Explosive Ordnance Disposal) teams. The use of refinements such as telephone warnings, code-words, hoaxes and threats enable the terrorist to create further disruption, while showing an apparent concern for the safety of civilians.

In Northern Ireland the British Army and Royal Ulster Constabulary gained much valuable experience in dealing with terrorist devices of all types. The IRA employed car bombs, culvert bombs and other types to varying effect, and for years there was a deadly game of cat-and-mouse as the bombers developed ever more sophisticated triggers and anti-handling devices, while the EOD experts developed techniques for dealing with each new version. In recent years the number of IRA bombs has declined significantly, but new threats have emerged with, for example, animal rights activists sending devices through the post.

Countering the bomb threat presents the security services with an enormous problem. Two of the terrorists' main aims are to create media attention and disruption to normal daily life. Yet to counter the threat it is necessary to use the media to warn the public to be alert, and to disrupt normal life by restricting access and conducting time-consuming searches. Even then the terrorists have the initiative, with the ability to choose the method, time and place of an attack. It takes only a moment to make a call claiming a bomb has been placed at a certain airport or railway station; it may take hours or even days to search the target thoroughly enough to be sure no bomb is present.

Recent developments in technology, however, promise to swing the balance more in favour of the security services. For a long time the only way to be certain that no device was present was by physical search. Metal detectors and X-ray scans can detect many devices, particularly those with large and easily recognisable metallic parts. But it is possible to construct a bomb with very little metal, and with its various parts shaped to look innocent when X-rayed. Everyday objects such as cameras, radios and tape recorders contain a maze of wiring and metal parts, among which a bomb might easily go unnoticed. Explosives themselves can easily be moulded to look like innocent items such as food or drink.

Metal detectors, X-ray devices and physical searching still have an important part to play in security at airports, conference centres and the like. But new technology such as ion 'sniffers' and backscatter X-ray imaging provides powerful tools to improve security while reducing the disruption to travellers. As the technology is improved and becomes more sensitive, it will eventually be possible to screen people entering and leaving, say, a shopping centre for bombs and explosives without them realising that any security measures are in place – although it may still be desirable to carry out an overt search as a deterrent.

One problem that the new technology has already encountered arises from it being, if anything, too effective. The Rapiscan 1000 caused some controversy when it went on trial at Orlando Airport, Florida. A backscatter X-ray device, it effectively sees through the subject's clothes, creating an accurate picture on screen of the naked subject – together with any weapons, explosives or contraband that he or she may have concealed about them. Civil liberties groups have complained that this is an intrusion, although in practice many passengers seem happy to submit to the scan in return for a faster check-in, with some commenting that it is preferable to the familiar 'pat-down' method.

PASSENGER SCREENING SYSTEMS

Rapiscan Secure 1000

The Secure 1000 by Rapiscan Security Products uses the relatively new X-ray backscatter technology to take an image through a subject's clothing. In a conventional X-ray machine, X-rays are passed through the subject and collected by a receiver on the far side. Denser materials, such as metals, absorb a large proportion of the rays, and therefore show up as a dark area on the image. With the backscatter technique, however, sensitive X-ray detectors are placed on the same side as the beam, and measure X-rays reflected back from the subject. Sophisticated algorithms process the data to create an image of the surface facing the machine. The image is displayed on a monitor, which can be some way from the machine and, crucially, can be in a closed room where the – potentially embarrassing – images may be seen only by the operator.

Rapiscan point out that their Secure 1000 Body Scanning System is a safe, non-intrusive screening system, which shows up metallic and non-metallic objects concealed on a person's body. This enhances security, while reducing the need for physical 'hands-on' searching.

The Secure 1000 allows the operator to detect threats by imaging explosive materials such as dynamite and C-4, as well as plastic weapons, glass vials and syringes, packaged narcotics, bundled paper currency and even wooden objects.

The device takes up a floor area of 1.1m², weighs 295kg and requires a clearance height of 204cm. In appearance, it is rather like a wardrobe, with a mat on the floor on which the subject stands. Each scan takes three seconds, with two scans needed per person: one back and one front. The field of view is 81.3cm wide and 203.2cm high. The image is displayed on a 13-inch high-resolution monitor.

With any scanning technology there are inevitably questions raised about exposure levels and safety. The Secure 1000 scores highly in this area, with an emission of only 3 microREM per scan – equivalent to approximately twenty minutes of exposure to naturally occurring background radiation. By comparison, a typical medical chest X-ray results in an exposure of up to 10,000 microREM, and even watching TV provides 500 microREM per hour.

It would appear that any concerns over backscatter technology will be overshadowed by the huge improvement in security and throughput at passenger terminals that it can provide. We may expect to see this technology rapidly becoming part of daily life at airports and the like, and perhaps even moving into other areas such as shopping centres, public buildings, offices, schools and colleges.

Barringer Sentinel II Explosives-detection Portal

The Barringer Sentinel II is a walk-through portal-type 'sniffer' for detecting explosives carried by an individual. It is in use at a number of US airports to screen passengers and guard against a suicide bombing similar to that attempted by the notorious 'shoe bomber', Richard Reid, on 22 December 2001.

The Sentinel II uses the same explosives-detection technology that is also employed to screen luggage and freight. It makes it possible to screen people quickly and non-invasively for the presence of an explosive device.

The Sentinel II walk-through portal can screen about seven people per minute for a variety of substances and may be used in facilities other than airports, such as office buildings, sports arenas, and other areas of high traffic.

Like Barringer's other detection devices, the Sentinel II uses Ion Mobility Spectrometry (IMS), which performs a real-time chemical analysis and essentially identifies a 'fingerprint' of a target substance. The company is, naturally enough, reluctant to divulge details of precisely what concentrations of which substances the device will detect. They do say, however, that even if a person has only a minute concentration of explosives, drug residue, or chemical agent on his or her skin or clothing, the substance will be detected.

The Sentinel II makes use of a sample pre-concentrator originally developed at the US Department of Energy's Sandia National Laboratories. This technology effi-

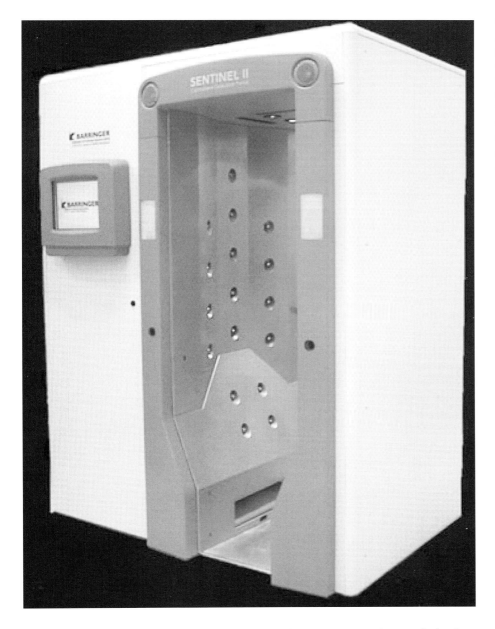

The Barringer Sentinel II can screen seven people per minute for traces of explosives on their skin or clothing; it is suitable for use at airports and other areas. Photo: Barringer.

ciently traps the target particles and vapours from a large volume of air, then directs the concentrated chemical sample to Barringer's Ionscan detector for analysis, which makes it possible to detect very low concentrations of explosive chemicals.

PW Allen Walk-through Metal Detector

Despite the development of highly sophisticated screening systems using technology such as backscatter X-ray imaging, there is still a place for the more straightforward metal detector portal, which is in use at hundreds of airports and other potential targets around the world.

Much has been made of the fact that it is possible to construct a weapon or explosive device that will pass through a metal detector undetected. In reality, however, a metal detector provides a powerful deterrent, and will detect the vast majority of threats. It also provides a point of intense psychological pressure for the potential hijacker or bomber, where properly trained security staff can expect to identify signs of stress and pull the subject aside for a more rigorous search.

The 600-371 Walk-through Metal Detector from PW Allen is an example of this type of detector. It follows the typical portal design, with an aperture 198cm high and 75cm wide. The detector uses advanced pulse-induction technology, with microprocessor control and sophisticated signal processing, making it highly sensitive while avoiding false alarms. It is simple to operate, with straightforward on/off, volume and threshold controls on the fascia – protected by a keylock to prevent tampering. There is also a hidden PIR on/off switch.

The alarm indication is by audible signal which is proportional to the target detected, as well as an LED column display showing target size and a separate size indication on an LCD panel. The detector can also trigger a remote alarm.

The unit is of lightweight, modular construction, and can be quickly dismantled, transported and set up where required. An autoset programme automatically optimises the unit's sensitivity for the working environment, avoiding the need for lengthy set-up procedures. It is designed to work on mains power, with an internal rechargeable battery that takes over in the event of mains failure, and can operate the unit for up to eight hours.

Rapiscan Metor 200 HD

Another example of the walk-through type of metal detector is the Rapiscan Metor 200 HD. Rapiscan is one of the leading manufacturers of walk-through metal detectors, and their products are used by many of the world's most demanding users. Rapiscan say that more than 40,000 Metors are currently in daily use in a diverse range of applications, some of which have been in operation for more than two decades.

The Metor 200 HD High Discrimination Detector is designed specially for demanding high-traffic screening applications. It detects weapons efficiently and discriminates against harmless personal possessions. Therefore traffic flow can be maintained at an optimum rate in locations where fast throughput is essential.

An important feature of the Metor 200 HD is that its detection area is divided into eight zones. Targeted objects are independently detected in the different zones, and signals from harmless distributed objects do not combine to produce unnecessary alarms. A display shows the operator the zone or zones in which an alarm has occurred, helping to locate the offending item. A remote zone display unit may operate at a distance of up to 65m from the detector. It shows the position of detected items and generates an audible alarm.

Specifications

Operating temperature	−10°C to 55°C
Humidity	Up to 95 per cent, no condensation
AC Power	90–264v AC/45–65Hz
Battery	24–35v DC
Alarm	Audible/visible alarm with alphanumeric display and zone display. Relay contact for remote alarm
Sensitivity adjustment	100 sensitivity steps per program. Each zone is individually adjustable (0 to 255 per cent) with respect to overall sensitivity level
Calibration	Automatic or manually set
Reset time	Adjustable
Interference suppression	Digital filtering by signal processor and user selectable frequency selection
Self-test	User-friendly diagnostics identify fault conditions
Network connections	Connectible to the Metornet security monitoring system (RS422)

Rapiscan Metor 28 Hand-held Metal Detector

A walk-through metal detector is only part of the screening process. Any indication – whether from the walk-through device itself or from the operator's suspicions being aroused in some other way – needs to be followed up with a more detailed search of the suspect. For this, a hand-held metal detector is invaluable. It makes it possible to pinpoint quickly any metallic objects that may have set off the walk-through detector, without using intrusive methods.

An example of the hand-held type is the Rapiscan Metor 28. This lightweight device has a unique angled design so that security staff can thoroughly scan an individual, while keeping their hands away from the subject's body.

The Metor 28 will detect ferrous and non-ferrous metal objects down to the size of a small key, but does not affect pacemakers and magnetic tapes. It is powered by a standard 9v battery, and gives an audible alarm signal as well as a visual indication via an LED. Where the audible signal would be hard to hear, or inappropriate, a headset can be used.

Specifications

Operating temperature	0°C to 50°C (32°F to 122°F)
Humidity	0 to 95%, no condensation
Power supply	Standard 9v battery or rechargeable NiMH battery

Battery Life	Alkaline battery 45h
	Rechargeable NiMH battery 20h
	Recharge time for NiMH battery 12h
Alarm Indications	Audible and visual alarm indication.
	Optional headset is available
Sensitivity	Three sensitivity settings
Detection performance Level 1:	small handguns and knives
Level 2	razor blades, handcuff keys
Level 3	.22 calibre bullet, metal shanks
Total weight	260g with battery
Dimensions	410 x 140 mm (16.35 x 5.5in)
Grip	33 x 33mm (1.3 x 1.3in)

PW Allen Dual-Purpose Hand-held Metal Detector

PW Allen offer a range of hand-held metal detectors for personnel search. The Dual-Purpose model is the most versatile, offering two sensitivity settings. On normal sensitivity it is ideal for personnel search; set to high sensitivity it becomes a general purpose metal detector capable of detecting extremely small metallic objects, as small as a 4mm section of 20swg wire.

Two models are available, one with the high sensitivity setting pre-set to the maximum level, the other with a control to adjust the sensitivity. Both are supplied with a wrist strap and batteries.

The detector has a circular probe at the end of a wand-type handle. The overall dimensions of the unit are 365 x 35mm, with a probe width of 105mm.

LUGGAGE SCREENING SYSTEMS

The bombing of PanAm Flight 203 in the sky over Lockerbie, Scotland, on 21 December 1988, killed 259 on board and eleven on the ground. This terrible attack underlines the importance of screening luggage for explosive devices. As with the screening of passengers, there are contradictory aims at work: the luggage needs to be checked thoroughly and effectively to minimise the chance of any device getting through the net, but delays are unpopular and impact the airlines' profitability.

Given unlimited time, every piece of luggage could be hand-searched and confirmed as 100 per cent safe. In practice, screening systems have long been a compromise, with the need for safety being balanced against the need for efficient movement of passengers and their luggage through the system and on to their destination.

Like personnel screening, luggage screening systems have benefited from advances in technology in recent years. Modern units using technology such as ion scanning and backscatter X-ray imaging allow a high throughput as well as providing a high detection rate – meaning that aircraft take off on time, while the risk of a bomb going undetected is extremely low.

The 11 September 2001 attacks led to a reappraisal and tightening of security at airports in the US and around the world. The US Aviation and Transportation Security Act of 2001 called for 100 per cent screening of all checked baggage by the end of 2002. In response, the FAA extended Raytheon's contract to install explosives detection systems in all the United States' 438 commercial airports by 31 December 2002. At the same time, elsewhere in the world, similar improvements were being made to baggage checking procedures and equipment. Thankfully, although the 11 September attacks did not involve explosives in luggage, the response has meant that the chance of a repeat of the Lockerbie tragedy is much reduced.

Rapiscan 500 Series Conventional X-ray Machines

Modern luggage X-ray systems do far more than simply provide a simple 'view through' picture of items being scanned. In the Rapiscan 500 series, for example, advanced X-ray technology coupled with state of the art image processing provides a new level of image quality. The 500 series machines provide the industry standard four-colour palette, allowing operators quickly to identify materials by general material type (organic/inorganic). Operator training programmes ensure that operators can gain the maximum information from the images displayed on the system's screen.

Rapiscan Model 524 X-ray Machine

An example of a typical X-ray inspection system is the Rapiscan Model 524. It is a compact design, well suited to security checkpoint areas such as airports, court-houses, embassies and prisons. The system offers a tunnel opening of 810mm (31.9ins) wide by 850mm (33.4ins) high to accommodate large package sizes.

The Model 524 uses Rapiscan's Enhanced Performance X-ray (EPX) technology to identify material with the specific characteristics of explosives and narcotics. Gold, currency and agricultural products can also be identified by means of EPX.

The system also addresses the human factor, which can be the weakest link in any security system. The system inserts images of threat objects, at predefined settings and intervals, into otherwise clean bags – allowing supervisors to monitor the operator's response. This is an important aspect of security screening of passengers and luggage; in early September 2002 an undercover TV crew from Meridian TV in the UK managed to smuggle a replica pistol, wrapped as a gift, and a pair of scissors, on to flights from Gatwick and Southampton airports. The director of security for the British Airports Authority confirmed that the system of inserting 'dummy threats' was in use as a way of monitoring operator performance, and was quoted as saying: 'Our detection rates are significantly better than anywhere else in the world. But there is no such thing as 100 per cent security. We are all human.'

Specifications

Penetration	27mm steel guaranteed, 29mm typical
Material Separation	Low Z, Medium Z, High Z to 0.5 Z accuracy
Monitor	17-inch SVGA colour, high refresh, non flicker
Power	110v AC 6A or 230v AC 3A Dimensions
Length	3,514mm (138.35ins)
Height	1,295mm (51.00ins)
Width	1,352mm (53.20ins)
Tunnel Size	550mm (W) x 850mm (H). (21.65 x 33.40ins)
Approx. Weight	Net: 560kg (1,232lbs)
Conveyor Speed	0.22m/sec (44ft/min)
Conveyor Load	50kg (110lbs)
Operating Temperature	0°C to 40°C
Relative Humidity	5 to 95 per cent non-condensing

Rapiscan Model 527 X-ray Machine

Like the Model 524, the Rapiscan Model 527 is an X-ray security inspection system designed to provide security inspections of checked baggage and small cargo. With a tunnel opening of 1,000mm (39.37ins) x 1,000mm (39.37ins), large-size packages can be quickly and easily scanned. The Model 527 can be used as a stand-alone device or integrated into an existing baggage conveyor system with automatic detection capabilities.

Like the 524, the Model 527 uses EPX and TIP technology, and is based on an Intel Pentium computer processor. Multiple X-ray units may be linked to a remote search area for additional review.

Specifications

Substantially the 527 is the same as Model 524, except as follows:

Dimensions

Length	3,936mm (155ins)
Height	2,090mm (82.3ins)
Width	1,388mm (54.6ins)
Tunnel Size	1,000mm (W) x 1,000mm (H). (39.37 x 39.37ins)
Approx. Weight	Net: 1,400kg (3,080 lbs)
Conveyor Speed	0.2m/sec (40ft/min).
Conveyor Load	150kg (330lbs)

InVision CTX 5500 Explosives Detection System

InVision's CTX 5500 DS is the most widely used FAA-certified Explosives Detection System (EDS) in the world. It is ideal for stand-alone applications yet powerful enough for integration into airport baggage handling systems. In addition to explo-

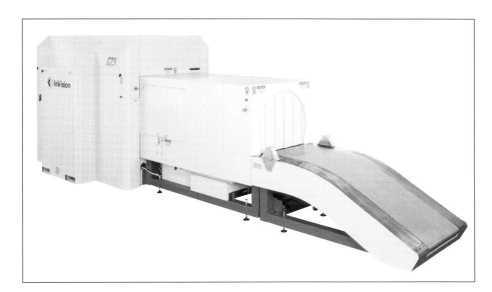

The InVision CTX 5500 DS is a sophisticated explosives detection system used in airports around the world to screen passenger luggage for explosives, narcotics and other banned items. Photos: InVision

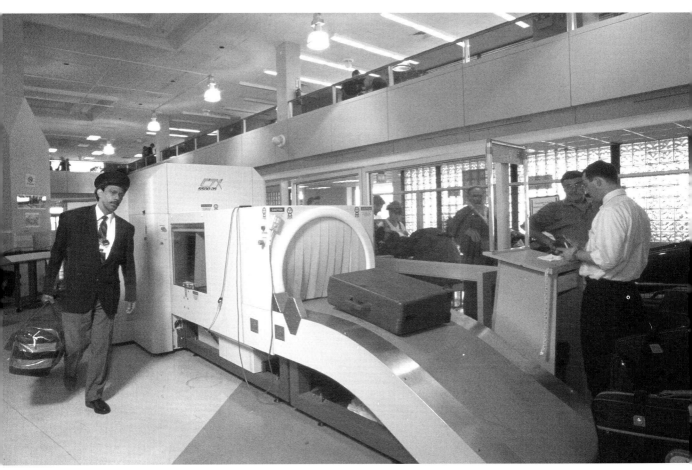

 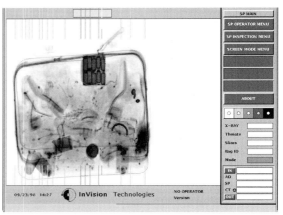

The InVision CTX 5500 DS system uses CT (Computed Tomography) to scan bags with a rotating X-ray source and show a detailed picture of the contents on a monitor screen. Photos: InVision.

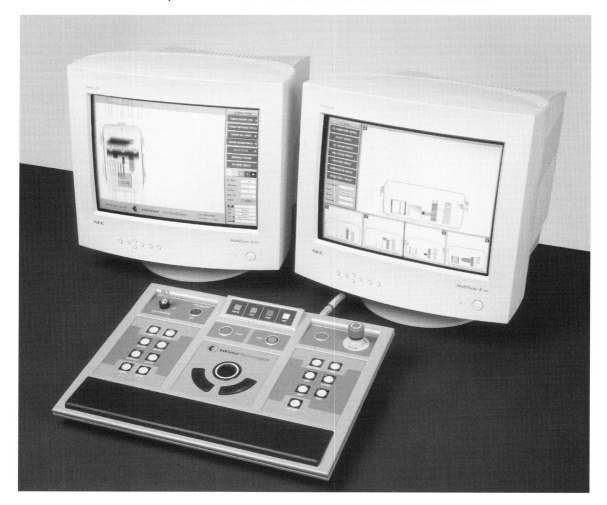

sives detection, the CTX 5500 DS may be configured to detect other types of contraband material.

Like all InVision CTX EDS machines, the CTX 5500 DS uses technology derived from medical Computed Tomography (CT) to quickly locate and identify explosive devices concealed in checked baggage. As the conveyor moves each bag through the machine, the system produces a scan projection X-ray image. From this image, the powerful onboard computer determines which areas need 'slice' images, taken by the rotating X-ray source.

Using sophisticated computer algorithms, the CTX 5500 DS system analyses these slice images and compares their properties with those of known explosives. If a match is found, the system alarms and displays the object on the screen. By viewing the screen images that highlight suspected explosives and bomb components, an operator can determine whether a threat exists, and then follow established protocols for threat resolution.

The CTX 5500 DS system has a FAA-certified throughput of 362 bags per hour, with a low false alarm rate. Its Dynamic Screening (DS) capability offers additional flexibility by allowing manual or automatic switching between various screening modes suited for different threat and load conditions.

With hundreds of systems deployed worldwide, InVision's CTX systems offer FAA-certified, field-proven technology backed by an expert team of training and support professionals to help large and small airports alike meet today's stringent explosives detection requirements.

InVision CTX 9000 DSi Explosives Detection System

The CTX 9000 DSi system is the world's fastest FAA-certified Explosives Detection System (EDS). It is FAA certified at 542 bags per hour, but can support even higher throughputs.

The CTX 9000 DSi system was designed by InVision from the ground up for integrated airport installations. Its 1m wide conveyor coordinates with standard airport baggage handling systems and requires minimal space for built-in installation.

Like the CTX 5500, the CTX 9000 DSi uses technology derived from medical Computed Tomography (CT). Four active radiation-shielding curtains enable the system to achieve its high baggage throughput rates while complying with all US and international radiation emissions regulations. The gantry rotates at 120rpm, enabling a slice image to be generated within half a second. This contributes to the system's high throughput capacity.

The system incorporates a powerful air-conditioning unit to ensure high performance and reliability even in hot, dusty and humid airport environments. The self-contained unit forces cool, filtered air through the entire system in a closed circuit.

The InVision CTX 9000 DSi system is able to scan more than 550 bags per hour. Photo: InVision

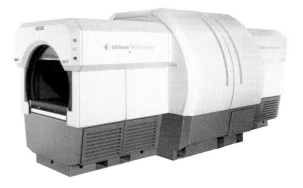

The InVision CTX 9000 DSi system uses the same technology as the company's CTX 5500, but has an even higher scanning rate throughput. Photo: InVision

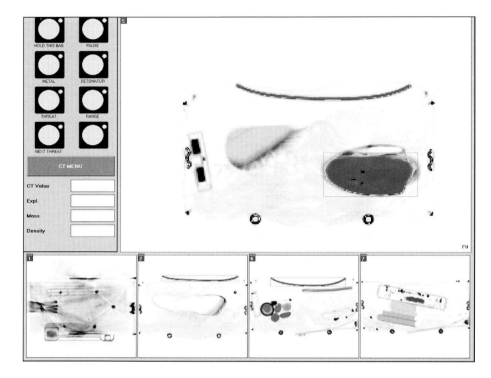

MAIL AND PACKAGE SCANNING SYSTEMS

Immediately after the 11 September 2001 attacks in the USA, rumours began to circulate of anthrax being distributed in the mail. Although many suspected threats turned out to be hoaxes or false alarms, several people were killed or injured by anthrax spores sent in letters and packages. At the time of writing, it is still not proven whether these attacks were instigated by those responsible for the 11 September attacks, or the work of an opportunist.

The use of biological agents in mail is a relatively new development, but terrorists have long used mail as a way of delivering explosive devices and hazardous materials to their targets. Hazardous items have included bombs, incendiary devices and sharp objects such as razor blades, needles and broken glass, as well as psychological threats such as packages claimed to contain blood contaminated with HIV.

Terrorists have displayed considerable ingenuity in devising packages that will pass a cursory inspection and travel intact through the postal system, but still injure the recipient when opened. Some years ago, animal rights terrorists in the UK developed a device based on a commercially available rat-trap, with pieces of razor blade set into the mechanism. Others have hidden explosive devices in innocent-looking containers such as a VHS video library case, or the type of cardboard tube used to mail posters and large documents.

All of these devices can cause psychological distress, personal injury or death, and considerable disruption to a business. Although more and more business is

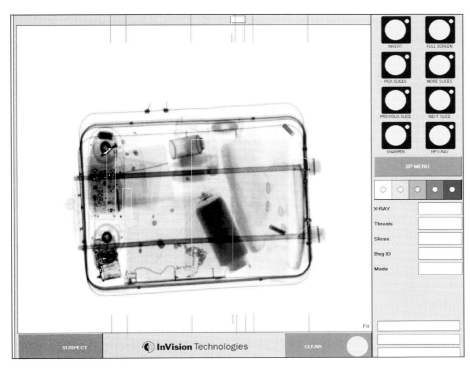

being done electronically, the mail system is still essential, and no one can guarantee they will not become a target. It is important for businesses to remember that victims of mail devices are often not the targets themselves, but those whose work requires them to handle mail – post-room workers and secretaries, for instance. There are considerable health and safety implications for any company that does not take the threat of hazardous mail seriously.

Todd Research Package Screening Systems

Todd Research, based in the UK, is an expert in package screening whose range of equipment and services include:

- Mail-room units (from desktop to conveyor) to screen incoming letters and parcels
- Portable detectors for abandoned cases and packages
- Gateway detectors for monitoring personnel
- Suppression blankets for containing devices once identified
- User training and demonstration of equipment, seminars and training videos

Todd Research TR Detector 8

The Todd Research TR Detector 8 is a large-capacity X-ray screening unit incorporating sophisticated materials recognition technology. It is designed for screening baggage, cases and large quantities of mail, and will help detect explosives, narcotics, weapons and concealed items. The system comprises an operator control console, conveyor unit and dual monitors. It is controlled by an integrated PC operating system.

A pre-set colour code is displayed when a specific material type is detected:

- Brown – indicates presence of an organic material (paper, card, food stuffs, drugs, explosives)
- Green – indicates presence of an inorganic/composite material (high density plastics, alloy metals, minerals)
- Blue – indicates ferrous and non-ferrous metals of higher density (steel, iron, some alloys)

The optional ADS (Advanced Detection Software) can be programmed to alarm and place a coloured frame around a large quantity of a certain material; for example, areas highlighted yellow may indicate the presence of drugs, while areas highlighted red may indicate the presence of explosives.

The system is versatile and can be used in loading bays, mailrooms and reception areas to screen incoming goods for staff protection and outgoing goods for theft control. It will accurately identify hazards, contraband, weapons and stolen property. This is easier and more certain with dual monitors: the colour monitor detects materials and densities while the black-and-white monitor detects silhouettes and outlines. The system is consistent and fast, causing minimum delay to the organisation's incoming and outgoing mail.

Specifications	
Overall length	3,000mm
Width	1,295mm
Height	1,945mm
Capacity	Items up to 900mm wide x 750mm high x unlimited length
Power supply	Single phase 220–240v 50/60Hz. 110v 56Hz on request
Film safety	Up to ISO 1600

PW Allen Letterbomb Detector

Internal security specialists PW Allen offer a desktop-sized Letterbomb Detector that will quickly screen packages up to telephone directory size. It detects virtually all known letterbomb detonating devices, regardless of the type of explosive used. No special training is required, and packages are simply passed through an opening in the detector. It is programmed to ignore normal items of office stationery such as paper clips, staples and metal tags, but sounds an alarm when a detonating device is detected. A test card is supplied with the detector. This can be passed through the detector prior to use to confirm that it is functioning correctly.

Specifications	
Capacity	2.25ins (58mm) thickness
Length	16ins (40cm)
Width	18ins (45cm)
Height	9ins (22cm)
Weight	17 lbs (8kg)
Power supply	220/110v AC 50/60Hz (switchable)
Back-up battery	12v DC
Operating temperature 0°C to 40°C	

PW Allen X-Ray Parcel Bomb Detector

For larger packages and parcels, PW Allen offer an X-Ray Parcel Bomb Detector, with a large capacity chamber that can handle most parcels and bulk mail as well as briefcases, holdalls and handbags for visitor screening. The unit will clearly display bomb components such as batteries, detonators and wiring, as well as dangerous items such as razor blades, glass, syringes and drugs. There are two models available: one displays the image on a fluorescent screen, which is viewed via a moulded inspection visor; the other displays the image on a black-and-white video monitor.

Specifications	
Chamber size	48 x 49 x 45cm (HxWxD)
Unit size	89 x 55 x 51cm (HxWxD)
Floor stand	38 x 55 x 51cm (HxWxD)
Weight	160kg
Power supply	230/120v AC 50/60Hz (switchable)
Resolution	36AWG

VEHICLE AND CARGO SCANNERS

Just as it is necessary to screen passengers and personal luggage at borders and ports, vehicles and cargo must also be screened for explosives, weapons, drugs, contraband and concealed personnel. Modern systems can be used, in scaled-up versions, to scan entire trucks and cargo containers – allowing effective checking without undue disruption to the flow of legitimate traffic.

Rapiscan 2000

The Rapiscan 2000 Series is a range of fixed-site X-ray systems for screening extra-large cargo. System sizes range from air cargo pallets to truck loads as large as 4.5 metres high, 3.5 metres wide and 25.0 metres long, with a maximum weight of 60 tons. Cargo can be screened independently or while remaining loaded on a truck. This effectively counters the pathways for drugs, arms smuggling and fraud in cargo shipments at ports and border crossings.

The X-ray scanning process is quick and efficient, expediting the movement of goods. The use of high-energy X-ray systems has proved to be more effective than manual searches for comparing contents rapidly with the manifest. It removes the possibility of breakage and pilferage associated with manual inspection. Manual searches are labour intensive, slow and unpopular with shippers.

These large X-ray scanners operate in a similar way to Rapiscan's 500 series, used to check aircraft passenger baggage. The cargo, still on a fully loaded truck, is carried through a fan-shaped beam of high-energy X-rays that pass through the cargo and on to arrays of detectors. Excellent picture quality and maximum penetration offers high throughput with high reliability.

Barringer Sabre 2000

The Sabre 2000 is an extremely versatile hand-held device that can detect and identify more than forty explosives, chemical warfare agents and narcotic substances. It has a huge range of potential applications, including checking vehicles approaching potential target areas, bomb searches, and sensitive site security.

The unit is truly portable, weighing less than 5.8 lbs, including the ninety-minute battery. It may be operated by non-technical personnel, and gives results in seconds. It can be brought on to a ship to sample cargo, or kept in a vehicle for instant detection capability.

The Sabre 2000 offers both particle and vapour detection. Vapour samples are simply collected from the target area – a vehicle interior, for instance – by drawing in ambient air. Particle samples are collected with a swab and then introduced into the detector.

Samples are analysed using IMS (Ion Mobility Spectrometry), and the device can simultaneously detect and identify more than thirty substances in seconds.

Specifications	
Substances detected	
Explosives	RDX, PETN, TNT, Semtex, NG, Ammonium Nitrate and others
Drugs	Cocaine, Heroin, THC (Cannabis) Methamphetamine, Ecstasy, Date Rape Drug (GHB) and others
Chemical agents	Nerve and blister agents, such as Tabun, Sarin, Soman, Cyclosarin, Agent VX and Vx, Nitrogen Mustard 3, CL2, HCL, NH3, and others
Analysis Time	15–20 seconds
Warm-up Time	Less than 10 minutes
Dimensions	13 x 4 x 4.5ins (33 x 11.5 x 13cm)
Weight	Under 5.8lbs (2.6kg) with battery
Power	Standard 90-minute battery. Optional DC and AC adapters and long-life battery pack available

BOMB DISPOSAL 6

In the previous chapter we looked at equipment to detect a terrorist IED (Improvised Explosive Device) – in addition to weapons and contraband – and prevent it being smuggled on to an aircraft, etc, either in luggage or concealed on the bomber's person. But what happens when a suspected device is found – perhaps during the checks described earlier, as a result of a warning from the terrorists themselves, or due to a member of the public reporting an abandoned package in a public place?

The unenviable job of investigating a suspected device and making it safe falls to the EOD (Explosive Ordnance Disposal) or IEDD (Improvised Explosive Device Disposal) specialists – often referred to in the media as 'bomb disposal', although their job goes well beyond that literal description.

Media reports and Hollywood films have contributed to a public perception of EOD specialists as brave, even reckless individuals tackling terrorist bombs with a pair of nail scissors: as the timer ticks down towards zero the hero must make an inspired guess as to whether to cut the red wire or the white one; if he guesses wrong, not only will he be blown to smithereens but half the city will be flattened.

Real life, of course, is very different. The EOD team's priority is to protect human lives – including their own. Also important, but further down the list, come the need to prevent damage to property, gain intelligence about the enemy's methods and capabilities, preserve forensic evidence, and allow normal life and/or military operations to resume as quickly as is safely possible.

The threat facing the modern EOD team is a complex one. Terrorists may choose from a wide variety of different bombs, from a small package sent through the mail to a large device in a car or truck. These may be specifically targeted at a particular individual – such as the bomb used to assassinate Earl Mountbatten on 27 August 1979, which was hidden on his boat and detonated by remote control from a vantage point on the shore. Or they may be aimed at causing the maximum disruption and economic damage – such as the IRA's attacks on the City of London in 1992 and 1993. Another possibility is a 'projected' device such as an improvised rocket or mortar.

Terrorist bombs may use various methods of detonation, depending on the purpose of the device. Bombs designed to kill an individual will most likely use a 'booby-trap' type mechanism, as in a parcel bomb, or some means of remote control – either by command wire, radio signal or some kind of light beam. Commercial equipment, such as cellphones and pagers, can also be adapted to function as bomb triggers. Indeed, a modified cellphone has been used as a very effective instrument of assassination in its own right; the bomber can call the target and get him to confirm that the device is held against his head before sending the detonation signal!

Bombs intended to cause disruption and damage are more likely to be controlled by a timer, such as the IRA's City of London bombs referred to above. There are exceptions, of course: the device planted in a Brighton hotel in 1984,

Troops at a checkpoint search a vehicle for concealed explosives. Photo: Author's collection.

months in advance of the Conservative Party conference, was intended to assassinate the Prime Minister, Margaret Thatcher, but used a timer mechanism. An adapted video timer was rigged to detonate the device when Mrs Thatcher should have been in her bedroom, although in fact she was still working and survived the attack.

Terrorists have become highly sophisticated, and it is now quite possible to encounter devices with a variety of complicated anti-handling circuits intended to target the EOD specialists themselves. Such circuits may employ a number of different sensors to trigger the device – a mercury tilt-switch has often been used, but other possibilities include light sensors (to detect when a lid is removed, for instance), PIR sensors similar to those used in intruder alarms, and magnetic switches activated by the proximity of a tool made of ferrous material.

There is also the ever-present possibility of a device containing chemical, biological or even nuclear agents. Following the 11 September attacks, intelligence sources raised the possibility of a 'dirty' bomb, designed to spread radioactive material, being used against a major US or European city.

The modern EOD team has access to some very specialised, high-tech equipment, including sophisticated robots which can be sent in to investigate a suspected device while the operator remains at a safe distance. Portable X-ray equipment can be used to investigate the inner workings of a device without dismantling it. And an explosive disrupter can tear the device apart before the mechanism has time to operate (the 'controlled explosion' often reported in the media).

Despite all this, however, there is still a place for some very low-tech equipment in the EOD team's armoury. The 'hook and line' set, for example, has long been a standard piece of EOD equipment. This is basically a simple length of rope, with a variety of attachments and accessories so that it can be used, for instance, to pull open a car door.

EOD robots

No matter how skilled an EOD expert may be, it is always preferable not to approach a suspected device – and for years the EOD robot has been the preferred method of investigating any threat. Perhaps the best known example is the Morfax 'Wheelbarrow', a remotely controlled EOD vehicle that first saw operational service in 1972 and was used extensively in Northern Ireland at the height of 'The Troubles' there, when terrorist bombs became a part of everyday life.

A tracked remotely controlled vehicle, the original Wheelbarrow was driven by two reversible electric motors, powered by two on-board 12v lead-acid batteries. The operator controlled the vehicle through a 100m umbilical cable, and used a monitor to view the picture from the on-board CCTV camera. Later versions used radio control to avoid the need for a cable, making the Wheelbarrow more manoeuvrable and versatile. Improvements to the drive system over the years made it possible to manoeuvre the Wheelbarrow up stairs and over various obstacles.

A variety of boom arms and extensions could be fitted, with a wide selection of tools enabling the operator to tackle various tasks remotely. The Wheelbarrow could be fitted with a disrupter for disarming IEDs, and a Browning automatic shotgun which could be used for tasks such as opening car boots.

EOD robots are an extremely versatile tool, with possibilities that go way beyond EOD work. A glimpse of the future was offered in 2002 when an Israeli EOD robot was pictured in newspapers taking a failed Palestinian suicide bomber into custody. Some of the explosives carried by the man had detonated, leaving him lying stunned in the road. The EOD robot drew up, extended its boom and grasped the man's wrist, then proceeded to check him over for further explosives. The US Joint Robotics Program is working to develop various 'hazardous duty' robots for tasks that include patrolling and sentry duties, mine clearance, and the monitoring of areas contaminated with biological or chemical agents (more information on this programme can be found at www.jointrobotics.com).

Telerob tEODor EOD robot

Telerob, of Ostfildern in Germany, manufacture the highly sophisticated tEODor, one of the new generation of EOD robots which have grown up from the early vehicles like the original Wheelbarrow. Essentially the tEODor's job is the same as that of the earliest EOD robots; it allows an operator to remotely examine and manipulate a suspected explosive device, and place and fire a disrupter to neutralise the device. Modern technology and years of practical experience, however, have enabled Telerob to improve the vehicle's performance substantially. The tEODor is a very versatile, capable, precision tool permitting the EOD operator to carry out delicate tasks from a safe distance.

The basic unit is a two-tracked vehicle. The running gear is very manoeuvrable, with good off-road capability and the ability to climb gradients steeper than 60 per cent. It has robust steel tracks that never need retightening, and are composed of individually replaceable segments. The high-torsion drives operate in infinitely variable mode with four-quadrant control in forward and reverse, enabling the vehicle to

The back and front of the Telerob tEODor is a modern EOD robot, with a very versatile manipulator arm and an on-board tool magazine that allows the operator to select the tool required. Photo: © James Marchington.

Specifications				
Vehicle		**Control console**		
Length	1,300mm	Dimensions	440mm W	
Width	680mm		x 220mm H	
Height	1,100mm		x 230mm D	
Weight	360kg	Weight	8kg	
Speed	0-50m/min			
Gradient	<62%	**Control station**		
Turning circle	1,460mm	Dimensions	700mm W x	
			1,100mm H x	
Manipulator			600mm D	
Tower rotation	+/– 210°	Weight	70kg	
Carrying load	100kg			
Reach	2,800mm	**Remote control**		
	vertical,	Data channels	433mHz–	
	2,400mm		435mHz,	
	horizontal		80 channels	
Gripper	300mm	Video channels	2.3GHz,	
capacity			5 channels	
Gripper force	600N			

move with great precision. Automatically activated safety brakes keep the vehicle from slipping on steep gradients or steps.

Where early EOD robots had a simple boom, the tEODor has a sophisticated six-axis manipulator arm with a reach of 2.8m, which can be moved into a variety of configurations – enabling it to look into awkward spaces, under vehicles and over obstructions.

An important feature of the tEODor is the on-board tool magazine, enabling the operator to change tools quickly while the robot is in position; there is no need to drive the vehicle back to the control post in order to change a tool. The tool magazine contains a selection of standard tools such as tearing hooks, window-breakers and battery-operated drills. As the manipulator arm collects a new tool from the magazine, the electrical contacts for controlling the tool are automatically established.

The tEODor can deploy an X-ray system around a suspected explosive device, passing the image back to the operator in real time for a rapid evaluation of the threat.

Among the tools on offer is a wide array of special ballistic systems and other equipment for deactivating IEDs. These include a LIN freezing device and a water-jet cutting system as well as the TEL 220, Telemach, Dynergit, Richmond RE 70, PigStick, HotRod and Remington Police shotgun.

Control of the tEODor can be via radio or a 200m fibre-optic cable. The cable has a sophisticated cable management system, with a cable drum that has an automated wind-up mechanism. The operator's stand is designed to serve as a mobile operations centre. It has its own power supply and can be set up anywhere within seconds.

A large TFT monitor provides an overview of the area of operation. The tEODor carries four cameras in its basic configuration: two drive cameras, an overview camera with 72x zoom, and a gripper camera. A stereo camera and an extra overview camera on an extending mast are available as options. All cameras are colour and are equipped with variable lighting.

Key vehicle data such as battery voltage, temperature of electronic components and gripping pressure are displayed on the control console. The operating controls are designed to be simple and precise to use, with extensive use of pictograms, and just two main joystick-type controllers.

Telerob offer the tEODor in various packages, which can include a fully fitted EOD van, operator training and support.

Remotec Mk8 Plus II

The Remotec Wheelbarrow Mk8 Plus II is produced by Remotec UK, a subsidiary of Northrop Grumman, and is a development of the familiar Wheelbarrow, referred to above. It has seen service in the Falklands and Bosnia as a mine-clearance vehicle, and is used by a number of EOD units around the world.

The Mk8 Plus II has seen many improvements on earlier Wheelbarrow variants. It is a rubber-tracked vehicle, with the ability to change its track geometry, so shifting its centre of gravity. This contributes to the robot's particularly good rough terrain capability. It can carry a variety of cameras, weapons, disruptors, manipulators, mechanical grabs and explosive or chemical detection equipment. There is a modular weapons mounting system allowing great versatility in configuration to deal with a variety of threats.

A new digital control system gives the user proportional control over the actuators. This offers more precise, positive control of the robot's movements. New communications links, and developments of the video and audio system, provide better information from the vehicle.

The Mk8 Plus II can be controlled by radio link, with a range of 200m in urban areas, or up to 1km line of sight in open country. Alternatively, it may be controlled by a cable or a fibre-optic link of up to 200m.

The Remotec Revolution is the latest development of the 'Wheelbarrow'. It has a turret that can rotate through 360°, and is fitted with four cameras. Photo: Remotec.

Specifications			
Length	125cm	Power	24v maintenance-free
Width	65cm		gel-type batteries
Operational weight	315kg	Reach	3.6m
Speed	0–5 kph	Lift	Extended 30kg
Turning circle	Own length		Retracted 150kg

Remotec Revolution

The Revolution is the latest incarnation of the Wheelbarrow. Retaining many of the tried and tested features of the Wheelbarrow MK8 Plus II, it is equipped with a turret, so that operational equipment can be rotated through 360° around the chassis. This enables the decks to be completely interchangeable.

The turret and articulating link are used to support a bridge, on to which can be fitted a boom and modular weapon-mounting system (MWMS), making it possible to mount a number of disruptors and a variety of additional fittings. Another new feature is that there are four cameras mounted, with all four views simultaneously viewed at the control point. The images can be viewed as picture-in-picture, split, vertical or horizontal. This equips the vehicle to be used for surveillance tasks as well as its typical IEDD role.

Remotec Super M

The Super M is the latest development in the Wheelbarrow Mk7 series of EOD robots. These vehicles have seen more active service than any other Remotec EOD vehicle. They have been in service in around forty countries, with over 500 vehicles being produced.

The Remotec Super M is the latest version of the Mk7 series, which have seen active service in around forty countries world-wide. Photo: Remotec.

Specifications		Power	24v maintenance free gel-type batteries
Length	121cm		
Width	67cm		
Operational weight	204kg	Reach	2.7m
		Lift	Extended 6.5kg
Speed	0–3 kph		Retracted 112kg
Turning circle	Own length		

The Andros Mark V-A1's unusual articulated track configuration gives it outstanding ability to negotiate obstacles like stairs, kerbs and ditches. Photos: Remotec.

The Super M is a friction-drive rubber-tracked vehicle with a speed of 0–3 kph. The track geometry is fixed. The top hamper and accessories are the same as those on other Remotec robots, allowing the Super M to be fitted with the latest EOD weapons and countermeasures. Remotec offer an upgrade service whereby older Mk7s can be upgraded to the latest Super M specification.

Remotec Andros family

Remotec also produce the Andros family of hazardous duty mobile robots. The largest and most powerful in the range is the Mark V-A1. This robot has an unusual configuration of articulated tracks, which allow it to manoeuvre over rough terrain and obstacles, climb stairs and cross ditches up to 24ins wide.

The Mark V-A1 is sealed to operate in any weather conditions, and in areas of high temperature and humidity. It can operate on almost any surface, including grass, gravel, mud and sand. The Mark V-A1 can be fitted with a wide variety of manipulators, video cameras, audio equipment and EOD disruptors. It can also mount various SWAT weapons, including a 12-gauge shotgun, window breaker and gas dispenser.

Specifications	
Length	115cm
Width	72.4cm
Height	110cm
Operational weight	275kg
Speed	0–3.2kph
Climbing ability	45° stairs/slopes, 41cm high ledge, 61cm wide ditch
Power	2 x 65AH 12v batteries
Reach	162cm
Lift	Extended 27kg
	At 45cm reach 45kg

Variants on the Andros Mark V-A1 include the Wolverine, which includes all of the proven Andros capabilities on a simpler six-wheel-drive chassis. Wolverine has an operational time of over eight hours, and will operate in all types of environments including rain, snow, sand and high humidity.

The Andros F6a is a compact version of the Mark V-A1. It has a higher speed capability, with a top speed of 5.6kph. It is also narrower, at 44.5cm, enabling it to be used in confined spaces, such as aircraft. It uses the same patented articulating track design to negotiate obstacles and cross rough terrain.

Another reduced size version of the Mark V-A1 is the Mini-Andros II. This too uses the articulated track design and is environmentally sealed to permit its use in a wide range of conditions. It has a 2 metre reach and uses a modular design to permit quick changing of tools. This model is 60cm wide, weighs 86kg and has a top speed of 1.8kph.

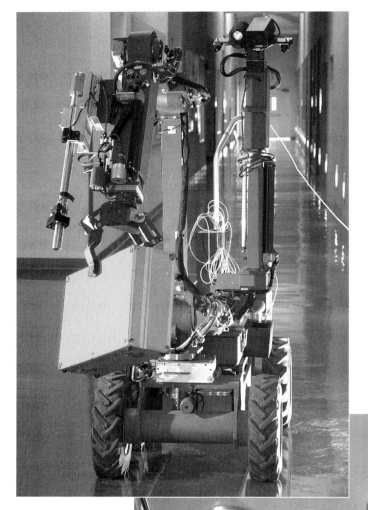

EOD Suits and Tools

Although it is generally preferable to deploy a robot to investigate a suspected IED, there will always be occasions when the only option is for an EOD specialist to approach the device – perhaps because of its inaccessible position, or because there is no robot available within a realistic timescale, or when more delicate procedures are required. In such a situation, the technician will use a protective EOD 'bomb-suit' to protect him as far as possible against injury or death should the device detonate. The suit is also used after a device is believed to have been deactivated by a robot, in case there is a second device hidden nearby.

The design of an EOD suit is inevitably something of a compromise between protection and retaining sufficient mobility and vision to complete the task in hand. A suit giving total protec-

Sandia National Laboratories have adapted this Remotec Wolverine EOD robot with 'SMART' software to automate many of its basic functions, enabling the operator to concentrate on decision-making. Photos: Sandia.

tion would be useless if the operator could not see or move to investigate the device.

The dangers from a nearby explosion come in four main categories: fragmentation, heat, overpressure and impact. Perhaps the greatest threat comes from fragments of the bomb and surrounding objects, which can enter the body at supersonic speeds. The high temperatures created by an explosion can cause burns to the body. The pressure wave from an explosion can cause severe damage to the lungs and eardrums, and cause trauma in other organs. Finally impact: the effect of the blast on the body can cause the head and upper body to accelerate at different speeds, potentially damaging or even breaking the neck and spine.

The PW Allen EOD Bombsuit is designed to protect against fragmentation, heat, overpressure and impact, the four main dangers to the human body from an explosion. Photo: © PW Allen.

PW Allen Advanced EOD Bombsuit and Helmet

PW Allen's Advanced EOD Bombsuit is built to meet the demanding US MIL-SPEC 622E standard, rather than the less strict NATO STANAG 2920. It consists of a jacket, leggings, groin cup and rigid ballistic panels, and is constructed of Kevlar, with an outer anti-static cover of 50/50 Nomex and Kevlar. The design is based on the results of extensive tests carried out by the US DoD (Department of Defense) and counters the four main threats outlined above.

Lightweight composite ballistic panels protect the wearer's upper torso, shoulders, neck, arms and legs from fragments, while maintaining lightness and manoeuvrability. Additional rigid ballistic panels give added protection to the chest, lower abdomen and groin areas. These panels have been tested with fragments at a velocity of up to 1,667m/sec.

The outer covering of Nomex/Kevlar mix is flame retardant and protects the user against burns. The ballistic panels are designed to limit the effects of overpressure on the body, and the collar completely encloses the neck area and overlaps the helmet for added protection. The suit is fitted with an articulated spine protector to protect against the

effects of impact, while the raised collar overlapping the helmet limits the movement of the head relative to the body.

The helmet is an integral part of the EOD Bombsuit. It is made of a lightweight but immensely strong fibre, which offers protection against fragments with speeds of over 683m/sec. It weighs just 3.6kg complete with visor, and the ergonomic design allows ease of movement and good visibility. The visor is made of laminated acrylic and polycarbonate, to give clear, undistorted vision and good protection against multiple fragment strikes.

The helmet incorporates a forced-air ventilation system and a communications system of microphone and speakers that is compatible with hard-wired or radio systems. The battery pack uses standard 9v batteries and provides up to five hours' use of the ventilation system.

The suit can quickly become very warm when worn in a hot climate, which is at best uncomfortable for the operator, and at worst could pose a danger of dehydration and heat exhaustion. For this reason, PW Allen also supply a liquid cooled undersuit, which can be worn under the bombsuit. It consists of a Nomex suit with a network of capillary tubes stitched into it. The tube system is connected to a water reservoir and

The PW Allen EOD Bombsuit has lightweight ballistic panels to protect the torso, shoulders, neck, arms and legs, while maintaining lightness and manoeuvrability. Photo: © PW Allen.

pump that circulates cold water around the suit, cooling the surface of the body.

The suit comes in three parts: a long-sleeved shirt that can be used on its own, a hood, and a pair of trousers. The pump and cooling unit is worn strapped to the leg of the bombsuit. The ice water bottle has a capacity of 2 litres, and when full will give 40–60 minutes of cooling, after which time it can be changed for another bottle. The miniature DC pump is powered by rechargeable NiCad batteries, and has a five-speed electronic control, allowing the cooling to be adjusted between 0 and 300 Watts of heat transfer.

There is a special wireless radio system designed to be used with the PW Allen Bombsuit. This is a full duplex system which produces a very low level of RF radiation when transmitting, to minimise any risk of creating induction currents in a bomb's

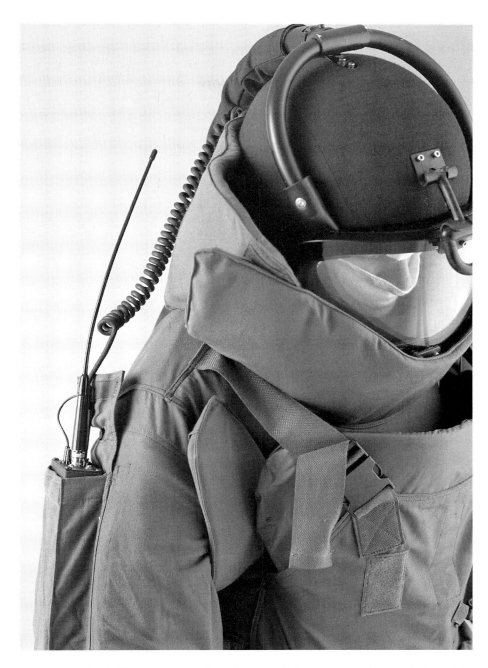

The EOD Bombsuit communication system integrates with the suit's helmet, and can be used in conjunction with the forced-air ventilation system. Photo: © PW Allen.

detonating circuit. The user can switch off transmission upon reaching a device, while still being able to receive incoming signals. The radio system may be used in two-way or three-way configuration, enabling two EOD operators to communicate with each other as well as with a base station. The system uses frequencies between 130 and 250Mhz and has an output power of less than 100mW into a 50ohm antenna. A recording receiver can be used in conjunction with the system.

A purpose-designed radio communication system is used with the PW Allen EOD Bombsuit. It is very low-powered to minimise the risk of inadvertently detonating a device. Photo: © PW Allen.

Alternatively the EOD team may use a hard-wired communications system, which is used in conjunction with the bombsuit helmet. The system can be used with standard firing cable, and connects the bombsuit helmet to a headset and boom mic with an amplifier unit.

Hook and line systems

It is often desirable to move a suspected IED from its original position, in order to examine it more closely, to obtain access for the equipment required to neutralise the device or, more rarely, to move it to an area where it presents less of a hazard if it should detonate. An example might be a terrorist weapon discovered in a 'hide', which could be attached to a booby trap. Where this cannot be done by a robot, the time-honoured and highly effective method is to use a 'hook and line' to pull the device into a more favourable position. The hook and line system is also useful for examining a suspect vehicle, making it possible to open car doors, boots and the like with minimal risk to EOD operators.

In its simplest form, a hook and line can be improvised from commonly available materials such as string or light rope, washing line fittings and the like. However, professional EOD teams use specially developed hook and line sets designed for the purpose. These offer a range of fittings that experience has shown are useful and effective, and overcome many of the problems commonly found when handling IEDs. The set also includes non-elastic rope, an important factor.

PW Allen offer a range of hook and line (or HAL) sets, each designed for a specific type of task. The Mk 4 HAL set, for instance, is a single line kit for removing IEDs from buildings. It contains a variety of components for attaching a line to a suspected IED and anchoring snatch blocks to floors, walls, window and door frames. The snatch blocks are self-opening to enable an IED to be manoeuvred along a complex route in a single operation. The 120m line means that the moving of the IED can be carried out from a safe distance. The kit includes a sledge so that the IED may be more easily manoeuvred across rough ground, or up or down stairs. The sledge also reduces the likelihood of the device snagging on corners. A telescopic pole, which extends to 3 metres, can be used to attach a line to the suspected device. All the components fit into a compact carrying case, with the line on a separate reel, and the entire set can be carried easily by one man.

PW Allen's HAL kit Mk 2 is intended for search and disposal of IEDs in vehicles. The set contains hooks, ropes and wire slings, pitons, seizers, crocodile grips, vice jaw grips, suction pad anchors, shock cords and snatch blocks. Two colour-coded 120m lines are included. There are various special components for gaining access to a vehicle: hooks and grippers can be used to open doors, glove compartments, etc. The kit is supplied in a metal case, with separate reels for the lines.

There is a separate set available of specialised vehicle access tools. This includes a remote window breaker, vehicle door button pusher, key/handle clamp and vehicle door handle lifter. Each tool is designed to perform its specific task reliably and without time-consuming rigging, reducing the risk to the EOD technician.

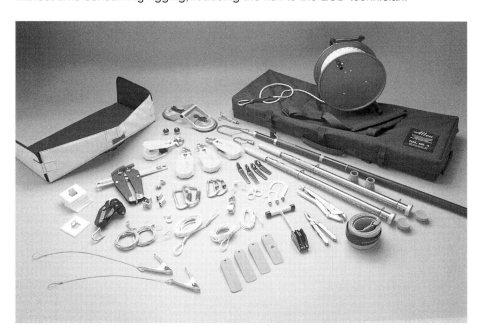

The Mk 4 HAL set from PW Allen is a single-line hook-and-line kit for removing suspected IEDs from buildings. Snatch blocks mean the device can be manoeuvred along a complex route in a single operation. Photo: © PW Allen.

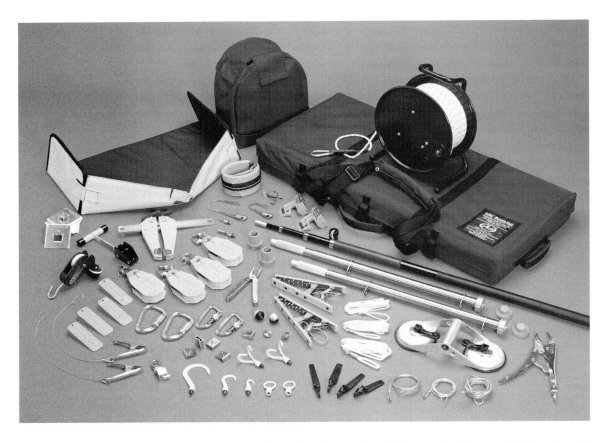

The PW Allen BombTec is a comprehensive two-line hook-and-line kit with components for moving a suspected IED from a building or vehicle. Photo: © PW Allen.

Another kit, the HAL Mk 3, is a heavy-duty kit for moving larger objects and vehicles. It contains a reel of 150m 3,670kg low-stretch line, various slings, ground anchors, a shackle, hooks and snatch blocks. The line may be attached to a suspect vehicle or container quickly and securely with the minimum of disturbance, and the object moved to an area where it presents less of a hazard and can be dealt with.

PW Allen offer various other HAL kits, including the HAL BombTec, a comprehensive two-line kit for devices located in buildings, vehicles or open areas. Another set, the HAL Special Operations Kit, is a lightweight and highly portable rigging kit for tactical situations; it is contained in a custom-designed backpack that can be carried by one man, leaving both hands free to handle a weapon or other equipment. Also available are a lightweight tripod for objects up to 90kg, a heavy duty tripod for objects up to 750kg, and a tactical procedures manual that gives detailed instructions on using the various hook and line systems.

EOD Disrupters

Once a suspected IED has been located and identified, the problem remains of how to disarm the device so as to make it safe, without detonating the main charge. A variety of disrupters are available for this purpose, each with different characteristics making it suitable for specific tasks.

Perhaps the simplest type is a conventional shotgun shell, which is used to fire a charge of lead shot into the device. Carefully aimed, this can remove the firing mechanism from an IED before it has time to detonate the main charge. The Browning recoil-operated 5-shot automatic shotgun was once the favourite tool for this job, often fitted to an EOD robot such as the Wheelbarrow.

A shotgun is quite likely to cause an IED to explode, however, and nowadays this job is more likely to be done by various types of water jet disrupters, such as the recoilless disposable type sold by PW Allen. Looking rather like a spotlamp, the recoilless disrupter contains a specially shaped liquid container and a retaining shell. The device is loaded with 250ml of water and up to 46g of plastic explosive. A conventional detonator is fitted in the detonator well. When fired, the unit disintegrates, projecting a very high velocity jet of liquid, which will disrupt many types of IED at a range of up to 2 metres – at this range the jet will penetrate 15mm of plywood. This type of disrupter may be emplaced close to the device, using its own wire legs, or attached to an EOD robot and manoeuvred remotely into position.

PW Allen also sell a disrupter intended specifically to deal with IEDs in vehicles. This device, the Disposable Car Boot Disrupter, is shaped like a briefcase, and is designed to be loaded with around 13.6 litres of water and 250g of explosive. The case is shaped so that the water surrounds the explosive charge, providing a tamping effect to increase the amount of energy imparted to the water jet; the jet itself consists of around 6.8 litres, or around half of the total volume loaded into the device. The case is 106mm high, so it can be easily slipped under a vehicle by an EOD robot.

Typically, the loaded case will be placed under the boot of a vehicle suspected of containing an IED. When fired, the disrupter projects a powerful jet of water upwards

The PW Allen Disposable Car Boot Disrupter uses explosives to produce a powerful jet of water, blowing open the boot of a car and ejecting the contents. Photo: © PW Allen.

The IED Disrupter Kit from PW Allen will penetrate a thin-walled IED with a low probability of detonating the device. Photo: © PW Allen.

with such force that the bottom of the vehicle is penetrated and the IED is ejected through the boot lid or the roof. The jet of water is highly effective at disrupting the detonating circuit of an IED without causing it to activate; detonating cord is severed by the jet without initiation. The spare wheel is normally ejected, and the petrol tank is ruptured and emptied without ignition.

Another type of water jet disrupter is the cartridge-fired type, typically mounted on an adjustable arm so that it can be aligned precisely with the suspect device. PW Allen's version of this is sold as their IED Disrupter Kit. It is designed to penetrate thin-walled IEDs with a low probability of causing detonation. The kit includes a barrel, breech assembly and stand, together with the reel and firing cable and a quantity of cartridges. A cartridge consists of an aluminium case fitted with an insulated centre contact (the case itself acts as the second contact). It contains an electrically fired igniter, propellant and a closure disc. The end is swaged and the cartridge is sealed.

The PAN Disrupter was used to disarm the shoe bombs worn by Richard Reid on a transatlantic flight from Paris to Miami in December 2001. Photo: Sandia.

The disrupter is loaded with a cartridge and arranged so that the barrel is aimed at the appropriate part of the IED. The stand has a counter-weight on its lower arm, and the arms are friction jointed so they can be set in position quickly and easily. The firing cable is 100m long, so the operator can retire to a safe position before firing. Firing is done with an Electronic Exploder unit. This contains a 9v PP3 battery and has a rugged reinforced nylon body that is waterproof and RFI shielded. Indicator lamps on the front of the unit show the status of the circuit. Pressing the prime button prepares the unit for firing; priming typically takes around 3 seconds and the indicator lamp shows when it is ready. Pressing the fire button will then initiate the explosion. The unit gives an output energy of 2.5 Joules with a peak output of 400v, 8.5A.

A similar type of disrupter, commonly used in the US, is the PAN or Percussion-Actu-ated Nonelectric Disrupter, developed by Sandia National Laboratories. This was used to deactivate the shoe bombs Richard Reid allegedly tried to detonate on board a transatlantic flight from Paris to Miami shortly before Christmas 2001. Reid was arrested in Boston, where Massachusetts State Police bomb squad members Sgt Dave Thomp-son and Sgt Ed Anderson, assisted by the FBI, disabled Reid's shoe bombs with a PAN Disrupter. The bombs were disarmed and their inner workings revealed without deto-nating them, so the FBI could use the deactivated bombs during criminal investigation.

The PAN Disrupter was developed in the early 1990s by Sandia bomb-disable-ment expert Chris Cherry and a team of Sandia researchers. Since 1995, when the PAN was licensed to Ideal Products of Lexington, Kentucky, it has become the primary tool used by bomb squads throughout the USA to disable conventional, handmade-type bombs remotely.

For more solidly built IEDs, a water jet may not be suitable. For instance, one common type of terrorist IED is a pipe bomb, constructed from a length of heavy-duty tubing such as steel gas pipe with a cap screwed firmly on to threads at each end. A water jet disrupter might simply hurl the device some distance, deforming it and possibly detonating it, rather than deactivating it.

For this type of device, a more suitable approach is to use a disrupter firing a steel slug – rather like a powerful cold chisel – to smash open the casing of the IED. Typi-

Sandia National Laboratories bomb-disablement expert Chris Cherry shows a replica of Richard Reid's shoe bomb to the news media at a news conference. Photo: Sandia.

cally a pipe bomb contains propellant powder similar to that used in rifle and shotgun cartridges. The explosive force comes from the burning of the powder in an enclosed space, so once the casing is broken apart it cannot explode with any great force.

PW Allen's De-armer is designed to project a variety of steel slugs into this type of device, and is also used to destroy the fuses of air-dropped bombs and similar ordnance. It consists of a recoil-reducing barrel with a cartridge chamber into which a standard .50 calibre electric propelling cartridge is inserted. The breech is closed with a breech plug, and the slug loaded into the barrel. A variety of different slugs are available for different tasks, including chisel, fork and blade types.

The De-armer is then aligned with the IED, and can be fired via a cable from up to 500m away. On firing, excess gas is tapped off and used to counteract the recoil, reducing the recoil of the barrel part to about 5m.

IED Electronic Jamming

As terrorists become ever more sophisticated, it is vital not to overlook the possibility of IEDs being initiated remotely by some form of radio control. This could take the form of a simple RC circuit similar to those used in radio-controlled model cars and aircraft – some terrorist devices have actually used RC model parts adapted to close a firing circuit. Alternatively, it could be a much more sophisticated system, perhaps using cellphone technology enabling the terrorist to detonate the device from anywhere in the world simply by calling the number of a GSM phone built into the device.

Clearly it is important to isolate any suspect device from incoming radio signals which might be used to detonate it while the EOD team are working on it. This is done with a variety of radio jamming equipment, most of which is specially built for EOD work. When selecting a suitable jammer, the EOD operator must consider the threat type (mobile phone, pager, radio frequencies known to be used), the type of deployment (mobile, transportable, fixed), available power source (e.g. 12 or 24v DC, 110 or 230v AC) and the skill and training of the personnel who will be using the equipment.

PW Allen's ECM Shield model 600-2121 provides jamming of RCIEDs (Radio Controlled Improvised Explosive Devices) across a broad range of frequencies, including frequencies known to be favoured by terrorist bomb-makers. The unit can be vehicle-powered and mounted, and can also be used to provide mobile jamming protection for VIPs in transit, military convoys and sensitive events. It effectively emits a protective shield of electro-magnetic radiation, hardening the target to terrorist attack. It can also operate as a pre-detonation device for certain types of RCIED, detonating a device at a safe distance as the protected vehicle approaches. PW Allen also provide a range of other jammers for particular circumstances.

EOD Procurement Packages

Due to the nature of EOD work, users often require a package comprising anything from a fully equipped vehicle to a full solution including training and support. Suppliers such as PW Allen, mentioned extensively in this chapter, offer this kind of complete procurement package. Many governments and international organi-

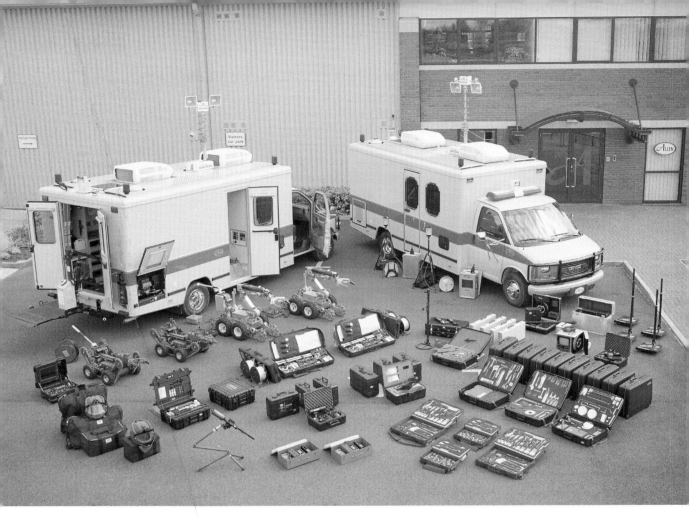

Suppliers such as PW Allen can provide a full 'procurement package' comprising all the equipment, training and support required for EOD work. The package is generally tailored to the customer's precise requirements. Photo: © PW Allen.

sations have used this approach, including the United Nations, humanitarian demilitarisation organisations, military and police. Naturally the package is tailored to the customer's precise requirements, and may include EOD suits, robots, support vehicles, and all the ancillary communications equipment, etc that the team will require.

For instance, in 2002 PW Allen supplied four specialist IEDD vehicles and equipment packages to a Middle Eastern security force. The vehicles were based on a GMC chassis and carried a full complement of specialist IEDD equipment to provide rapid response, search team transport, command and control, secure equipment storage, recharging and maintenance facilities. The package also included full 24/7 maintenance cover, and assistance with ongoing training of EOD teams.

Telerob, mentioned earlier in this chapter, also provide complete package solutions, and have supplied fully kitted-out vehicles to a range of security organisations including the armed forces of UAE and Indonesia, police in Germany, Nigeria and Uzbekistan, the air force of Argentina, and specialist internal security organisations in Kazakhstan, Saudi Arabia and Romania.

INTERNAL SECURITY AND COUNTER-TERRORISM VEHICLES

Counter-terrorist forces employ a large variety and number of vehicles in their work, ranging from the unmodified production saloon car for low-profile transport of personnel to tracked armoured vehicles. Both these extremes, however, really fall outside the scope of this book. We will concentrate on specially equipped vehicles, and restrict ourselves to the type of APC (Armoured Personnel Carrier) that might be deployed in an urban riot situation.

There is a natural revulsion to the use of 'tanks' against 'civilians' – witness the worldwide condemnation of China's use of main battle tanks in Tiananmen Square in June 1989. Any government concerned with its international image and democratic support at home will shy away from deploying tracked armoured vehicles against protesters on its streets.

A police force certainly needs the protection of armoured vehicles if it is faced with a hostile crowd that may conceal elements armed with firearms, petrol bombs and the like. At times of heightened tension in Northern Ireland, for example, APCs have become a common sight on the streets. But when a government resorts to using such things as tracked armoured vehicles or Light Strike Vehicles against a civilian

The ubiquitous Land Rover has seen service in many of the world's trouble spots, often with up-armouring to protect the occupants. White bodywork and UN markings contribute to a less aggressive appearance. Photo: Land Rover.

This up-armoured humvee was destroyed by a land mine that threw debris more than 50 metres, but the three-man crew suffered only minor injuries. Photo: US Army.

population, it is probably fair to say that things have gone beyond any real definition of 'terrorism'; we are now talking about civil war – although in time-honoured fashion the regime will likely decry its opponents as 'terrorists'.

In this chapter, then, we will narrow the definition of Internal Security (IS) vehicles to include only wheeled vehicles with sufficient armour to protect against threats up to the level of mines, bombs and .30 calibre armour-piercing ammunition. This does not, of course extend to .50 calibre anti-materiel sniper rifles such as the Barrett, heavy machine guns or shoulder-fired rocket launchers such as that old terrorist favourite, the ubiquitous RPG-7.

Internal Security Vehicles

Some IS vehicles are variants of armoured vehicles designed originally for the battle-field. It is important to recognise, however, that the requirements for IS are very different from those of open warfare. Typically an IS armoured vehicle will be operating in an urban area, in an unpredictable and rapidly changing situation where the occupants may quickly find themselves cut off from colleagues and surrounded by a hostile crowd who will use their ingenuity and anything at their disposal to attack the vehicle.

Even a quite genial crowd can turn hostile with terrifying speed, and there are always a few hard-core individuals who will take advantage of a legitimate protest to

Internal security vehicles should appear authoritative without being provocative. They must provide protection against weapons such as bricks and petrol bombs as well as firearms. Photo: © James Marchington.

A police Land Rover at an animal rights protest: military style vehicles would be considered inappropriate for this type of duty. Photo: © James Marchington.

cover their own attack on the security forces. An example was the Poll Tax demonstration in Trafalgar Square, London, on 31 March 1990. The vast majority of those present were content to demonstrate peacefully, but violence flared up nevertheless. One police vehicle, isolated by the crowd, beat a hasty retreat as a demonstrator thrust a heavy scaffolding pole through its window with sufficient force to kill or maim the occupants had it hit them.

The crew of an IS vehicle find themselves in an impossible position. On one hand, they need to protect themselves and control the crowd; on the other they must beware of using excessive force, which will inflame the crowd and be politically unacceptable. In contrast, on the battlefield an APC is likely to be operating in wide-open spaces some distance from an enemy who are in a known direction. If the crew find themselves surrounded by the enemy they can merrily let fly with every weapon at their disposal; there is no such thing as 'excessive force'. On a Belfast street, a single dead rioter is one too many.

The requirements for IS vehicles, then, are very different from those of battlefield APC/AFVs. An IS vehicle is often required to be highly visible (in contrast to the camouflage necessary on the battlefield). It should appear imposing and authoritative without being seen as too 'militaristic', which may prove confrontational and encourage an escalation of violence. It should resist a determined and prolonged attack at close quarters by rioters with a variety of implements, from screwdrivers to scaffold poles and petrol bombs – rioters whom, for political reasons, the vehicle's occupants may not be able to resist forcibly. Yet it should be fast and highly manoeuvrable, allowing the occupants to embus and debus quickly. The vehicle should also

Battlefield armoured vehicles, like this US Army humvee, are not best suited to Internal Security operations. Photo: US Army.

have adequate communications, including the ability to transmit video images and data as well as voice, preferably with antennae that are not vulnerable to attack from outside the vehicle.

The weapons deployed in IS situations are generally rather different from those used in warfare, of course. IS vehicles may be fitted with various 'less than lethal' weapons for crowd control, such as water cannon and tear-gas launchers, as well as or instead of conventional cannon and machine guns.

Discreet Operational Vehicles

So much for the armoured IS vehicle, but as already mentioned, police forces and counter-terrorist organisations make use of many other types of vehicle. These are often referred to as Discreet Operational Vehicles or DOVs. This category includes a huge range of vehicles, based on standard production civilian models, which are covertly armoured and/or fitted out with specialist weapons and equipment for surveillance, communications, etc.

Clearly a DOV has the advantage that it does not cause the political difficulties associated with the use of military-style APCs, and is less likely to provoke an escalation of, for example, a student demonstration. It also gives the initiative back to the counter-terrorist force, by making it harder for terrorists to determine what measures are being taken and to identify the location and capability of the forces ranged against them. Used to transport a VIP, a DOV can assist in making the target

The requirements for an internal security vehicle are very different from those of a battlefield APC. This type of protected vehicle was deployed in Northern Ireland. Photo: © James Marchington.

effectively invisible – providing greater security than any amount of armour and weaponry.

DOVs range from police patrol and pursuit vehicles, through VIP limousines and escort vehicles, to specialist surveillance, command and communications vehicles. Although many are converted and supplied 'as new', counter-terrorist forces have been known to purchase privately owned second-hand vehicles and convert them to their own specification. This tactic was used by undercover forces in Northern Ireland, for instance, so that counter-terrorist teams could operate without arousing suspicion in a region where a new or 'foreign' vehicle of any type would have attracted unwanted attention. The conversion work was carried out by the British Army's own specialists, rather than civilian contractors, reducing the chance of a security compromise.

Armoured vehicles can contribute to the safety of officers or VIPs, but few will withstand a direct hit from a weapon such as the RPG-7, a favourite of terrorists worldwide. Photo: © James Marchington.

DOV armour and blast protection

The armouring of any vehicle is inevitably a compromise between protection and performance. There is no such thing as total protection against every possible type of threat; given sufficiently heavy weapons, or the time to deploy sufficient force, any armoured vehicle can be compromised. The crucial thing is to assess the threat and provide adequate protection for the occupants – bearing in mind that good intelligence and SOPs will contribute more to security than any amount of armour.

Threat levels are graded according to the type of weapon likely to be used by an enemy or terrorist against the vehicle. Knowing the capabilities of the most powerful weapon that the terrorist can bring to bear, one can then apply armour that is capable of protecting the occupants. Unfortunately there is much confusion over the classification of ballistic threat levels. Different countries around the world apply different standards, with confusingly similar categories denoted by Roman numerals, while some companies appear to have invented their own classification system which by some curious coincidence makes their products sound as though they give higher levels of protection.

Anyone specifying an armoured vehicle (or body armour) should be careful to determine exactly what classification system is in use, and what testing method has been used. For example, a few millimetres of steel may prevent a high-velocity rifle bullet from passing through, but the spall thrown off the rear surface could be as dangerous to the occupants as a bullet fragment. It is important that the standards applied reflect the actual protection offered in real-life situations.

There are other factors to be taken into account, of course. The vision panels (i.e. windows) should provide the same level of protection as the vehicle panels – there is little point in having superior armour in the doors and body panels, only to be shot through the window. Special attention must be paid to the potential weak areas around door seals and the like. A properly armoured vehicle will have 'splash returns' around the full length of these areas, to catch any bullet or fragment that finds its way through the chink between the door and door pillar.

Perhaps the most reliable indication of ballistic protection is the NIJ standard commonly applied to body armour in the US and elsewhere (for details of these standards, see chapter 9). The NIJ standards are commonly used to describe the protection provided by vehicle armour, although in fact the NIJ standard does not apply to vehicles. A crucial part of the NIJ standards is the measurement of blunt trauma suffered by the wearer's body, directly beneath the point of impact. This is, of course, not applicable to vehicles. However the spall thrown off the back of the armour – or lack of spall – is crucial in a vehicle, and this is not specified in the NIJ body armour standards. Nevertheless, it is common to hear vehicles referred to a giving 'Level IV protection', etc, and in practice this is taken to mean that it gives adequate protection to the occupants if the vehicle is hit with the equivalent weapon.

It is, of course, a mistake to rely too heavily on the nominal protection of a certain type of armour. Only a fool would sit and watch as a terrorist aimed a pistol at his vehicle, thinking, 'That's OK, it's only a 9mm and I've got Level III armour.' For one thing, most types of armour are rated for a single hit at any one point. Although it is unlikely that two bullets will impact on the same point, there is always that possibility. Plus there is no guarantee that the terrorists have not acquired a more powerful weapon than one expected, or will not simply explode a massive land-mine beneath the vehicle as it slows for an obstruction. That said, effective armour is a valuable part of beefing-up security for a VIP, or providing additional protection for counter-terrorist operators – and is routinely used by VIP protection specialists and counter-terrorist organisations worldwide.

There are many companies around the world that provide armoured limousines and 4x4s. Each has its own favoured methods and materials, but the principles remain the same. The process of armouring and protecting a vehicle is likely to include the following:

- The passenger/driver area is lined on all sides (including roof and floor) with armour material to resist bullets/fragments
- All window glass is replaced with transparent glass/polycarbonate armour
- The fuel tank is adapted to resist explosion and protect it against bullets/fragments
- The battery and electrical system is hardened to protect it from damage by bullets or fragments
- Run-flat devices fitted to all wheels, including spare
- The suspension is replaced with a heavy-duty system to restore normal handling with the extra weight of the armour and other additions
- The engine is replaced with a more powerful unit to provide adequate performance bearing in mind the additional weight of the vehicle

Other modifications will depend on the user's requirements, but may include some or all of the following:

- Special radio communications equipment, weapons racks, etc fitted
- Strengthening of front/rear bumper area to protect vehicle in the event of it being used as a battering ram to force through a road-block, etc
- Removal of air-bag safety systems which would present a hazard by hindering escape in the event of an attack
- Exhaust modified to prevent tampering causing the engine to stall, or insertion of an explosive device
- Anti-tamper detection system fitted
- Auxiliary battery and electrical system fitted
- Auxiliary fuel tank fitted
- Smoke/tear gas dispensing system fitted
- Intercom/PA system fitted to enable communication from inside the vehicle without the need to open window or door
- Fire-extinguisher system fitted to engine, luggage and passenger compartments
- Compressed air system fitted to provide positive pressure clean air supply in the event of gas or chemical attack

Run-flat tyres

The tyres are one of the most vulnerable parts of a wheeled vehicle – a bullet or shrapnel fragment can quickly destroy a tyre, causing the driver to lose control and bringing the vehicle to a halt. Likewise, various types of device are designed to be

A cutaway shows the principle of run-flat tyres: if the tyre is damaged, the vehicle can run on the composite insert attached to the wheel rim. Photo: © James Marchington.

Hutchinson make a variety of run-flat tyre inserts; this one is designed to withstand a mine, diverting the blast away from the vehicle and allowing the vehicle to continue driving. Photo: © James Marchington.

deployed on the road to puncture and deflate a vehicle's tyres. This is clearly unacceptable for an operational vehicle – so run-flat inserts are used in the wheels to enable the vehicle to continue if a tyre or tyres are damaged.

There are a number of different manufacturers of run-flat tyres, but the principle is much the same. An insert of composite material is fitted to the wheel, and the tyre fitted over the top. The insert is basically a 'solid tyre' fitted inside the pneumatic tyre. If the tyre is damaged, it will collapse – but the vehicle will continue to run on the insert. The occupants may have a less comfortable ride, but at least the vehicle can continue with its task, whether that is to whisk a VIP away from a threat, continue a pursuit, or press ahead with an attack.

Hutchinson SNC, of Persan in France, manufacture a range of run-flat inserts. Their CRF is intended for use with a one-piece drop centre wheel and tubeless tyre. It consists of several sectors made of a composite material, locked together with nuts and bolts with opposite threads and secured with a thread sealant. It enables a vehicle to continue, with full driving capability, for 80km or more, despite a flat tyre. There are special variants for high-speed vehicles (in excess of 180 km/h) and for off-road vehicles.

Bomb sensors

The possibility of a bomb being attached to a vehicle while unattended is a constant threat for VIPs and security services personnel. A bomb can be constructed in a

Jankel Armouring of England manufacture a range of armoured vehicles, with protection up to 7.62mm rifle ammunition as standard; higher levels of protection are available. The vehicles are based on standard commercial chassis. Photo: © James Marchington.

weatherproof container, such as a plastic lunchbox, and include a powerful magnet which allows it to be attached to the underside of a vehicle in seconds. The British WWII veteran and politician, Airey Neave, was killed on 30 March 1979 by such a bomb, planted by the INLA on his car while it was in a car park under the Houses of Parliament in London. The device contained a timer and a mercury tilt-switch; once the timer ran out, the device was armed and any movement of the car could activate the tilt-switch and detonate the bomb. It detonated as Neave's car negotiated the ramp up from the car park to ground level.

Talos, from Vindicator Technologies in Austin, Texas, is a vehicle bomb detector system which can be fitted to any type of vehicle. It is designed to give a warning if it detects a device attached to the vehicle, or if the vehicle has been tampered with since it was left.

Such a system is not a replacement for standard security procedures such as guarding and visual inspection, but it does give an added layer of protection that can improve the security of high-risk individuals.

The Talos system is powered by the vehicle's battery, and includes a control unit and eight sensors strategically placed around the vehicle. A display, normally placed on the dashboard where it can be viewed on approaching the vehicle, indicates the system status. The system arms twenty seconds after the last door, hood or trunk is closed, and performs a self-test. If any door is tampered with, or an IED is attached to the vehicle, the system will show an alert.

APCs

Jankel Armoured 4x4 Vehicles

Jankel Armouring, of Weybridge in England, produce a range of specialist protected vehicles based on mass-produced commercial chassis including the General Motors K Series and the Ford F-450 Super Duty. This type of vehicle bridges the gap between up-armoured civilian vehicles such as the Range-Rover or G-Wagen, and conventional military-style APCs – providing similar levels of protection to a military APC, but at a significantly lower cost and with a less provocative appearance.

Jankel has supplied vehicles to a wide variety of users, including newsgathering organisations, police forces and specialist counter-terrorist and hostage rescue teams. Their vehicles can be fitted with specialist rapidly deployed ladder configurations for hostage rescue assault operations – enabling the vehicle to be driven straight up to a hijacked aircraft, first storey window, etc, to allow the team rapid access.

Jankel vehicles come with protection to the level of 7.62x51 NATO Ball as standard. This can be supplemented as required to give protection to 7.62x51 AP, engine bay protection, and underbody blast protection against anti-personnel mines, hand grenades and anti-vehicle mines.

The standard specification includes a 1,500kg payload capacity, automatic transmission, power steering, power-assisted ABS brakes, long-range fuel tanks and air conditioning. The GM chassis can be fitted with an 8.1 litre V8 petrol engine or a 6.6

A Jankel Guardian armoured vehicle, based on the GMC K Series chassis, as supplied to the Metropolitan Police for Airport duty. Photo: © James Marchington.

litre Duramax V8 diesel. The Ford chassis has the option of a 6.8 litre Triton V10 or a 7.3 litre Power Stroke V8 diesel.

The Metropolitan Police in London recently took delivery of three Jankel Guardian vehicles for use at Heathrow Airport. The vehicles are based on the GMC K Series chassis, with the 6.5 litre turbo diesel engine. The special equipment package includes light bars with amber lights for airport use and blue/red for police use, plus a matrix sign at the rear that can display messages for traffic control. There is an intercom and PA system so that officers inside can communicate with people outside without compromising their own safety.

Inspector Mike Jukes of Heathrow Police was quoted as saying: 'We are really pleased with these new vehicles. They bring us up to date, providing us with a diverse range of facilities we need for the modern day demands of policing Heathrow. The armoured vehicles have been made to our specifications and I hope will prove invaluable in the fight against terrorism and other crime.'

Alvis Tactica

Alvis Vehicles Ltd, of Telford in England, manufacture a range of armoured vehicles, including tracked vehicles such as the Warrior and Scorpion. The company's Tactica family is a range of 4x4 wheeled vehicles used by military and security forces in a variety of roles including: patrol vehicle, APC (with or without turret), ambulance, bomb disposal, water cannon, assault vehicle, command vehicle, and emergency/rescue vehicle.

The Tactica family have what Alvis describe as a 'non-aggressive profile': they are box-like in shape, at first glance looking more like a bus than a military APC. This, combined with appropriate colouring and markings, can make the Tactica suitable in police and security roles where a more aggressive-looking vehicle would be inappropriate.

The Tactica provides a high level of protection to the crew, with armoured protection against 5.56mm and 7.62mm ball at point-blank range, as well as anti-personnel mines, firebombs and other improvised devices. The vision areas are protected to the

A Jankel Aigis 5-door utility armoured vehicle, as supplied to the British Army for peacekeeping duties with KFOR. Similar vehicles have been produced for NGOs, TV news crews and the like. Photo: © James Marchington.

same level. Additional protection is available to protect against armour-piercing rounds, mines and shell fragments. Run-flat tyres are fitted as standard and the engine and wheels may be protected with a fire extinguisher system. Weapons such as water cannon can be fitted either on pintle mounts or in a one-man turret.

Despite the high level of protection, the Tactica provides good mobility and comfort for the crew. The vehicle will accept a range of turbo-charged diesel engines to suit the customer's requirements. These will give road speeds up to 120km/h. Permanent four-wheel drive with lockable differentials gives good cross-country performance. Full-width protected vision areas, comprehensive instrumentation, a small turning circle and power-assisted controls reduce driver fatigue.

Specifications (Alvis Tactica APC 14-seat variant)	
Crew	2 + 12
Configuration	Permanent 4x4
Length	5,600mm
Width	2,200mm
Height	2,350mm
Ground clearance	300mm (axle)
Combat weight	10,000kg
Payload	3,400kg
Engine	Mercedes OM906LA
Driver position	L or R
Max road speed	120km/h
Max road range	650km
Max gradient	60 per cent
Max side slope	35 per cent
Armour type	High hardness steel to 7.62mm NATO Ball
Ventilation	Twin air-conditioning
Smoke extraction	Twin electric fan
Internal lighting	Day and night systems

Alvis Scarab

The Alvis Scarab was designed as a highly versatile go-anywhere scout and liaison vehicle. As well as its military applications, it is well suited to the armoured scout and patrol car role in internal security operations.

The Scarab is based on the Mercedes Unimog engine and running gear, which gives it good mobility and reliability, and simplifies maintenance and repair. The vehicle's protection is higher than other vehicles of its type; it is protected against 7.62mm AP ammunition all round, with armour against heavy machine gun fire across the frontal arc. Mine protection is built-in against mines up to blast mines containing the equivalent of 7kg of TNT; an enhanced mine protection kit is available.

The Scarab comes in various configurations, the most basic being the Scarab Command, which carries a crew of up to five people and can host a full range of

The Alvis Scarab APC is a versatile scout and patrol car suitable for a variety of Internal Security applications. It is based on the Mercedes Unimog engine and chassis. Photos: Alvis.

The interior of the Scarab APC. The vehicle is protected against 7.62mm AP ammunition all round, and mines containing the equivalent of 7kg of TNT. Photo: Alvis.

surveillance and communications equipment. The Patrol variant has a one-man turret that may be mounted with a 7.62mm or 0.5in machine gun.

Specifications	
Crew	3–5
Configuration	Permanent rear-wheel drive, selectable 4x4
Length	5,283mm
Width	2,405mm
Height	1,900mm
Ground clearance	480mm (axle)
Combat weight	Up to 11,100kg
Payload	2,500kg
Engine	Mercedes OM906LA 6-cylinder injected diesel, with 6-speed automatic gearbox.
Max road speed	110km/h
Max road range	600km
Approach/departure angle	44/42 per cent
Static tilt angle	45 per cent
Vertical obstacle	350mm
Armour type	To 7.62mm AP all round, to 12.7mm AP (horizontal attack) over frontal arc.

Panhard VBL

The Panhard Véhicule Blindé Leger (VBL) was developed in response to the French Army's need for a new light reconnaissance/anti-tank vehicle, and first entered service in 1990. In the intelligence/scout role the VBL is a capable IS vehicle, providing good protection and mobility for a crew of two or three.

The VBL can be fitted with a 7.62mm machine gun and/or a 12.7mm machine gun. Standard equipment includes nuclear/biological/chemical (NBC) protection and passive night vision equipment. It can also be fitted with a full range of surveillance and communications equipment.

The VBL is fully amphibious, and can be fitted with a single propeller mounted at the rear of the hull, providing a water speed of 5.4km/h. It is fitted with a central tyre-pressure regulation system and power steering, and there is a range of other options including an air-conditioning system. The vehicle is extensively used by the French Army, and has been exported to many other countries including Mexico, Nigeria, Oman and Portugal.

Specifications	
Crew	2–3
Configuration	Permanent 4x4
Length	3,800mm
Width	2,020mm
Height	1,700mm
Ground clearance	370mm
Armament	Depending on configuration. Options include 7.62mm and 12.7mm machine guns, cannon and grenade launchers, ATGMs and SAMs
Combat weight	3,500–4,000kg
Power pack	Peugeot XD 3T turbo-charged diesel, 95hp, through automatic gearbox
Max speed	100km/h on road, 5.4km/h in water
Max range	600km, 800km with optional 20 litre tank
Max gradient	50 per cent
Side slope	30 per cent
Vertical obstacle	0.5m
Fording	0.9m
Options	NBC protection, air conditioning, amphibious propulsion, various electronic packages for GPS, radio comms, etc.

Shorland S600

The story of the Shorland S600 ISV begins with the armoured Land Rovers developed more than thirty years ago by Short Brothers of Belfast – the name 'Shorland' is a contraction of 'Shorts' and 'Land Rover'. These vehicles were widely deployed by the security services in Northern Ireland, and are typified by the Mark 4 and Series 5 armoured Land Rovers. These were based on Land Rover's Series III and 110 vehicles, with armour, gun ports and a variety of weapon options.

Years of practical experience led to a number of improvements. The S55 Patrol Car, for instance, had a gutter beneath the junction of the bonnet and windscreen to divert burning petrol from an improvised firebomb, and prevent it entering the engine compartment. The roof was designed so that a bomb landing on it would roll off. Side and rear doors were arranged to allow quick debussing and embussing, even for personnel carrying a weapon and specialist equipment.

Following a series of company take-overs, the Shorland S600 is now produced by Tenix in Australia. It is no longer based on a Land Rover chassis, but on the Mercedes-Benz Unimog. It combines protection, enhanced situational awareness and the ability to negotiate man-made obstacles, barriers and narrow streets in urban environments, making it ideal for internal security operations such as riot control. Six Shorland S600 Police ISVs were recently supplied to the Belgian Police, and the vehicle is in service with various other police and security forces around the world – including twenty-two S600 vehicles, in six variants, which were delivered to the Kuwait National Guard.

The Shorland S600 carries up to twelve personnel, together with their equipment, in a good standard of comfort with low levels of vibration and noise – helping to minimise fatigue on extended operations. The Police ISV variant can be fitted with a broad range of options for urban operations, including powered sliding doors, barri-cade removers and surveillance and recording equipment. Other optional extras include grenade launchers, public address equipment, a variety of weapons mounts, thermal imaging systems, GPS and night driving aids.

The Shorland S600 provides effective protection for both crew and engine from multi-strike attack by weapons in the 5.56mm SS109 and 7.62mm NATO categories. The hull is capable of withstanding blast and fragmentation effects from grenade or mine detonations.

The S600 retains the cross-country performance of the Mercedes-Benz Unimog chassis on which it is based. This ensures that the S600 can accomplish missions in hostile environments, yet still fulfil high-speed convoy escort duties on primary roads. It is recognised by Mercedes-Benz as an 'approved' use of their Unimog chassis, and retains the Mercedes-Benz guarantee on the engine and running gear.

Hotspur (Penman)

The name of Hotspur has long been associated with armoured vehicles, many of them based upon Land Rover components. The Hotspur Hussar, for instance, was originally designed as a military APC in the mid-1980s, and over the following years a number of variants appeared for internal security uses such as prisoner transport, EOD and riot control.

The Hotspur Hussar IS vehicle was based on Land Rover components, using a third, driven axle to give a 6x6 configuration with the capacity for a large payload and excellent cross-country performance. The vehicle carries a crew of two plus ten to twelve passengers, fully equipped as necessary for the operation.

The Hussar provides protection up to 7.62mm NATO ball at 25m. The driver and front seat passenger/navigator are provided with adjustable louvres over the front and side windows. There are access doors at either side and double doors at the back. Gun ports and vision blocks at the sides and rear allow the crew to observe in all directions and to fire weapons from within the vehicle if necessary.

The vehicle is powered by a 3.5 litre Rover V8 petrol engine and measures 5.75m long, 1.85m wide and 2.28m high.

In 1989 Hotspur Armoured Products was purchased by Penman Engineering, who have retained the Hotspur name for their range of discreet and overt armoured vehicles. The Hotspur Hussar is still made, and is in service with police, paramilitary and border patrol forces worldwide. The latest variant has a capacity of ten fully equipped personnel under armour, and uses 90 per cent Land Rover components, providing low running costs and ease of maintenance. A 4x4 Hotspur armoured Land Rover is also available in a range of designs and options.

Penman recently announced that it had won a contract for the supply of five armoured Land Rovers to transport personnel engaged in humanitarian mine-clearance operations in Kosovo. The Land Rovers provide full ballistic protection and are fitted with additional AP mine protection shields on the underside.

At first glance this appears to be a regular Land Rover 110, but in fact it carries protection up to 7.62mm rifle ammunition and has anti-mine shields on the underside. Photo: Penman Engineering.

MacNeillie specialist police vehicles

S MacNeillie & Son Ltd, of Walsall in England, are specialists in converting commercial vehicles for police applications. Working from an original commercial motorcycle, car, 4x4 or truck, the company will produce a fully equipped police vehicle, road-ready to enter service immediately as an operational vehicle.

Naturally the company are reluctant to discuss details of the specifications, but the range of vehicles they produce includes riot and crowd control vehicles, prisoner transport, dog vans, communications vehicles, mobile armouries, lightly armoured armed response vehicles, and heavily armoured vehicles for specialised firearms units.

The conversion work for a specific vehicle may include installing light bars, strobes, sirens, PA systems, radios and police livery. The work is carried out to the highest standards. The company has ISO 9001 accreditation and follows a stringent in-house quality control system to maintain top build quality.

Land Rover armoured vehicles

Land Rovers have long been a workhorse of the military, police and security services in the UK and in many other countries around the world. In their standard, off-the-shelf configuration, Land Rover 90s and 110s, and more recently the Discovery and Range Rover, have often been used as patrol vehicles and for transporting personnel and equipment regardless of difficult terrain and conditions.

The Land Rover chassis has also been the basis of many specialist IS vehicles, including armoured vehicles, as described earlier in this chapter. Land Rover themselves offer armoured versions of their vehicles, such as the Demountable Armoured System (DAS) Defender. This variant allows the user to fit or demount armoured panels and glass screens to a prepared general service vehicle, transforming a standard vehicle to an APV within a few hours. The DAS provides all-round protection up to European B6+ level (5.56x45mm SS109 steel jacket at 980m/s). It can also be provided with additional anti-personnel mine protection if required.

At a recent military vehicle exhibition, Land Rover displayed a new discreetly protected version of their Range Rover, incorporating the latest armouring techniques and materials, with ride and handling specially tuned to compensate for the extra weight.

The Land Rover Discovery is just one of many vehicles that is converted to police use, with the fitting of lights, strobes, sirens, PA, radios and police livery. Photo: © James Marchington.

Motorcycles are widely used for police work: they are adapted to carry equipment such as radios and strobe lights. Photo: © James Marchington.

Land Rover This vehicle is configured for internal security operations in Northern Ireland. Photo: © James Marchington.

From the outside the vehicle looks indistinguishable from a normal Range Rover, but it has been developed by Land Rover Special Vehicles, working closely with Armour Holdings Group, to resist attack from pistols, rifles, machine guns and hand grenades. Its 4x4 chassis and off-road ground clearance allow a quick getaway from attack or ambush. As Land Rover point out, unlike conventional armoured limousines the Range Rover can be driven across all terrains, including unforgiving urban obstacles such as high kerbs or even steps. The stiff monocoque body and independent suspension give excellent road holding, enabling the protected Range Rover to evade most threats.

It is available in four levels of protection, up to the European B6+ standard described above. A variety of armouring materials are used, including steel, Kevlar and other non-metallic compounds. The glass is plasma cut and up to 40mm thick. Special 'splash' protection prevents bullet fragments entering the passenger compartment around the door and window edges. The vehicle's battery and fuel tank have extra protection, and the tyres all have run-flat capability.

To ensure that the protected version handles like a Range Rover, Prodrive Ltd have extensively retuned the air suspension, chassis and braking systems to cope with the extra weight and demands likely to be placed on the vehicle. Options include an internal oxygen system, darkened privacy glass, an intercom system, covert emergency lights and siren. Prices for the protected Range Rover start at £165,000, and the vehicle is available with either a 4.4 litre V8 petrol engine or a 3 litre turbo diesel.

From a distance, this Range Rover appears to be a normal production vehicle. However, it has been armoured to resist attack by pistols, rifles, machine guns and hand grenades, and has a specially adapted suspension system. Photo: © James Marchington.

RIOT CONTROL AND NON-LETHAL WEAPONS

8

This book is primarily concerned with the fight against terrorism. The weapons and equipment featured have been developed for bona fide security services – so that they can counter and prevent attacks on innocent people. Few people would take issue with the use of an EOD robot to deal with a terrorist bomb, or a radio so that officers can keep in touch with one another. The whole area of riot control and non-lethal weapons, however, is fraught with ethical arguments.

On one hand, anyone in a democracy has the right to peaceful protest, and it is the duty of the security services to defend that right. On the other hand, peaceful protests have a habit of turning ugly, and being hijacked by an extreme minority – at which point the role of the police switches to one of protecting persons and property, and preventing further breaches of the peace.

Policing any protest is an unenviable job. The police are faced with a volatile crowd who are highly mobile and unpredictable. Left alone they may well cause trouble, but any successful attempt to maintain control will be criticised as 'provocative' and 'heavy handed'. Protective clothing, shields and batons are associated with repression, but if the situation degenerates from mere rowdy protest into a riot, police may find themselves facing a hail of bricks, paving slabs, petrol bombs and worse; not to wear protection would be sheer folly.

The line between peaceful protest and violent disorder can be a fine one; police have the unenviable task of maintaining order. Photo: © James Marchington.

US Marines practise prisoner handling techniques during riot control training. Photo: US Marine Corps.

Opposite page: A traffic monitor webcam captures the scene near Trafalgar Square in London on 1 May 2002; in the event, the day passed with relatively little violence. Photo: Author's collection.

This publication, entitled *Bodyhammer*, is freely available for download from anarchist websites; it is a detailed tactical manual on how rioters can combat police and security forces.

It is undeniable, however, that items of crowd- and prisoner-control equipment are capable of being misused. A programme provocatively titled *The Torture Trail*, broadcast on Channel 4 in the UK in January 1995, highlighted the use of equipment such as electro-shock batons for torture of prisoners in countries with a deplorable human rights record. This kind of misuse makes for sensational headlines, but it is true to say that in the hands of a repressive regime, any military or counter-terrorist equipment can be misused.

It is not the job of this book to judge the ethical and moral issues surrounding the policing of protests and civil unrest, or indeed the manufacture and supply of internal security weapons and equipment. The weapons and equipment are presented here to illustrate what is available and in use by various police and security services around the world. How and when the equipment is used, and the safeguards put in place to prevent its misuse, will no doubt continue to be debated fiercely for many years to come.

In recent years we have seen the rise of anti-capitalist protests which have shown a tendency to turn violent. The protest in Seattle in November 1999 is seen as a watershed. Some 100,000 demonstrators protested at the opening ceremony of a meeting of the World Trade Organisation. Most of the protesters remained peaceful, but gangs of masked rioters began smashing shop windows and overturning street stalls. Police used baton rounds, OC and CS gas in an attempt to disperse the crowds. A state of civil emergency was declared, 500 people were arrested and damage was estimated at £12.5m. Police were later criticised for using what were seen as heavy-handed tactics.

The ill-feeling that arose after Seattle contributed to the ugly scenes at protests the following year: the World Economic Forum's annual meeting in Davos, Switzerland, in January, and the meetings of the World Bank and the International Monetary Fund in Washington DC in April, and in Prague in September. The next year, 2001, saw more shocking scenes of violence in the streets. Police used water cannon, baton rounds and CS gas to disperse protesters at the Summit of Americas in Quebec City in April.

Trouble was expected in several European capitals on May Day 2001. Most of the planned events were relatively peaceful, but violence erupted in the Kreuzberg district of Berlin, where petrol bombs were thrown and cars set on fire. In London, police applied a new tactic to control the anticipated protest. They manoeuvred a core of 150 protesters into Oxford Circus, blocked all exits and simply held them penned in for seven hours in what became known as 'the kettle' – the idea being that people at boiling point could be allowed to simmer there until they had run out of steam. This approach attracted some criticism, but there was considerably less damage and violence than the previous year.

Worse was to come. At the European summit meeting in Gothenburg, Sweden, in June 2001, police fought running battles with protesters and at one stage fired live ammunition, hitting three protesters. The following month, at the G8 meeting in Genoa, a demonstrator was shot dead by police. Although several thousand anarchists had travelled to Genoa specifically to cause trouble, media coverage focused on the 'heavy handed' approach of the Italian police, especially a police raid on a school which was being used as a base by protesters.

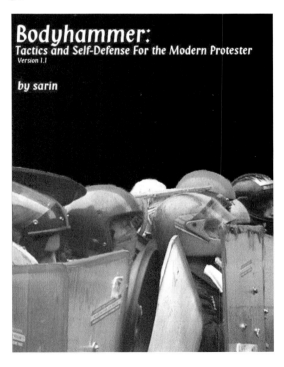

The anti-capitalist/anti-globalisation movement continues to gather momentum. It seems inevitable that there will be further violence at protests in the future – played out under the glare of the media spotlight, with pundits and politicians always ready to criticise police methods as too brutal or provocative.

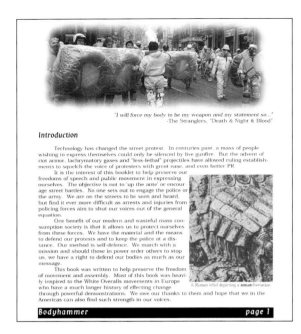

"I will force my body to be my weapon and my statement so..."
-The Stranglers, "Death & Night & Blood"

Introduction

Technology has changed the street protest. In centuries past, a mass of people wishing to express themselves could only be silenced by live gunfire. But the advent of riot armor, lachrymatory gases and "less-lethal" projectiles have allowed ruling establishments to squelch the voice of protesters with great ease, and even better PR.

It is the interest of this booklet to help preserve our freedoms of speech and public movement in expressing ourselves. The objective is not to 'up the ante' or encourage street battles. No one sets out to engage the police or the army. We are on the streets to be seen and heard, but find it ever more difficult as arrests and injuries from policing forces aim to shut our voices out of the general equation.

A Roman relief depicting a *testudo* formation

One benefit of our modern and wasteful mass consumption society is that it allows us to protect ourselves from these forces. We have the material and the means to defend our protests and to keep the police at a distance. Our method is self-defence. We march with a mission and should those in power order others to stop us, we have a right to defend our bodies as much as our message.

This book was written to help preserve the freedom of movement and assembly. Most of this book was heavily inspired to the White Overalls movements in Europe who have a much longer history of effecting change through powerful demonstrations. We owe our thanks to them and hope that we in the Americas can also find such strength in our voices.

Bodyhammer **page 1**

Part III:
Shield varieties, their construction and other equipment

Garbage can/barrel shields:

The easiest shield to make is often one that is mostly premade for you. Found street items can often work wonderfully making construction quick and easy. Plastic garbage cans are the easiest with lids turning into instant shields and the cans themselves requiring little more than being cut in half. Orange construction barrels are a little bit more difficult to obtain, but can similarly be used – however they tend to be much more rounded and hence difficult to grip in a one-armed style.

Protesters crouch behind garbage can shields in Quebec City, April 20, 2001.

Construction:

With a can lid, you should be all set. That is unless you don't want the awkward to use handle, which is not optimal for protecting yourself or advancing, but will do fine if you aren't particular. If you desire a better grip, follow the above instructions. Furthermore, keep in mind that the handle is on the opposite side of what you might prefer. It should be attached so that the concave rounded side is what points outward.

Ideal for tower shields, the body portion of a plastic trash can be used for two or three shields depending on the size of the can and the desired width. Larger, industrial trash containers or barrels tend to be taller and will cover more area. With a saw, remove the bottom of the can and any handles on the side. Then cut the can into the desired portions. Size it up against your own body to find the desired width. Since the can is rounded, applying one-armed handles on the inside of the shield will be a little bit trickier. While it works fine in that manner, trashcan shields are also perfect for the two-handed grip style. If you are using it in this manner and plan on being in the front line of a Tortoise formation, consider using a hot knife to cut a small slit a few inches from the top to peer through.

Tip: Do not forget for all shields about the need to place foam or another material along the part of the shield which you arm will reside behind. This should run from your knuckles at the grip down to your elbow on a one-armed shield.

Inflatable shields:

Quick to construct, easy to transport, inconspicuous and adding an extra bounce, inflatable shields are a very clever variant. On the opposite extreme of an imposing shield wall,

Bodyhammer **page 7**

Pages from *Bodyhammer*, downloadable from anarchist websites.

Police tactics for dealing with demonstrations and protests are continually being refined – not least because the protesters themselves are constantly developing new tactics. The internet has provided anti-capitalist and anarchist movements with a powerful means of communication and organisation; riot tactics and techniques are discussed on message boards, protests are planned, and anarchist websites provide advice for would-be protesters. The following extracts are taken from two such sites, and give an idea of the level of tactical sophistication police may face:

Wedge Charge

This method, requiring much coordination is derived from a classic Viking method of charging. It requires a good deal of discipline, not to mention an awful lot of courage on the part of the person in front. This method also requires the space to make for a near running charge to provide maximum disarray and psychological intimidation against opponents.

A wedge will have one or two persons in front, using the two-handed method with as large a shield as possible. The two lines that follow to the right and left of the focal point slightly angle their shields to the outside direction.

Once in position a countdown to a charge should be given and the charge should be made at a quick pace of short steps to keep tight, as full sprinting will lose cohesion. The wedge works by focusing on one point and pressing upon it while the two angled sides deflect forces attempting to aid the one point and widening the breech. It also keeps a degree of cohesion for those attempting to break through. A normal flat line of attack may open a hole in one or two places, but they are difficult to expand upon and to even notice for reinforcements to converge upon.

Another advantage of the wedge is that if a person in the lead is about to be nabbed, there is immediate support behind him or her to pull them back away from arrest. It is then critical to remain close to the person in front of you. A wedge need not be more than 7–11 persons across or about 4 persons deep. Extra bodies can be used to fill the inside of the wedge, and form a solid line behind it – although at the ready to push through the breech.

Extreme self-defense tactics

When facing an opposing force that is hell bent on breaking laws and violating your rights by viciously attacking you, any code of self-defense allows for extreme measures. By this we mean to include the throwing of projectiles and use of bludgeon weapons which serve to distract and disorientate the opposition so that the demonstrators might regroup or escape.

While injury to others is never a facet to embrace in self-defense, we must recognize this possibility as it has happened in the past, and will probably occur again. If the police are prepared for the worst, so should we. While this is not the place for a moral treatise, the general philosophy is that we are fighting for life and freedom, and so long as we don't fight for death and oppression as our enemies do, we have moral fortitude on our side.

Grease guns, smoke and paint bombs and other items don't necessarily injure and also can provide tactical advantages in disorientating the police. But, as this is a booklet concerning self-defense tactics, we won't get into specifics on more aggressive street fighting manners. And hey, how much do you need to know about throwing a brick?

BATONS, SHIELDS AND ARMOUR

The basic equipment of a riot officer has remained substantially unchanged for decades; indeed it is similar in form and function to that of the medieval battlefield. The officer is equipped with a full set of head-to-toe protective clothing, a shield and a baton. Modern, lightweight materials have replaced the heavy materials of old, giving improved protection, reducing fatigue and allowing greater freedom of movement.

Some of the developments have made new tactics possible. The modern type of interlinking riot shield means that a group of officers can quickly assemble a formation to protect against an attack with bricks, petrol bombs, catapults and even airguns and shotguns. A group of officers can link shields overhead to protect against missiles dropped from bridges, rooftops, etc. A phalanx of officers with interlocked shields can move in to split up a group of protesters. A wall of interlocked shields also provides an effective barrier behind which specialist teams can prepare to deploy. Yet the formation can break up instantly to allow swift movement as the tactical situation demands.

Communications have been improved greatly too. Modern radio systems, linked to headsets built into each officer's helmet, allow instant two-way communication between officers on the ground, and up and down the command chain. An officer

US Navy riot control training: note the range of protective equipment used, including full-length transparent polycarbonate shields, knee and shin protectors, helmets and visors. Photo: US Navy.

who finds himself cut off from his colleagues can quickly call for backup. Commanders, aided by CCTV and observers in helicopters, are more aware of the developing situation, and can direct their forces accordingly.

Tactics for the use of equipment like shields and batons have been developed and refined over many years of practical experience, and forces such as the British police run sophisticated training programmes for riot officers and commanders. Drills

and procedures are developed to define the appropriate level of force for a given situation. These are supported by the equipment manufacturers themselves.

Monadnock, makers of the ubiquitous PR-24 baton, for instance, issue a chart showing the body classified into green, amber and red areas. 'Green' areas are least vulnerable to serious injury, while 'red' areas – such as the head and neck – carry the highest risk and should not be struck unless the rioter is in the process of causing serious injury to the officer or another person.

A crowd control situation may at times look like a medieval battlefield, complete with mounted 'knights in armour', but the reality is very different, at least on the police side – a highly rehearsed, carefully controlled deployment aimed at minimising injury and violence while dispersing rioters and arresting the ringleaders.

US Marines training in the use of shields and batons for riot control. Note the use of interlocked shields to present an impenetrable wall to the rioters. Photo: US Marine Corps.

Monadnock PR-24 Baton

Monadnock Lifetime Products Inc has been manufacturing police batons for more than thirty-five years. The company's PR-24 side-handled baton revolutionised police

The expanding baton is widely carried by police officers for defensive use, but is not normally used for riot control. Photo: © James Marchington.

self-defence and restraint tactics, and has been widely adopted worldwide. The side-handle, or Trumbull Stop Handle, to give it the correct name, makes possible a number of moves and restraints that could not be achieved with a traditional truncheon-type straight baton.

Made of advanced polycarbonate material, the PR-24 and its derivatives are immensely strong and come with a lifetime warranty against breakage under any conditions. The baton absorbs energy and reduces shock, and will not warp or dent.

The Monadnock range also includes a selection of straight batons (without the side-handle), and various extending friction-lock batons. The extending version takes marginally longer to deploy, but is more convenient to wear, particularly if the officer needs to get in and out of vehicles during the course of his work. It can also be perceived as less threatening when the officer is on general duties.

Arnold riot protection equipment

Arnold Engineering Plastics, based in Northampton in the UK, manufacture a comprehensive range of protection equipment for riot officers. The company's literature points out that under current health and safety legislation, Chief Constables have a legal responsibility to provide officers with personal protective equipment that complies with the relevant standards 'when risks to their health and safety encoun-

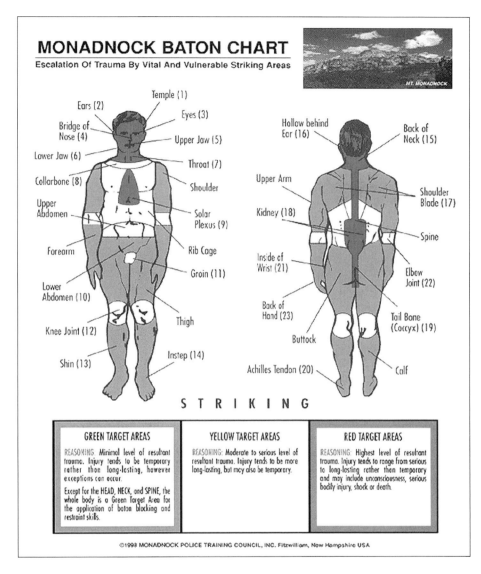

This chart is issued by Monadnock, makers of the PR-24 side-handled baton. It classifies areas of the body according to how vulnerable they are to serious injury if struck. Picture: courtesy of Monadnock Lifetime Products

tered during the course of their duties cannot be avoided or sufficiently limited by technical means of collective protection or by measures, methods or procedures of the work organisation'.

The company has been closely involved in developing new standards for personal protective equipment, through its membership of a British Standards Institution sub-committee on protective clothing and equipment for use in violent situations.

Arnold Engineering Plastics' range of body protectors bear the CE mark, and are constructed from high-impact ABS thermoplastic mouldings lined with impact-absorbing foam laminate. The outer skin is user friendly for extra comfort. Straps are riveted to the ABS moulding with non-rust rivets, and fastened with Velcro. These protectors are very light in weight, but provide a high level of protection against impacts from missiles such as stones, bottles, etc.

The range includes: the AL1 Shin Protector which protects the ankle and shin; the ALK2 Shin/Knee Protector which gives complete protection for the ankle, shin and knee; the ATH1 Thigh Protector which protects the front and side of the thigh and is designed to be worn with a Shin/Knee Protector; the AFE1 Forearm/Elbow Protector; and the AUA1 Upper Arm Protector which is designed to be worn with the Forearm/Elbow Protector and covers the area between the elbow and the shoulder. An alternative Shin/Knee Protector, the ALK3, is a lightweight equivalent of the ALK2 and is designed for officers in more mobile operations.

The company also manufactures a range of riot shields. These are made from transparent polycarbonate or high-impact plastic materials which are virtually inde-structible yet light to carry, minimising fatigue for officers who might spend several hours on duty in a riot situation.

The AM2 Riot Shield is a full body shield commonly known in the UK as 'The National Shield'. It was originally designed jointly with the Metropolitan Police and is used by all UK police forces. Designed primarily for a defensive role, it is manufac-tured from 4mm thick transparent polycarbonate. It is 1,655mm high by 600mm wide, and weighs 6.4kg. A taller version, measuring 1,829mm high, is also available.

The AR1 Riot Shield is an example of a shield designed to be used in an offen-sive mode. Supplied to a number of UK police forces and prison authorities, it is circular and non-transparent. It is manufactured from high-impact ABS, measures 540mm in diameter and weighs 1.40kg. It is supported on the arm with a ring and handle.

The AC1 Riot Shield is another 'offensive' shield. It is rectangular in shape, curved, and made from 3mm thick transparent polycarbonate. The AC1 measures 900mm by 600mm and weighs 2.3kg. Like the other shields, it is supported on the arm with a ring and handle, enabling the officer to retain it while using both hands to make an arrest.

Horse protection

Arnold's also produce a range of equipment to protect the most vulnerable areas of the horse during public disturbances and riots. The range includes a visor, constructed from 3mm thick clear polycarbonate sheet and formed to fit around the head to protect the eyes and surrounding area. It is attached by Velcro straps to the bridle and Nose Protector. The Nose Protector itself is constructed from rigid ther-moplastic lined with impact-absorbing foam and covered with black leather. Velcro straps are fitted to attach the protector to the bridle.

A Front Leg Protector protects the areas of the pastern, fetlock, cannon and knee. It is constructed of impact-absorbing stretch foam with the added protection of rigid ABS and extra foam for the more vulnerable areas. It is secured by webbing/elastic straps with Velcro fastening. The Hind Leg Protector is of the same construction as the Front Leg Protector but smaller in size, covering the cannon and back tendon areas up to the hock.

Mounted officers can be a valuable resource in crowd control, but it is necessary to provide protection to the more vulnerable parts of the horse's body. Here, US soldiers prepare for possible disturbances at the Salt Lake City Olympics. Photo: US DoD.

NP Aerospace helmets, visors and body armour

NP Aerospace manufacture a range of helmets, including a number of designs that are in service with British armed forces – such as the GS Mk6 Combat Helmet, Para Helmet, Tank Crew Helmet and Flying Helmet. The company's AC 400 helmet is similar to the US PASGT-style helmet. It offers a high degree of ballistic protection for minimal weight; it weighs 1.2kg and has a V50 protection rating of 450m/sec (17 grain fragment). The harness and suspension system are simple to adjust, and give good comfort and stability. The helmet is designed to allow the use of the latest communications headsets, ear defenders and respirators.

In common with most of the company's helmets, the AC 400 may be fitted with a transparent polycarbonate, hinged visor. This provides protection for the eyes and surrounding area, while maintaining good visibility all round. It can also be used in conjunction with a respirator, communications equipment, etc.

NP Aerospace manufacture the British Army in-service body armour, and can provide lightweight body armour designed to defeat a range of ballistic threats. A range of sizes, with double side adjustment, ensures that all sizes of officer are catered for. The body armour can accommodate a bullet-stopping plate to provide protection up to NIJ level IV – more on body armour in Chapter 9.

Avon AR10 respirator

The AR10 respirator, manufactured by Avon Rubber, is the police equivalent of the company's highly successful S10 military respirator, which is in service with Britain's armed forces. The AR10 is shaped to give a good seal against the face, providing protection against riot agents such as CS gas. Adjustable straps allow it to be deployed quickly, and adjusted for comfort and a good seal. Two circular, high-impact polycarbonate lenses give a wide field of vision and resist misting.

A speech-transmitting diaphragm makes it possible for officers to communicate by speech while wearing the respirator, and there is provision for a radio communications harness. The filter canister may be fitted to the right or left, or the respirator

Petrol bombs thrown by rioters are just one of the many threats that officers on riot control duty need to be protected against. Photo: Author's collection.

may be worn with two canisters. It provides a low breathing resistance, making the respirator more comfortable for the user to wear for extended periods.

Armadillo tactical riot shield

The Armadillo is a tactical, interlocking riot shield that not only protects an individual officer, but allows a group of officers to make up a formation that is highly protected yet mobile. Since its introduction in 1985, the Armadillo has made it possible to develop new methods and tactics for controlling and dispersing rioters, and arresting ringleaders. The Armadillo system is also used in prisons worldwide, where it enables officers to control and restrain violent prisoners more safely.

The Armadillo shield consists of a rectangular sheet of transparent polycarbonate. This material is immensely strong, and will resist attacks from stones and other missiles, hammers and axes, and even shotguns.

Running vertically up each side of the shield is a curved channel, roughly semi-circular in cross-section. This channel may be quickly interlocked with the equivalent part of an adjacent shield, so that a line of officers can quickly lock their shields together to form a solid wall, without the usual gaps between the shields that could be penetrated by a heavy missile or a determined push by the rioters. A second line of officers can raise their shields above their heads and interlock them in the same way, providing a sloped roof that protects themselves and their colleagues in the front rank against falling missiles, petrol bombs, etc.

Other, more complex formations have been developed for specific riot control tasks – yet any of these formations can be broken up instantly and each officer remains protected by his individual shield, able to redeploy quickly as directed.

CS (Tear Gas)

Police and security forces worldwide make use of CS gas tactically in riot situations – to disperse rioters, or to drive them away from selected areas. CS gas, commonly known as tear gas, was specifically developed for riot control at Britain's Chemical and Biological Defence Establishment at Porton Down.

CS, or O-chlorobenzylidene malononitrile, to give it its chemical name, is classified as a 'non-lethal incapacitant'. In its raw form it is a white solid, which can be incorporated into liquid sprays or burned to form a whitish gas. It acts quickly and is extremely irritating to the nose, throat and eyes. The victim's nose and eyes stream, and he or she feels nauseous, disorientated and short of breath. The vapour is absorbed by sweat in areas such as the crotch, armpits and neck, producing a burning sensation. The effects take from twenty to sixty seconds to appear, and last for about ten minutes after the victim has escaped from the vapour.

In a riot situation, CS is typically deployed by means of hand-thrown and vehicle-discharged grenades, and by 38mm cartridges fired from a special-purpose shoulder-fired riot weapon. It may also be incorporated into the water discharged from a water cannon, or discharged from knapsack-type sprayers. All these methods are somewhat reliant on suitable weather conditions – a strong wind

US Marines
practising riot
control
techniques,
wearing
respirators to
protect against
CS gas. Photo:
US Marine Corps.

blowing from the rioters towards the riot control officers would make the use of CS inadvisable.

A typical hand-thrown CS grenade is the CS Grenade Mk4. This consists of a cylindrical metal body similar to a food can. Inside are blocks of CS smoke composition and an igniter pellet. At the top of the grenade is a spring-loaded striker mechanism operated by a fly-off lever. To use the grenade, one withdraws the safety pin, taking care to hold the lever against the side of the grenade. The grenade is then thrown; the lever flies off, allowing the striker to operate after a delay of one or two seconds. The smoke is emitted through apertures in the top of the grenade. The grenade is 138mm high, with a diameter of 65mm, and weighs 490g. Typically it might be thrown a distance of approximately 30m.

The vehicle-discharged type of CS grenade works on a similar principle, but contains a propellant charge to fire it from the launcher tube on the vehicle. This charge, when fired, also ignites the CS composition. A standard vehicle grenade is designed to fit into a 66mm discharger, with an electrical jackplug connector at its base. The grenade is fired electrically, and the entire grenade exits the discharger barrel, leaving the launcher ready to be reloaded immediately if required. The grenade travels a nominal 80m from the vehicle. CS smoke is emitted through a series of holes around the body of the grenade, discouraging rioters from picking up the burning grenade and throwing it away, or back at security forces.

CS Cartridges are produced in 37/38mm or 40mm calibres, to be fired from riot guns such as the Schermuly 38mm MPRG (Multi-Purpose Riot Gun), the Heckler & Koch 40mm MZP-1, and the Federal M203A 38mm Riot Gun. Some types of CS cartridges can be fired from 40mm military grenade launchers such as the M203, which is mounted under the barrel of an M16 assault rifle. Riot guns are generally simple, break-barrel single-shot smoothbore weapons. The Schermuly MPRG, for instance, has a fixed foresight and flip-up rearsight, marked for ranges of 50, 100 and 150m. The trigger is double-action, so squeezing it cocks and fires the weapon.

A variety of cartridges is available; a typical basic CS cartridge is contained in an aluminium canister. This houses the primer, ejection charge, and a projectile containing a delay fuse, igniter pellet and CS smoke-producing composition. Maximum range is approximately 130m (with the gun fired at 45 degrees) and the projectile burns for approximately twenty-five seconds.

Another type of cartridge is the multi-burst variety, which contains a number of separate sub-munitions. On firing, these fan out and scatter in a random manner, giving a dispersion of CS smoke over a wide area, burning for approximately twenty-five seconds. The range of multi-burst CS cartridges is somewhat less than the single projectile type, typically 80-100m.

OC Pepper, Mace, etc

Although not generally used as a riot-control agent, mention should be made here of the various 'pepper' or OC (oleoresin capsicum)-based sprays and self-defence products. The term 'mace', often used generically, is in fact a brand name and

A volunteer is hit with OC 'pepper' spray during trials conducted by the US Navy. Pepper sprays have proved useful for self-defence, but are of limited value in riot control, where CS gas is usually preferred. Photo: US Navy.

The pump-action shotgun can be used as a less-than-lethal weapon for riot control, either with specially developed 'bean bag' type kinetic energy projectiles, or regular birdshot. Note the throat microphone worn by the officer with the shotgun. Photo: US Navy.

correctly refers to Mace Brand pepper/tear gas spray, which combines OC and CN (a type of tear gas) in either aerosol or foam.

Such sprays are widely used by law enforcement officers around the world, and in some countries are available to the general public as self-defence weapons. In the self-defence role they have proved extremely effective at disabling an attacker for long enough to enable a victim to escape. For law enforcement use, they can also allow an officer to overpower a violent criminal and take him into custody. Experiments have been carried out using these active ingredients for riot control, but for good practical reasons CS remains the preferred agent in the vast majority of cases.

Kinetic energy riot weapons

Sub-lethal kinetic energy weapons – 'rubber bullets' or 'baton rounds' in common parlance – are widely used in riot control, despite the associated problems of injuries and escalation.

Experience in Northern Ireland and elsewhere has shown that baton rounds may be used successfully to disable rioters in the act of throwing petrol bombs, etc, and can be extremely effective in breaking up a riot and dispersing the rioters. It has also shown that baton rounds are susceptible to abuse by individual officers unless their use is very tightly controlled.

The basic baton round is fired from a 38mm riot gun as described above. It consists of an aluminium cartridge case containing a primer, propellant charge and a projectile of plastic or rubber, weighing approximately 135g. It may be fired with reasonable accuracy at point targets up to 90–100m away (i.e. at individual rioters or ringleaders). The kinetic energy of the projectile is such that it is not recommended for use on human targets at less than 30m unless the safety of security force personnel is threatened.

A development of the basic baton round is a Multi-Baton Round, which contains three smaller projectiles in place of a single, larger one. Each of the three projectiles weighs 45g. When fired, they spread out in a cone pattern, giving a spread of about 3m across at 40m. Each baton's impact is considerably less forceful than that of a standard round. This type of munition is clearly not suited to use against individual rioters, but can be effective against a group, either to keep them at a distance from security forces or to disperse the group and force them to withdraw.

A variety of other kinetic energy projectiles have been developed, including rubber balls and shot-filled bags, with varying degrees of success. Some of these projectiles incorporate an indelible marking dye, so that rioters can later be positively identified.

Electro-shock weapons

Electro-shock weapons have limited use in riot control situations, and security forces generally shy away from their use due to the political repercussions of using such technology against civilians. Such devices include electric cattle-prod type batons, hand-held stun guns and the pistol-shaped Air Taser – which uses compressed air to fire two dart-type electrodes attached to 5 metres of fine wire, at a velocity of 135fps.

The darts are fired simultaneously into an attacker, and a 50,000V charge produces a current that overrides the central nervous system and incapacitates the attacker. The M-18L model, for instance, comes supplied with eight 1.5v AA batteries, air cartridges and laser sight. It weighs 18oz. The weapon can also be used as a conventional stun gun, by simply touching the assailant with the electrodes.

Sub-lethal weapons

There has been much work in recent years on advanced sub-lethal or 'less-than-lethal' technologies for riot control. There are clear advantages in a system that allows the security forces to deter or disable rioters without causing them serious, lasting harm.

Various ideas have been investigated – including sticky foams, entanglements, chemical irritants and calming agents, foul-smelling gases, fogs and smokes, dazzling devices and directed energy weapons using microwave radiation or ultra-sonics. These latter would enable riot control forces to target an individual ringleader or bomb-thrower, applying a measured dose of energy without affecting people near by, even those standing beside the target.

No doubt the search for a 'magic bullet' will continue, but advanced sub-lethal weapons have proved highly controversial and disappointing in their effectiveness. One factor often overlooked is that such weapons are not used in a laboratory. Rioters do not cooperatively stand still and let themselves be hit with whatever device is being used, and their colleagues react angrily to the use of such weapons – seeing them as justification for scaling up their own armoury and the degree of violence they are prepared to use against the police.

The psychology of a riot is a complex thing, but understanding the motivation of the rioters is crucial to its control. Anything that gives the police overwhelming power to control the riot, and prevent the rioters making their protest, is likely to escalate the situation. Paradoxically, in order to control a riot, it may be necessary to allow it to become slightly out of control.

Any new riot control weapon is likely to be denigrated by politicians, the media and the protesters themselves as an infringement of their right to protest. For the time being at least, the most effective means of riot control remain the tried and tested use of well-trained officers equipped with good protective equipment and supported by horses, protected vehicles, CS gas and baton rounds – with the ultimate recourse to military weapons where this proves necessary.

BODY ARMOUR

9

It is a fact of life that counter-terrorist operations sometimes involve officers placing themselves in the line of fire. Whether it is a border control guard questioning travellers, or a hostage rescue team storming a building, bullets may fly and people may get hit. In such situations, body armour can provide valuable protection, dramatically reducing the injuries sustained by an officer unfortunate enough to be hit by a bullet or fragment. In extreme cases, it can quite literally make the difference between dying and walking away.

Personnel are exposed to many different kinds of threat besides bullets. In the course of their duties, they may be attacked with a wide range of blunt, sharp and pointed objects, from iron bars to knives and hypodermic needles. And for anyone travelling in a vehicle, especially on operations, there is always the risk of being involved in an RTA (Road Traffic Accident).

Body armour can protect against these threats too, but of course in real life things are not as clear-cut as Hollywood would have us believe. Body armour is not 'bullet-proof'. Being hit by even the lightest bullet is a thoroughly unpleasant experience, not to mention dangerous, regardless of what body armour is worn. And while it is possible to make body armour with a high level of protection, it becomes bulky, uncomfortable and tiring to wear, reducing the officer's efficiency.

The level of protection worn is determined by operational requirements. Here a US solider trains in MOUT (Military Operations in Urban Terrain), wearing eye protection and a Kevlar helmet. Photo: US DoD.

The choice of what body armour to wear is always a compromise. The decision is based on the threat faced by the officer, the length of time he or she will be exposed to the threat, and the degree of encumbrance and discomfort that can be tolerated for that time, bearing in mind the operational requirements: will the officer need to climb through awkward openings, abseil, run, drive a vehicle, operate special equipment, fire a weapon, etc?

The equation produces a different answer for different types of operation. Someone manning a security checkpoint may be on duty for many hours at a time, day after day, and face a relatively low risk of attack. A SWAT team storming a building held by terrorists, on the other hand, faces a high level of risk – there is a good chance they will be shot at. And although they may need to climb awkwardly through windows, run and shoot, the operation is unlikely to last long. In this case, a high level of protection is called for.

For centuries warriors have worn special clothing to protect them from the weapons of their enemies. The history of warfare shows protection and weaponry leapfrogging one another: medieval metal armour offered a high level of protection, at the price of much reduced mobility, until firearms appeared on the scene and swung the balance in favour of lighter protection and greater speed and manoeuvrability.

For many years, soldiers hardly bothered with ballistic protection, since nothing existed that was practical to wear and still offered any worthwhile level of protection.

A US Army assault team moves in towards a target building. Note the special knee and ankle protection worn by the soldiers, as well as ballistic vests, helmets and eye protection. Photo: US DoD.

It was far more important to be able to run fast and get behind cover. There are stories of soldiers in WWI and II who owed their lives to items such as a metal cigarette case that had deflected a bullet; some even suspended metal plates over the most treasured parts of their anatomy. But it was not practical to cover the entire torso with anything strong enough to stop a bullet.

Advances in synthetic fibre technology during the twentieth century swung the balance once again. It became possible to produce immensely strong materials, woven from fibres such as Kevlar – a synthetic material that is around five times stronger than steel, and was originally developed by DuPont as a substitute for steel belting in vehicle tyres.

Materials like Kevlar could be made into clothing that was practical to wear, and gave previously unattainable protection against ballistic threats such as bullets and fragments. So body armour was reborn, and since the early 1970s has become widely available to police officers, SWAT teams, and others involved in the fight against organised crime and terrorism.

The first recorded incident of a US law enforcement officer's life being saved by body armour was on 17 May 1973 in Detroit. Officer Ron Jagielski was working on a drugs case. He and several colleagues approached a building that had been under surveillance. As he went towards the front door, a .38 Special bullet was fired through it and hit him in the chest. The bullet was later found embedded in his ballistic vest; without body armour he would almost certainly have died.

By 1 January 2001 it was estimated that body armour had saved the lives of 2,500 US police officers. Of this total, 42 per cent were connected with accidents such as car crashes, and 58 per cent with an assault of some kind. Of the assaults, 40 per cent involved firearms, 12 per cent cutting or stabbing, and the remaining 6 per cent some other kind of assault. The data is collected by the IACP/DuPont Kevlar Survivors' Club, and published in *Police Chief* magazine in the US.

One of the objectives of the club is to promote the wearing of body armour by police officers on duty. A study in 1987 showed that although 65 per cent of US police officers surveyed owned body armour, only 15–20 per cent actually used it. The reasons for not wearing body armour included concerns about comfort and weight, but also misconceptions about the protection it offered. Clearly education is important here: even the most advanced body armour is no protection if it is left behind while the officer is on duty.

How body armour works

'Soft' body armour consists of many layers of ballistic fibre such as DuPont's Kevlar, Twaron Products' Twaron, or Honeywell's Spectra. A vest offering Level III-A protection (9mm sub-machine gun) may include as many as thirty layers of Kevlar. The ballistic layers are made up into a suitable vest shape, usually in two main panels – back and front – which are curved to conform to the user's body shape. The ballistic material is contained within an outer layer of material such as ballistic nylon, which provides protection from everyday wear, and also protects the ballistic fibre from sunlight, water, etc, which could degrade its performance over time.

The layers of material may be stitched together around their perimeter, or stitched across at intervals in a quilt pattern; the stitching appears to make no difference to the vest's performance. The vest is fastened by elasticated straps with Velcro hook-and-loop patches – not metal buckles and fasteners, which could become secondary projectiles if hit.

When a bullet strikes a ballistic vest, it becomes caught in the web of fibres, which absorb and disperse the impact energy. As the bullet progresses, successive layers of Kevlar fibre become involved, helping to disperse the bullet's force across a larger area. Energy that would have been focused on an area the diameter of the bullet is spread out across a much wider area – preventing the bullet from penetrating, and reducing the 'point force' it applies to the wearer's body.

Terminal ballistics is a complicated science, and it is not feasible to go into the detail here. The important point, however, is that body armour prevents the bullet entering the wearer's body, and spreads out its energy across a wide front, lessening the damage that would otherwise be done to the tissues beneath. The bullet's energy is still transmitted to the wearer's body, however, and can easily knock him off his feet.

Even though body armour is very effective at dispersing the impact energy, there is still a focus of energy at the point of impact. This force can be sufficient to cause injury – known as 'blunt trauma'. Blunt trauma injuries can be life threatening, and anyone struck by a bullet, even if wearing body armour, should receive medical attention in case there is damage to internal organs that is not apparent from outside.

Testing of body armour is designed to assess the blunt trauma inflicted on the wearer when it is hit by a variety of typical projectiles. The body armour to be tested is fixed to the front of a panel containing a special ballistic clay. Rounds are then fired over a chronograph into the vest, so that their velocity can be measured. Each round creates a dent in the clay that corresponds to the degree of blunt trauma that would have been experienced by someone wearing the vest. The depth of indentation is measured and compared to published standards, to give an indication of the armour's effectiveness.

Protection levels

There are many different ways to classify body armour, and various standards are used in countries around the world. Additionally, manufacturers may quote their own ballistic protection standards; sometimes, one suspects, to make their armour look better than that of the competition. The most widely accepted standard, however, is that produced by the US National Institute of Justice (NIJ), which first developed standards for body armour around thirty years ago.

The NIJ testing procedure classifies body armour according to the type of ammunition it can protect against. Armour is graded from I to IV, ranging from .22 LR and .380 ACP up to .30 AP. In each case, in order to pass the test the maximum indentation in the ballistic clay should be no more than 44mm (1.73in). The test standards lay down the number of rounds to be fired at each body armour panel, and the angle at which the bullets must hit the panel.

The testing procedure also demands that the armour is tested wet as well as dry. Experience has shown that a wet vest is as much as 20 per cent less effective than the same vest when dry. The reason has never been proved, but it is thought that the water may act as a lubricant, allowing the bullet to slip more easily between the fibres. Even the dampness caused by perspiration can significantly reduce the effectiveness of body armour, especially when working in a hot, humid climate.

Details of the NIJ standards are shown in the table below:

Threat level	Calibre and bullet type	Typical weapon equivalent	Bullet weight	Velocity
I	.22 LR	'Saturday night	2.6g	329 m/s
	.380 ACP	specials'	8.2g	322 m/s
	FMJ RN			
IIA	9mm FMJ RN	9mm semi-auto pistol	8.0g	341 m/s
	.40 S&W FMJ	.40 semi-auto pistol	11.7g	322 m/s
II	9mm FMJ RN	9mm semi-auto pistol	8.0g	367 m/s
	.357 Mag JSP	.357 Mag revolver	10.2g	436 m/s
IIIA	9mm FMJ RN	9mm SMG	8.2g	436 m/s
	.44 Mag SJHP	.44 Mag revolver	15.6g	436 m/s
III	7.62mm NATO FMJ	Sniper rifle	9.6g	847 m/s
	7.62mm x 39	AK47 Kalashnikov		
	5.56mm FMJ	M16		
IV	.30 cal AP	AK47 or similar w/armour-piercing ammunition	10.8g	878 m/s

Abbreviations:

AP	Armour Piercing	RN	Round Nose
LR	Long Rifle	JSP	Jacketed Soft Point
FMJ	Full Metal Jacket	SJHP	Semi-Jacketed Hollow Point

Another way of testing body armour is known as V50. This involves firing bullets or fragments at varying speeds (velocities – hence the 'V') at the armour on test. The test determines the speed at which the projectile has a 50 per cent chance of penetrating the armour (hence the '50'). In other words, at the rated velocity, one fragment in two will penetrate the armour.

The V50 method is helpful to manufacturers in testing their body armour, and comparing one type or batch or armour against another. It is little help to the user in choosing which armour to use, however, as it takes no account of the blunt trauma effect – and a one-in-two chance of having a bullet go through your armour is little comfort!

Up-armouring panels

So-called 'soft' body armour – that is, armour made from layers of fibre such as Kevlar – can only provide protection up to Level III-A, equivalent to a 9mm SMG. To protect against more powerful threats, such as assault rifles, sniper rifles and the like, it is necessary to add plates of solid material, which can be inserted in special pockets built into a ballistic vest. These are commonly known as 'hard' body armour, to distinguish them from the textile-based 'soft' types of armour.

Typical materials for these ballistic panels are ballistic steel or ceramic material. A .308 Winchester FMJ round (7.62 x 51mm NATO) will be stopped by $\frac{1}{4}$in of ballistic steel, or $\frac{1}{2}$in of ceramic, giving Level III protection. For Level IV protection, to defeat a .30-'06 AP round, it is necessary to have $\frac{1}{2}$in of ballistic steel, or $\frac{3}{4}$in of ceramic.

Such plates are heavy, inflexible and cumbersome. They are tiring and tiresome to wear for any length of time, and would not normally be used as regular daily wear. However, for officers exposed to a high threat level for a short time, they are invaluable. They are standard wear during hostage rescue operations and the like.

RBR Armour produce a range of ceramic plates which are widely used worldwide by police and military forces. The company has refined the shape and curvature of its plates to follow the shape of the human body more closely, making them more comfortable to wear and allowing better mobility. A relatively recent development is their 'Armour Light' plate, which is considerably lighter than earlier designs for the same level of protection. An Armour Light plate measuring 250 x 300mm and giving NIJ Level III protection weighs only 1.8kg.

Also available from RBR Armour is a 'German Standard SK2' plate, which is an armoured steel plate designed to defeat specialised armour-piercing handgun ammunition. This can be inserted into a special pocket on a 'soft' ballistic vest to give a greatly increased level of protection.

Stab and slash resistance

Bullets and fragments are clearly a major risk in anti-terrorist operations, and the main purpose of body armour is protection against such objects. Body armour, however, also offers a degree of protection against other threats, from improvised thrown missiles like bricks and stones, to knife attacks. As stated above, of the 2,500 lives said to have been saved by body armour, 12 per cent of these incidents involved stabbing or cutting, rather than firearms or other ballistic threats.

A study carried out in Europe by DuPont Life Protection showed that attacks on police officers were split 50 per cent blunt trauma (attacks with blunt weapons such as iron bars, etc), 35 per cent stab/puncture (including knives, hypodermic needles, etc) and 15 per cent firearms.

The stab/slash threat is highest for officers serving in prisons, but any officer on counter-terrorist duties is potentially at risk of being attacked with a knife or improvised stabbing/slashing weapon.

Regular ballistic materials offer some protection against pointed and edged weapons, such as a knife or ice-pick. The layers of ballistic material resist the blade, dissipating the force so that the blade is less likely to penetrate the vest and enter the wearer's body.

A ballistic vest, nevertheless, is primarily designed to resist a bullet, and could potentially be defeated by a knife or similar object. A sharply pointed weapon, thrust with enough force, may slip through the layers of ballistic material more easily than a bullet. In order to defeat such threats, it is necessary to incorporate more tightly woven fabric that will prevent a sharpened point from penetrating.

DuPont have carried out a good deal of work on blunt trauma and stab resistance, and have developed their own testing methods. One test for blunt trauma, for instance, involves dropping a 4kg sabot with a blunt point, to apply 60 joules of striking energy to the armour's surface; a pass requires an indentation of no more than 25mm behind the armour.

The NIJ collaborated with the Office of Law Enforcement Standards (OLES), the US Secret Service and the UK Police Scientific Development Branch (PSDB) to create a separate standard for stab- and puncture-resistant armour. The new standard, Stab Resistance of Personal Body Armour, NIJ Standard 0115.00, was released in September 2000.

DuPont MTP

In November 2001 DuPont launched a new flexible armour system designed to give combined protection against the range of threats typically faced by police officers: knife, bullet and blunt trauma. The new system uses a development known as Kevlar MTP (Multiple Threat Protection), and has become the first flexible body armour system to meet the UK PSDB standards for stab, spike and bullet resistance.

MTP is a modular system incorporating Kevlar Comfort AS299, a patented high performance, stab-resistant material. It uses a high energy-absorbing Kevlar NFT fibre, woven in a special construction and coated with a resin system from the aerospace industry. This makes it the lightest knife-resistant material available, and also protects against sharp-tipped objects such as hypodermic needles.

The MTP system involves layers of Comfort AS299 and soft fabric layers of Kevlar NFT strategically placed throughout the Kevlar MTP vest, to provide a high level of blunt trauma protection. This provides a lightweight system that gives the wearer previously unheard-of protection against all the major threats he or she is likely to face: bullets, knives and blunt trauma.

Horses for courses

As already mentioned, the selection of body armour is always a compromise. Body armour is not 'bulletproof', but it does provide a degree of protection against defined threats. Greater protection, however, comes at a price; the armour becomes more awkward and inconvenient to wear. At the extreme, very heavy armour worn for extended periods could lead to long-term medical problems such as back trouble and damage to knee and hip joints.

It is necessary to match the level of armour to the threat, bearing in mind the circumstances and the length of time the officer will be exposed to the threat. In practice, Level I armour is not generally recommended, since it protects only against the lowest velocity pistol ammunition. Level IIA is a good choice where concealability and comfort are important. Level II, which protects against the more powerful 9mm pistols as well as .357 Mag, is considered a good balance between comfort and protection for general police duties.

Level IIIA is the highest protection rating available in soft body armour. It is tested to 9mm FMJ at 1,400fps, to cover rounds fired from a 9mm SMG such as the MP5. It is generally too bulky, uncomfortable and restricting for general daily use, but is advisable for high-risk situations such as hostage rescue operations, etc – often with the addition of ceramic up-armouring panels to give added protection.

NP Aerospace

NP Aerospace, based in Coventry, England, designs and manufactures a large range of protection equipment, including shields, ballistic visors and body armour. The company specialises in thermoset and composite materials, and is one of the largest thermosetting moulding companies in Europe. It has developed ways to improve the strength-to-weight ratios of products from bicycle frames to combat helmets. NP Aerospace supplies the British Army with in-service body armour, and also equips news organisations, aid agencies and the like.

The British Army in-service body armour is combat proven and is available in six sizes with double side adjustment to cater for all builds. It weighs 2.5kg, and is designed to allow good levels of comfort and freedom of movement, so that the soldier can fight effectively whilst protected.

CA/BA Body Armour

NP Aerospace CA/BA Body Armour is a lightweight body armour designed to defeat a range of ballistic threats up to NIJ Level IIIA. It is designed for overt use by police firearms teams and the like. The armour is fitted with pockets that can accommodate a plate to provide protection up to NIJ Level IV. The armour weighs 5.5kg, plus the weight of any ballistic plates fitted. CA/BA Body Armour is rated V50 >600 m/s.

Ballistic Plates

NP Aerospace offer a wide range of bullet-stopping ceramic plates which can be used in conjunction with their body armour. Plates are available in sizes from 100 x 150mm to 250 x 300mm, to NIJ Level III and IV. The following table shows the range of options available, and the weight of the different plates:

Size	Threat Level III	Threat Level IV
100 x 150mm	1.2kg	1.4kg
250 x 200mm	–	2.5kg
250 x 300mm	3.2kg	3.4kg

CPV 700

NP Aerospace's CPV 700 is a tight-fitting discreet body armour that may be worn covertly under a uniform or civilian clothing. It is easily adjustable to fit snugly against the body, and provides protection against a wide range of handgun threats. It can be supplied in NIJ II or NIJ IIIA variants, weighing 3kg and 4kg respectively.

CPV 800

The CPV 800 body armour is designed specifically for use by Special Forces swimmers, and employs materials that are unaffected by water. All threads and materials have been selected to resist the effects of saline environments. The CPV 800 is available offering protection to NIJ level II (3kg) or NIJ IIIA (4kg).

CPV 900

CPV 900 is a special-purpose body armour which provides built-in buoyancy as well as ballistic protection against threats to NIJ Level IIIA. The jacket weighs 7kg, and provides 10kg of buoyancy. It will support a trooper while he awaits rescue from the water. Ballistic plates can be added to increase the protection to Level IV.

CPV 1000

The CPV 1000 is the standard-issue jacket for BBC journalists operating in conflict zones. It is specifically designed for use by journalists and other non-combatants, and comes in a range of non-threatening colours. It is fitted with pockets designed to take notebooks and video cassettes. The jacket weighs 5.5kg and gives protection to NIJ Level IIIA. There are pockets for two ballistic plates to uprate the protection to NIJ Level IV.

RBR Tactical Armor

RBR Tactical Armor, Inc. has its head office in Virginia, with manufacturing facilities in North Carolina and in the UK. The company produces a range of body armour and related products, and has supplied US special operations groups and tactical teams, as well as military, police and internal security forces around the world.

100 Series

RBR's 100 Series is a range of discreet ballistic undervests, designed to be worn under normal clothing. The 101 vest, for instance, is a classic style of undervest with adjustable elasticated straps on the sides and shoulders, and a pocket to accept a 125 x 200mm shock/anti-stab plate. RBR suggest wearing a Coolmax T-shirt underneath this item, as the T-shirt absorbs perspiration and transports the moisture along the fibres, keeping the wearer cooler and more comfortable. The 101 vest has wrap-around sides to give particularly good coverage of the torso. A female version of the vest is also available.

The 100 series is available with ballistic protection to NIJ Level IIA, II, II+ or IIIA. The vests feature RBR's 'Memory Moulding' technology, ensuring a good fit and maximum freedom of movement and comfort. They may also be worn with RBR's TR2 Trauma Plates, which are designed to minimise the effects of blunt trauma.

The RBR 101 discreet ballistic undervest can be worn beneath normal clothing, and provides protection up to NIJ Level IIIA. A Coolmax T-shirt is recommended underneath to wick perspiration away from the skin. Photo: RBR.

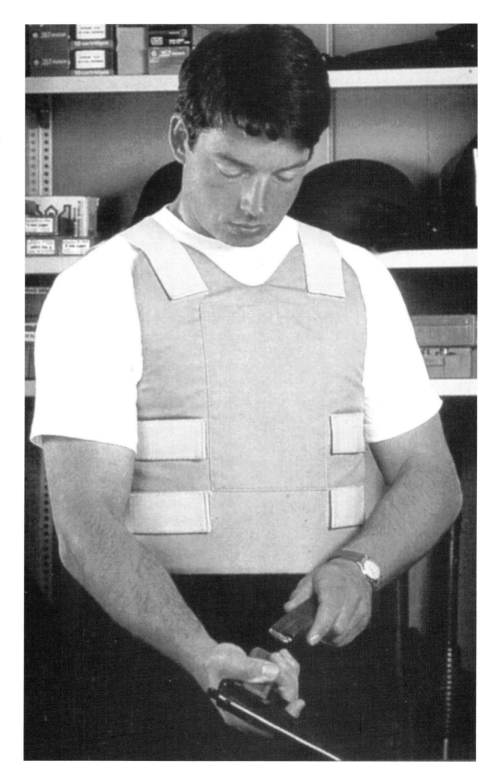

Another option that may be added is a shock or anti-stab plate, which upgrades the vest to give extra protection against bullets and knife attack. A range of plates is available, in either steel or Aramid, in sizes 125 x 200mm, 200 x 250mm and 250 x 300mm.

200 Series

RBR's 200 Series of vests is their police and tactical range, and has been developed in close consultation with SWAT and tactical assault teams over many years. The 203-70 is the latest incarnation of the company's Modular Tactical Assault Vest, and is designed to give the operator the highest area of coverage without reducing mobility. The vest features a removable collar, internal groin protector and shoulder insert, making an extremely versatile system.

The pocket attachment system is Velcro-backed nylon webbing, which is compatible with the Blackhawk Tactical System, US Military ALICE as well as a wide variety

RBR's 200 series vests are designed for police and tactical use. The 202 shown here is available in male and female versions, and has side and shoulder adjusters for improved comfort. Photo: RBR.

The 203 is a military vest, with a raised collar for additional neck protection, and will accept an up-armouring ceramic plate. Photo: RBR.

of other load-carrying system pockets. This enables the user to build a pocket system to suit the particular mission.

The 201 is a simpler, uncluttered design which is ideal for multi-role police work, while the 202 (also available in a female version) has side and shoulder adjustment, and is designed to be worn for long periods of time. Another variant, the 204, offers the maximum area of coverage, extending low on the torso with shoulder pieces and an optional groin protector.

Standard features on the 200 series include ballistic protection to NIJ Level IIA, II, II+ or IIIA, 'Memory Moulding' technology, removable machine-washable cover, and pockets for up-armour plates to raise the protection level. Options include trauma packs, attachment points for communications systems, etc, and police identification tabs.

300 Series

The 300 Series is the military equivalent of the 200 Series, typified by the 304 Combat Body Armour – similar to the US PASGT vest but with waist adjustment. A 'Quick fit' Plate Harness, designated 311, makes it possible to hang an up-armouring rifle resistant plate in front of any ballistic vest, including front-opening military-style vests.

400 Series

The 400 Series is designed for aquatic environments; the 401 is a Ballistic Flotation Vest which provides buoyancy in the water as well as ballistic protection. This vest is designed to be used for harbour patrols, coastguard, customs and other officers whose work may involve the risk of falling into deep water as well as coming under attack with firearms. An 'Aqua Light' flashing strobe light can be fitted on the shoulder, and is activated by pulling a clearly marked tag, making it easier to find someone who has fallen into water in the dark.

The 204 offers maximum coverage, extending low on the torso, and has an optional groin protector. Photo: RBR.

The 405 is a special-purpose combat swimmer vest, and has been designed to offer minimum buoyancy. This, combined with special water-repellent treatments, makes it ideal for divers and other marine combat personnel. As with the other RBR vests, the 400 series vests are available in a range of NIJ Level ratings, and can be up-armoured with the addition of rifle-resistant plates.

500 Series

RBR's 500 Series is a range of covert overvests, suitable for executive protection and undercover counter-terrorist operations. The 501, for instance, has the appearance of

The RBR 405 is a special-purpose combat swimmer vest. It offers minimum buoyancy, and has a special water-resistant treatment to resist waterlogging.

RBR's 500 series vests are suitable for executive protection, and can be tailored to look like a regular waistcoat. Photos: RBR.

a quilted 'body warmer' type of vest as commonly worn in everyday civilian life, and comes in navy blue and olive drab colours. However, the vest can incorporate ballistic protection up to NIJ Level IIIA, giving front, back and side protection with multi-hit capability.

For more formal occasions, the 502 Executive Vest is tailored like a smart waistcoat, and covered with high quality suit fabric. Without close inspection, it is indistinguishable from a regular waistcoat of the type typically worn by corporate executives. A wide range of colours and styles is available, and spare covers can be supplied.

The 503 Police Jacket is cut to look like a traditional civilian windbreaker jacket, but provides a high level of protection with zip-out inner body armour and the option of steel or Aramid shock plates and anti-stab plates. The jacket is available in the full range of colours, including navy blue, royal blue, black, grey and sand. The back is loose fitting to allow unrestricted arm movement. Large retractable identification badges are fitted front and rear, allowing the user to remain covert yet quickly show highly visible 'police' identification when required.

10

ASSAULT AND RAPID ENTRY EQUIPMENT

At 7.23 p.m. on a Bank Holiday Monday, 5 May 1980, the British SAS (Special Air Service) stormed the Iranian Embassy in Princes Gate, London. The assault, named Operation Nimrod, was watched live by a massive TV audience, thrusting the SAS unwillingly into the media spotlight.

The siege had begun five days earlier, at 11.25 a.m. on 30 April, when six armed Iranians overpowered police constable Trevor Lock, who was on duty outside the embassy. Inside they took twenty-six hostages, mostly embassy staff, and began making their demands: the release of ninety-one political prisoners in Iran, and a plane to fly themselves out of the UK. During the tense negotiations that followed, press photographers and TV news crews set up outside the building; the crisis became a real-life TV drama.

When the body of a hostage, Abbas Lavasani, was pushed out of the embassy door, it was clear the time for negotiations was over. Twenty minutes later, the SAS assault team went in. Within fifteen minutes, five of the six terrorists were dead. All but one of the hostages, killed by the terrorists, were free. The SAS team were on their way back to Hereford, and the legend of 'The Embassy Siege' was born.

The aftermath of Operation Nimrod: five of the six terrorists died, and all but one of the hostages survived. Photo: Author's collection.

As they abseiled into position at the back of the building, one SAS trooper's rope became entangled. He was suspended above a burning window, and suffered serious burns before his colleagues were able to cut him free. Photo: Author's collection.

SAS soldiers move into position across the roof, armed with H&K MP5 sub-machine guns and wearing fire-retardant black coveralls, body armour and respirators. Photo: Author's collection.

It was not the first such operation; three years earlier, on 13 October 1977, a GSG9 team aided by the SAS had successfully stormed LH181, a Lufthansa Boeing 737 at Mogadishu. Significantly, stun grenades provided by the SAS were used to initiate the assault. Three of the four Palestinian terrorists were killed, and all the hostages were released.

Operation Nimrod was unique, however, in that it was watched live by millions on TV. British newspapers published detailed graphics showing how the assault had been carried out, together with photographs of the SAS teams moving into position on the embassy roof, abseiling down to the windows and placing frame charges, and finally handling the hostages (and one surviving terrorist) on the small patch of grass at the back of the building. In the months and years that followed, the whole area of CRW (Counter Revolutionary Warfare) attracted massive public interest, spawning a host of books, videos and films featuring dramatic scenes of hostage rescue.

In some ways the high profile nature of Operation Nimrod, and the continuing interest in hostage rescue, has been unhelpful to Special Forces and SWAT teams. The advantage of surprise is largely lost if hostage-takers know what to expect. They can obtain special protective equipment to prepare themselves for an attack supported with stun grenades, CS gas and 9mm SMGs. On the other hand, it sent a clear message to terrorists around the world, and has certainly acted as a deterrent against similar hostage-taking attempts. It has also encouraged a number of people

Two of the SAS team provide cover from the pavement at the front of the building. The assault was carried out in view of live TV cameras. Photo: Author's collection.

Speed, aggression and surprise are essential to any hostage rescue operation; abseiling gave the assault team access to the entry points with the minimum delay. Photo: Author's collection.

to seek a career in Special Forces at a time when recruitment has proved difficult – not all of them suitable, of course.

Before going into details of the equipment used in hostage rescue and similar operations, it is worth reiterating that, as elsewhere in this book, we have been careful to avoid giving details of equipment and techniques that could be of use to terrorists. All the information that follows is in the public domain, and available from unrestricted sources. Certain equipment and information has been deliberately omitted, in order not to compromise operational security.

All hostages are treated as potentially hostile: outside the back of the Embassy, the SAS team bind the hostages' hands with plasticuffs. Photo: Author's collection.

Surveillance

In any hostage situation, one of the security forces' first tasks is to gather information: about the terrorists, the hostages, the building or craft in which they are being held, and any other intelligence that may be relevant. One aspect of this involves drawing on other departments' resources – such as immigration records, police and security services files, architects' plans, etc. It is also vital to get a look inside the besieged building to ascertain the numbers and positions of terrorists and hostages, the type of weapons used, the terrorists' morale and state of readiness, and so forth.

After the Iranian Embassy assault, it was widely reported that various surveillance devices had been deployed. These included microphones lowered down the embassy chimneys, and miniature video cameras inserted in holes drilled through the walls from adjoining buildings. Indeed, the kidnappers quizzed PC Trevor Lock about the sounds of drilling (he blamed the sound on mice in the walls!) Aircraft heading for London's Heathrow Airport were diverted over the embassy so that the noise would mask the sound, and 'workmen' began drilling noisily in the street near by. The information gained from these devices was vital in preparing the assault plan, and undoubtedly helped to preserve the lives of the hostages and assault team members.

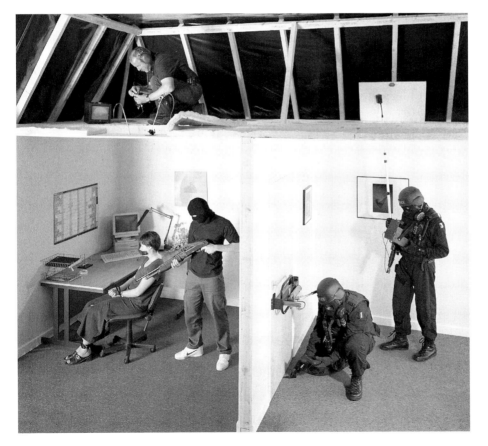

A wide range of surveillance devices is employed in any hostage situation, to help build up a picture of what is happening inside the besieged building or vehicle. All this information is very useful to the assault force. Photo: © PW Allen.

Today, more than twenty years on, the equipment available to security forces has become more sophisticated, smaller and more reliable than anything available at the time of the Iranian Embassy siege. The principles, however, remain much the same: specialised cameras and audio equipment are used to gain a clear picture of what is happening inside the besieged building, without alerting the kidnappers.

In general terms, the security forces will also ensure that they control communications in and out of the besieged building, whether by landline or by RF (radio frequency) communications. They will also take control of services such as water, gas

The PW Allen Under-door Viewer can be slipped through the tiny gap under a door, and provides a good view of the room on the other side. An adaptor makes it possible to examine the reverse side of the door for booby traps. Photo: © PW Allen.

and electricity into the building, as well as the supply of food, cigarettes, medical supplies, etc to the terrorists and their hostages.

Wall/ceiling scopes

There are various scopes available for viewing through a hole drilled in a wall or ceiling. A typical example is supplied by PW Allen, and comes as a kit that includes the endoscope itself, a mounting bracket suitable for various types of wall, drill bits and centring bushing, and a carrying case.

The endoscope probe measures 2.5mm in diameter (approximately 1/10in – about the size of a match head) and is available in lengths of 180mm and 280mm. It has an offset mirror that gives a 55 degree field of view, and can be rotated to cover an 85 degree view of the interior of the room under surveillance.

The scope gives a bright, sharp image that can be viewed directly through an eyepiece, or remotely by coupling the device to a video camera by means of an adaptor. It can also be used with an infra-red camera to provide an image if the room under surveillance is in darkness.

The through-ceiling scope is a shorter version of the through-wall scope. It is set up in the same way, being inserted through a 2.5mm diameter hole drilled in a ceiling tile or plasterboard ceiling. As with the through-wall scope, it provides an offset 55 degree field of view.

Under-door viewer

Another device for covertly viewing the interior of a room is the under-door viewer. PW Allen supply such a device, which slips easily under a door with a gap as small as 6mm. The device has a 55 degree field of view, and can be adjusted once in position to survey the entire interior of the room. The kit also includes a right-angle adaptor that provides a clear view of the inside surface of the door. This enables the user to examine any barricades or booby traps that may have been set up.

The under-door scope has a C-mount so that a video camera may be attached, or the picture can be viewed directly with a detachable eyepiece. As with the through-ceiling and through-wall scopes, the under-door scope can also be used with IR viewing equipment if the room is in darkness. An IR light source is available to provide illumination.

Peephole viewers

Many houses and flats have a peephole viewer on the main entry door. The optical design of this type of viewer allows a person inside to see clearly anyone standing outside the door, but it is hard to see through the other way, into the building. However, by using a scope with specially designed optics, it is possible to view the interior.

PW Allen supply two types of peephole viewer. One is a small-diameter scope, similar to a small telescope, that is held to the eye and looked through directly. The other consists of a miniature low-light video camera, with a specially designed video lens. The camera has a bracket that fits quickly on to standard interior and exterior door peephole viewers. The picture relayed by the camera can then be viewed on a monitor, or recorded for use as evidence. The angle of view depends on the optics inside the peephole viewer itself, but usually allows a good view of the room behind. The camera is powered by a standard 9v battery, or a mains adaptor.

Audio probes

When a terrorist group is holding hostages inside a building, craft or vessel, obtaining real-time pictures of the scene inside is clearly a huge advantage for negotiators, and for planning an assault. Pictures, however, tell only part of the story; having audio as well can provide a great deal more intelligence. Audio will help to assess the terrorists' state of mind as well as their level of preparedness and their plans – as they discuss events, give orders to one another, or argue among themselves. It will also help to determine how the hostages are likely to react when an assault takes place.

PW Allen supply an audio surveillance probe designed to be used in conjunction with their through-wall and through-ceiling video probes. It consists of a 4mm diameter stainless steel microphone probe that can run in the same drill bush mounting as the video probe.

The audio probe has an electric microphone characterised by its wide, flat frequency response, high sensitivity and low noise. It is ruggedly housed to withstand severe conditions, and being pushed through brick and plasterwork. The microphone is normally used in conjunction with the matched, battery powered amplifier and headphones supplied in the kit, but provided the microphone is connected to a suitable power source (0.9–1.6v DC) it may be connected to any compatible amplifier and recording equipment.

Dog collar camera

Sandia in the US have been evaluating the potential of a wireless video 'K-9' camera attached to a dog's collar for use in hostage negotiations and rescues. The project was inspired partly by the April 1999 Columbine High School attack, when officers lacked the reliable information they needed safely to enter school buildings. Work on the project, funded by the NIJ, began in April 2001.

The system consists of a camera attached to a collar worn by a trained police dog. The dog is sent into a building where terrorists or criminals are believed to be hiding. The video image collected by the camera is transmitted to a hand-held video receiver; the signal will pass through the walls of a target building.

The project received a field test rather sooner than planned. Shortly after the World Trade Center attack on 11 September 2001, NIJ project officials contacted Sandia to see whether the kits could be deployed rapidly to aid the Federal Emergency Management Agency's (FEMA) Urban Search and Rescue (US&R) teams as they scoured the rubble for survivors.

Sandia project leader Richard Sparks spent twenty-two days at the site helping the US&R teams outfit their search dogs with the cameras and radios attached to special collars. The kits were in use twenty-four hours a day for several weeks. The real-life situation provided valuable information about the K-9 cameras' potential uses

The 'K-9' camera is attached to a dog's collar and relays a picture back to an operator in real time. The system was used to search for survivors in the remains of the World Trade Centre after 11 September 2001. Photo: Sandia.

not only in law enforcement, but also in emergency response, and helped suggest needed improvements.

Other surveillance methods

In a hostage or siege situation, the security forces will remain flexible and use any surveillance equipment and methods that may prove useful in the circumstances. Any of the equipment described in Chapter 1 may be deployed as appropriate, to gain the maximum intelligence about the terrorists and hostages, and any physical information about the building and obstacles that may have been emplaced by the terrorists. For a

Abseiling from a helicopter provides one way for an assault team to reach their target quickly and retain the element of surprise. Photo: Author's collection.

Counter-terrorist forces must be prepared to tackle terrorists wherever they may strike. This British special forces team is pictured during training for an assault on a terrorist-held ship. Photo: Author's collection.

team planning an assault, details of a building's layout and construction (materials, thicknesses of walls, doors, etc) are vital in deciding how best to carry out the assault.

Snipers will be deployed early in the operation, positioned to provide good all-round surveillance of the target building, craft or vehicle. A good sniper will provide a constant flow of valuable intelligence about the terrorists' locations and actions, as well as details of weapons carried, level of alertness, etc.

All these sources of intelligence will be collected and collated at the command post, and will aid commanders in preparing their plans and choosing between the various options.

LADDER SYSTEMS AND VEHICLE PLATFORMS

When an assault is made on a building, craft or vessel, speed, aggression and surprise are vital to the success of the operation. The terrorists should have no idea that an assault is about to take place until the assault team are in and shooting. Even a few seconds' delay could give them time to kill hostages, detonate a bomb or fire back at the troopers.

Clearly this means that the assault team must be in place at the entry points, ready to enter immediately they are breached (in the next section we will look at the equipment employed rapidly to breach doors, windows and walls).

As millions saw in May 1980, abseiling from a roof is one way to gain access to windows above ground level. Once a team is in position on the roof, they can quickly and covertly drop to the level of the target window, emplace frame charges, throw in stun grenades and swing inside. Of course things do not always go smoothly, as in Operation Nimrod, where one SAS trooper became entangled in his abseil rope above a burning window. He suffered severe burns before his colleagues cut him down; to his credit he promptly entered the building and shot a terrorist dead.

The architecture of the Iranian Embassy lent itself to an assault. The building was not especially high, and there were balconies and balustrades on which the assault team could assemble ready to enter the building. Other types of buildings, not to mention ships, aircraft, trains and buses, present a range of problems. The SAS and other counter-terrorist forces constantly practise techniques for assaulting every kind of situation where their specialist skills might be called for. In conjunction with various manufacturers, they have developed a range of specialist equipment for the job. The equipment is designed to be as adaptable and versatile as possible, as there is no knowing where terrorists may strike.

Camlock PDE vehicle system

The PDE vehicle system has been developed by Camlock Engineering Ltd of Hereford, England, in conjunction with British Special Forces. The system may be fitted to a prepared vehicle in minutes, and can deliver fully equipped troopers at various heights, with the added advantage of cover from other personnel positioned on the vehicle. Camlock's ground assault ladders can also be carried on the vehicle, providing a highly effective system for Special Forces troopers to assault a variety of buildings, vehicles and aircraft. Naturally, a number of suitably equipped vehicles may be used simultaneously to attack the target at multiple entry points.

The system can be fitted to any suitable vehicle – typically a powerful 4x4 on/off road vehicle such as a Land Rover, Range Rover, Toyota Land Cruiser or Mercedes G-Wagen. The basis of the system is a rigid main deck, mounted on the roof of the vehicle. Clamp hand wheels secure the platform to the vehicle in seconds, and anti-slide pins prevent it slipping, even under heavy braking or acceleration.

The platform is fitted with grab handles and handrails so that personnel can cling on safely even if the vehicle has to travel over rough ground or perform sudden manoeuvres. Side ladders with sniper platforms enable additional personnel to be deployed at the sides of the vehicle, to provide cover for the main team. The side ladders are attached to the vehicle with heavy duty steel hooks and secured with ring-pins. There is a bonnet protector so that troopers can deploy quickly to the ground from the main platform by stepping on to the bonnet – the protector's surface is ridged to provide a good grip even in wet conditions.

The ladders are attached with special fixings that are easily adjustable, yet can be quickly locked in position with a cam-lock system (hence the name). This makes it possible to set up the system very quickly to assault a target with entry points at just about any height.

The Camlock PDE assault system, fitted on an NP Aerospace CAV100 armoured Land Rover. This combination can be configured quickly to deliver a fully equipped assault team to various entry points on a building, vehicle or aircraft. Photo: NP Aerospace.

Door, window and wall breaching equipment

Once the assault team is in position, it is essential to gain entry very quickly indeed, so that the terrorists do not have time to kill their hostages, attempt to escape or mount a counter-attack. There is a wide variety of rapid entry tools available for rapidly breaching the many different types of doors, windows, walls, etc that may be encountered.

As in Operation Nimrod, explosives may provide the fastest and most effective means of gaining entry. They have the added advantage that the sudden noise, blast,

Special Forces troopers practise abseiling to assault a building where terrorists are holding hostages. Photo: © James Marchington.

dust and smoke of an explosion can help to disorientate the terrorists – especially if charges are emplaced at multiple entry points around the target building and the detonations are synchronised.

Practical experience and trials have made it possible to predict accurately the size and type of charge most suitable for a wide range of different walls, doors, window frames, etc. Clearly it is important to gauge this correctly: too weak a charge will simply warn the terrorists of impending attack, while too strong a charge may injure hostages or members of the assault team, or leave parts of the building dangerously unstable. In his book, *Fire Magic*, former SAS trooper Barry Davies, BEM, describes how on an exercise he added the favourite ingredient 'P for Plenty' – and completely flattened the house they were supposed to be assaulting!

For a combat engineer skilled in such work, it is relatively straightforward to rig up a frame charge for a specific task, using commonly available materials and military explosives such as PW4 Plastic Explosive and Linear Cutting Charge. Knowing the thickness and type of material to be breached, he can refer to tables showing the correct weight and configuration required to achieve the desired result.

Explosive Wall Breaching System

PW Allen supply a purpose-made Explosive Wall Breaching System, which is designed to provide a rapid method of entry for Special Forces assault teams through walls and other obstacles. The unit consists of a plastic shell with a frame to support the explosive and a container for water to surround the explosive. The unit is placed

The PW Allen Explosive Wall Breaching System will blow a hole in a solid wall, large enough for the assault team to step through and attack the terrorists inside. Photo: © PW Allen.

against a wall and fired; the water tamps the explosive and directs the energy forward, cutting a hole in the wall.

The unit has two channels for explosive: one around the perimeter, which defines the size of the hole; and another vertical channel down the centre of the unit, which on thicker walls helps to push out the building material to leave a clean, open hole through which the assault team can enter quickly.

The amount and type of explosive used depends on the task. For a thin, internal wall a single length of detonating cord may be sufficient. For thicker, more strongly built walls, it may be necessary to use multiple lengths of det cord, or flexible linear cutting charge for a more directional effect. The water jacket surrounding the explosive helps to quench the hot gases and reduce the danger from fragments.

The Enforcer door ram allows a man to deliver a blow powerful enough to burst open most residential doors, even reinforced ones with multiple locks and bolts, in a couple of seconds. Photo: © PW Allen.

Door rams

The door ram is widely used by police and fire services around the world for breaking through inward opening doors quickly and with minimum fuss. There is a variety of sizes and designs available, but the principle remains the same. A good example of this type of tool is the Enforcer, supplied by Sigma Security Devices of Dover, England. Many thousands are in use worldwide. This 16kg steel ram consists of a tube with a solid block at one end. Two handles are fitted, the forward one of which has a D-shaped guard to protect the user's hand.

The Enforcer is designed to be used by one man, either left- or right-handed. It is swung against the door near the lock, providing an impact of more than 3.5 tons. This is sufficient to break open most residential doors, even reinforced ones, within a couple of seconds. Experience has shown that the Enforcer can open doors with up to seven different locks, bolts and chains at a single blow. The Enforcer measures 58cm long, and is also available as a kit with protective mitts and forearm protectors. A back pack is available for carrying the Enforcer while keeping both hands free for abseiling, climbing, etc.

The Disrupter, also supplied by Sigma Security Devices, is a more powerful version of the Enforcer, weighing 18kg. Like the Enforcer, it measures 58cm long. The design is improved, with the front handle further back. This ensures that impacts are higher and more effective, while also making the ram safer to use.

A smaller version, the Firecracker, is only 46cm long and weighs 16kg. It can be stowed and carried more easily, and may be used in more confined spaces such as corridors and small entry halls, yet packs the same punch as the Enforcer.

For very sturdy and reinforced doors, there is a Two-Man Enforcer, with a length of 140cm and weighing 33kg. This tool requires plenty of space to be swung effectively by two men, but generates huge power to open any inward-opening door.

The Ripper, supplied by PW Allen and other specialist companies, is a powerful tool for forcing entry through an outward-opening door. It will normally burst a door open on the first attempt. Photo: © PW Allen.

Door rippers and 'hooligan' tools

While a door ram is the answer to an inward-opening door, a different approach is required for outward-opening doors. A specially designed Door Ripper is supplied by Sigma Security Devices. This has a blade that can be slipped or driven with a hammer into the gap between the door and its frame. Pulling back on the handle will normally break any locks and bolts, and force the door open at the first attempt. A ratchet mechanism allows the blade to be worked behind the door to improve the leverage and overcome resistance. The Ripper weighs 6kg and measures 79cm long.

There is a large variety of 'hooligan' tools available for general purpose use in breaking open locks, windows, grilles, gates and the like. The standard Hooligan Tool measures 107cm long and weighs 6.4kg. It consists of a straight, high-alloy steel shaft, with a claw at one end and a dual head at the other.

The head has a sharp, tapered spike that can be inserted behind locks and latches, and a broad, flat 'duckbill' wedge for levering open doors and windows. The claw is designed to fit over locks and hasps, allowing them to be broken quickly. An alternative model has a can-opener type claw, which can be used to cut openings in vehicles and metal containers. The tool is particularly effective at breaking through windows. The glass can be knocked out quickly with the end of the tool, and the frame then ripped out with the hooked end.

Rapid entry personnel may also use a variety of more general purpose tools such as axes, sledgehammers and pry-bars, as well as specialist tools designed to overcome specific makes of locks and hinges. The pump-action shotgun, firing a special cartridge known as a Hatton Round, is also employed to breach locked doors by blowing out the locks or hinges.

Hydraulic and pneumatic door breakers

Where a door is strengthened and reinforced, it may take too long to break down with an Enforcer type tool. To be sure of gaining entry rapidly, and maintaining the element of surprise, a hydraulic or pneumatic door breaker can be used.

The Hydraulic Ram will exert 5 tons of pressure, reliably breaking open steel reinforced inward opening doors. The ram is placed over the door, at the level of the main lock. Pumping the handle forces apart a pair of jaws, which bite deep into the frame and secure the device, at the same time pushing the door frame apart and loosening any bolts, locks and catches. Once ready, a valve is operated to activate a ram that forces the door open. The manual hydraulic system is virtually silent in operation, and the entire operation can be completed in thirty to forty seconds. The Hydraulic Ram kit comes with three claws for all standard door widths, in a heavy-duty carrying bag, and weighs 25kg.

The Blower is a pneumatic door ram advertised as the most powerful door-breaking system in the world – it exerts 5 tons of force across the door frame, and 11 tons against the door itself. The first part of the Blower system is basically the same as the Hydraulic Ram. It has a pair of claws that are forced apart by a hand-pumped hydraulic system to embed themselves into the door frame at either side, exerting up to 5 tons of pressure. This then forms a firmly anchored cross-beam. A specially designed air bag is then slipped between the beam and the door itself, and inflated rapidly with compressed air from a cylinder. The sudden force of up to 11 tons will blow open just about any door, even heavily reinforced steel doors. The task takes less than one minute from start to finish, and is virtually silent until the final blow that bursts the door open instantly.

The Blower is supplied as a self-contained kit in a heavy-duty carrying bag, complete with air bag, air hose and compressed air cylinder with shoulder strap. It weighs 27kg and comes with three claw lengths: 40, 48 and 56 cm.

Stun grenades

When GSG9 and SAS troopers stormed LH181 at Mogadishu in October 1977, the assault was initiated by throwing in a number of 'stun grenades', designed to stun the occupants with a combination of a loud report and a very bright flash. The SAS had been experimenting with the devices, nicknamed 'flashbangs', as a means of adding to the surprise and disorientation of the terrorists. Barry Davies, BEM, describes in *Fire Magic* how he brought a case of stun grenades with him to Mogadishu and instructed the GSG9 troopers on their employment.

The stun grenade is designed specifically for use by Special Forces during hostage rescue. It is classified as a diversionary assault grenade, producing noise and brightness levels sufficient to induce disorientation in the terrorists. The grenade itself consists of a case with a firing mechanism and operating lever fitted to the top. It is roughly similar to a soft drinks can in size and shape – approximately 100mm high by 50mm diameter, with a weight of around 150g.

The grenade contains an ignition and delay mechanism, and a quantity of flash composition – typically a mixture of aluminium powder and potassium perchlorate. To operate the grenade, the trooper pulls the ring, taking care to hold the flip-up lever against the body of the grenade. The grenade is then thrown, allowing the lever to

Stun grenades are a combat-proven way of disorientating a group of kidnappers when assaulting a building or aircraft, giving the assault team a valuable advantage. Photo: Sandia.

flip up and operate the ignition system. After a short delay (approximately one second) the flash composition ignites, emitting a loud bang and bright flash via the blow-out base of the grenade.

An alternative version contains a number of sub-munitions to provide a 'fire-cracker' effect of multiple flashbangs. The first report starts within one or two seconds of initiation, followed by fifteen or so loud reports in quick succession over the next few seconds. This type of grenade is typically of similar dimensions to the 'single' type, or slightly larger, and a little heavier at around 175g.

There has been much work carried out over the years to reduce the risk to hostages from stun grenades. If a conventional stun grenade detonates close to a hostage it could cause permanent injury. Sandia National Laboratories in the US have recently developed a new type of stun grenade that reduces this risk.

The new flashbang creates the same blinding flash and deafening bang as a conventional stun grenade, but this is achieved with an airborne powder that fans out before igniting, making it less dangerous to hostages. The new grenade is also reusable, making it more suitable as a training aid.

The new grenade is made of plastic, and contains only metal powder, without any potassium perchlorate or other oxidising agent. The particles of powdered metal are

The new stun grenade developed at Sandia National Laboratories creates the same disorientating flashbang effect, but is less likely to injure hostages nearby. Photo: Sandia.

forced out like a burst of talcum powder through sixteen 1/4in diameter holes in the base of the canister. The ejected particles hang momentarily in the air, forming a sheet of metal dust about five feet in diameter, before igniting by combining with oxygen in the air.

The spread of the powder means that the pressure in the immediate vicinity of the device is lowered to a safer level. The canister remains undamaged, and may be reloaded for a few dollars.

CS and other gases

CS and other types of gas are options that will always be considered when an assault team is planning a hostage rescue operation. These carry a number of risks, however. Russian Alpha anti-terrorist personnel pumped incapacitating gas into the Palace of Culture Theatre in Moscow on 26 October 2002, where some fifty Chechen terrorists were holding around 800 hostages. Some of the terrorists were wearing explosives strapped to their bodies, and had threatened to detonate them if the theatre was attacked. The gas rendered the terrorists unconscious before they had time to carry out their threat.

The operation was a success, in that the siege was broken, the terrorists were killed and the majority of the hostages freed. More than 110 hostages died due to the effects of the gas, however, and many more were critically ill in hospital.

Protective clothing

In any hostage rescue assault operation, all the personnel are potentially exposed to a whole range of risks, from fire and explosion to bullets and fragments. It is important that they are protected, so far as is practical, against all these. The standard assault kit is nowadays instantly familiar from countless pictures, books and films. In addition to protecting the trooper from multiple threats, it also has a very intimidating appearance. This helps in psychologically overwhelming the terrorists.

Barry Davies puts it well in his book, *Fire Magic*:

> For maximum psychological advantage, these men are dressed to look evil … They advance rapidly towards the terrorists with the sole aim of blasting their brains out … A terrorist's instinctive first reaction is to stop the invading beast bearing down on him. It takes only micro-seconds to choose between resistance and surrender, but he will be dead before he ever makes that choice.

A further advantage of the anonymous black kit, with faces hidden by insect-like respirators, is that there is no chance of a trooper being identified if the assault is caught on film or video, as with Operation Nimrod.

The standard kit makes extensive use of fire-resistant Nomex material. GD Specialist Supplies produce a full range of flame-retardant underwear and overgarments, including a hood to cover the parts of the head not protected by the respirator. The assault suit incorporates felt pads on knees and elbows, to provide additional protection when it is necessary to crawl across hot surfaces, as well as protecting against blows and sharp objects.

The respirator of choice is the Avon SF10, which was developed from the military S10 specifically for Special Forces use. The SF10 incorporates an internal microphone and clip-on anti-flash lenses, and protects against CS and other irritant gases as well as aerosols and smokes. It is compatible with the CT400 communications system described in Chapter 3. Body armour, as described in Chapter 9, is worn.

An assault belt kit or assault vest is used to carry the various items of equipment needed for the operation: CS and stun grenades, pistol, spare magazines, communications equipment, forced entry tools, etc. Traditionally this type of load-carrying equipment was made of leather, but increasingly modern fabrics are being used, as in the Blackhawk range of tactical nylon equipment. This company, based in Chesapeake, VA, USA, offers a huge range of holsters, pouches, assault vests and similar equipment online at www.blackhawkindustries.com and in their catalogue.

The assault team wear black overalls, hood and respirators. This helps to protect them against explosions, fire and fragments, but also gives them an intimidating appearance, providing a psychological advantage. Photo: © James Marchington.

ANTI-TERRORIST WEAPONS

11

Anti-terrorist operations are often carried out in urban areas. This means that weapons must be chosen carefully, so as to do the job required without posing an unnecessary threat to civilians nearby. Photo: © James Marchington.

In the fight against terrorism, security forces employ a wide range of weapons. Most of the weapons used are standard military or police issue, although they may be adapted for a specific task where necessary. The demands of counter-terrorism work, however, are different from those of the battlefield. In all-out war, the enemy is generally in a known direction. There is nothing to be lost, and plenty to gain, by throwing as much destructive power as possible in the enemy's direction. There is no such thing as 'excessive force' on the battlefield; bigger is better. Counter-terrorist work, on the other hand, is often conducted on home territory, within range of civilian homes, businesses and property.

Public and politicians expect to see terrorists shot precisely and surgically, without stray bullets flying off and endangering innocent passers-by a couple of miles down the road. It is a fine ideal, but hard to achieve in practice. The result is that counter-terrorist forces tend to use weapons that allow a high degree of precision, such as sniper rifles, or have a very limited range, such as 9mm SMGs (sub-machine guns). The assault rifle, whether 5.56mm or 7.62mm, has limited use in counter-terrorism, as it is often too powerful and indiscriminate.

It is interesting to note that firearms have changed little in the last fifty years or so. Materials and manufacturing methods have been improved, but today's weapons still fire jacketed lead bullets from brass-cased cartridges containing a primer and propellant powder. The rounds are housed in a box magazine, and fed into the chamber by the operation of a bolt or slide. The ubiquitous H&K MP5 SMG – still favoured by most counter-terrorist forces around the world for hostage rescue – was first developed in the mid-1960s, and fires a round created decades earlier.

Special Forces are not slow on the uptake when it comes to adopting new technology. They were among the first to use GPS navigation, satellite communications, and a host of other new technology. But they stubbornly stick with the old tried-and-tested firearms such as the Vietnam-era M16 assault rifle, and the 1960s H&K MP5. This is not nostalgia; it is a choice based on sound, practical reasons.

In close quarter battle, what really matters is 100 per cent reliability, and a combination of shape, weight and balance that provide intuitive handling. Possessing the latest bit of clever technology is irrelevant. At the vital moment, when it is kill-or-be-killed, all that counts is having a weapon you can rely on to drop the enemy – fast. Just watch someone fiddling with the controls on one of the latest 'ergonomically designed' electronic cameras; if taking a photograph first meant life or death, you would choose a simple manual camera every time.

SUB-MACHINE GUNS

Heckler & Koch MP5 Series

Since it was first developed in the 1960s, the Heckler & Koch (H&K) MP5 sub-machine gun has become the favourite of anti-terrorist forces around the world. It is carried by police firearms teams, internal security forces, SWAT teams, hostage rescue assault teams and many others – including the British SAS and police, and Germany's GSG9. The sight of SAS troopers using MP5s to assault the Iranian Embassy in 1980 was a powerful advertisement, of course. But there is much more to it than that. The MP5 really is in a class of its own.

The MP5 is correctly described as a sub-machine gun. It fires what is basically a pistol round on fully automatic in a weapon designed to be held two-handed. But it is a million miles from the crude, inaccurate, 'spray 'n pray' weapons that are typical of sub-machine guns. The MP5 is a sophisticated weapons system that is really a high-quality selective fire carbine, which just happens to fire the 9mm Parabellum round.

The MP5 comes in a number of variants; it is really a family of weapons rather than a single weapon. It comes with a fixed or folding buttstock, and with the option of single-shot, three-round burst and fully-automatic fire. There is a special silenced model, and a short K (for 'Kurz' – 'short' in German) model. The various combinations of these options produce a long list of variants, all designated by a combination of letters and numerals. So an MP5 A5, for instance, has a telescoping buttstock, 225mm barrel and three-round burst option.

At the time of Operation Nimrod, the SAS had already decided that the MP5 was the ideal weapon for hostage rescue assaults. Its 9mm Parabellum round is sufficiently lethal at short range to produce an instant knock-down of a terrorist, especially if he/she is struck with multiple hits from burst or fully-automatic fire. Yet it does not carry the problems of over-penetration that would occur with rifle calibres, where rounds could pass through a wall or aircraft skin, possibly injuring a passer-by a kilometre or two away.

The MP5 sub-machine gun series is used worldwide by anti-terrorist forces as well as regular military units, internal security and police. Photo: Author's collection.

The MP5 is outstandingly accurate for a sub-machine gun, and can be fitted with various sighting and target illumination devices to aid target acquisition and aiming. The weapon is compact and handles well, making it simple to carry when undertaking difficult insertion techniques. It has also proved to be exceptionally reliable. With normal routine maintenance, a jam is virtually unheard of when using good quality metal-jacketed ammunition.

It is also well supported by the manufacturers, now part of Britain's BAe Systems, who provide a high level of after-sales service including spare parts, armourers courses, etc.

The MP5's mechanism is unusual for a sub-machine gun in that it fires from a closed, locked bolt – this enables it to achieve its excellent accuracy and reliability. The bolt is locked by a roller mechanism. The bolt is in two parts: the bolt head, which lies against the cartridge head; and the larger mass of the main body of the bolt. When the bolt is closed, inclined planes on the bolt body press against the rollers, pushing them outwards into recesses and locking the bolt head against the breech.

On firing, there is a slight delay as the main body of the bolt begins to withdraw, allowing the rollers to unlock. The two parts of the bolt then travel rearwards together, extracting and ejecting the spent case. Spring pressure drives the bolt closed again, collecting the next round from the magazine and loading it into the breech before the rollers lock again and the mechanism is ready to fire. That might sound like a long, slow process, but it happens in the blink of an eye, and the MP5 is capable of firing at a rate of 800 rpm (rounds per minute) – emptying a 30-round magazine in 13.5 seconds.

The controls on the MP5 have been designed so that they are simple and intuitive to operate. The cocking lever travels in a slot in the upper left quarter of the receiver, and has a large three-quarter moon knob that is easily operated even with gloved hands. The combined safety catch and selector switch is located above the trigger, and can be operated by the thumb of the trigger hand without changing your grip on the weapon. The magazine catch is at the rear of the magazine well, where it is easily operated by the thumb of the hand grasping the magazine.

The H&K MP5 uses a roller-lock mechanism to fire from a locked breech, giving it much better accuracy than a typical blowback-operated sub-machine gun. Photo: © James Marchington.

Opposite page: The H&K MP5 can be readily field-stripped and reassembled, without the need for special tools. Photo: © James Marchington.

213

The basic MP5 has open sights consisting of a blade and tunnel foresight and a rotating turret aperture rearsight. However, there are many specialist sighting systems that can be fitted. Photo: © James Marchington.

The basic sights are similar to those on the H&K G3 rifle from which the MP5 was developed. There is a blade foresight contained within a protective ring. The rearsight consists of a rotating turret offering apertures of different sizes to suit various conditions.

An entire industry has grown up supplying specialised sighting and target illumination systems for use with the MP5. Laser systems that project a red dot on to the target have become popular for anti-terrorist operations. In some circumstances simply shining the dot on to a kidnapper may be sufficient to persuade him to surrender, resolving the situation without the need to fire. Alternatively, the laser light may be invisible to the naked eye, but visible through night-vision goggles worn by the assault team.

There are many different night-vision scopes, optical scopes and other aiming devices that can be mounted on the MP5. This type of scope is popular with police firearms teams such as Britain's SO19, who may find themselves in a stand-off where they must cover a kidnapper at ranges up to 100 metres for some length of time. For hostage rescue assault operations, however, where snap-shooting is required, it is normal to use the standard fixed sights in conjunction with a target illumination device and perhaps a red dot laser sight; the longer-range accuracy provided by a scope is not required, and the scope would simply get in the way.

The SD variants of the H&K MP5 have an efficient silencer around the barrel, reducing the sound of a shot to something little louder than a twig snapping. Photo: © James Marchington.

Target illumination systems have come a long way since Operation Nimrod, when the assault team had D-cell Maglite torches fixed above their MP5s' receivers like telescopic sights. Nowadays the preferred torch is much smaller and gives a more precise, even beam. There are various mounts available which replace the standard MP5 fore-end to provide a housing for torches such as the Sure-Fire. The torch may be fitted with an IR filter, so that the beam is visible only through night-vision goggles, to give an added advantage to the assault team who will certainly have cut all electrical power to the target building or craft before initiating the assault.

Specifications	
Manufacturer	Heckler & Koch, West Germany (part of BAe Systems)
Model	MP5 series sub-machine gun (Specifications refer to MP5 A2 except where indicated)
Introduced	1965
Calibre	9mm Parabellum
Action	Roller-locked delayed blowback, selective: single shot/3-round burst/fully automatic
Feed	15- or 30-round box magazine
Rate of fire	800rpm
Sights	Blade and aperture open sights, rearsight with revolving turret to allow selection of aperture size. Various target illumination and laser pointer systems available
Weight	2.55kg
Length	680mm (telescoping butt variants 490mm with butt retracted, K variants 325mm)
Barrel	225mm (115mm on K variants)
Variants	MP5 A2 – Fixed stock, 225mm barrel
MP5 A3	Telescoping stock, 225mm barrel
MP5 A4	No buttstock, 225mm barrel
MP5 A5	As A3 with 3-round burst option
MP5 SD1	No buttstock, silenced
MP5 SD2	A2 type buttstock, silenced
MP5 SD3	A3 type buttstock, silenced
MP5 SD4	As SD1 with 3-round burst option
MP5K	Short variant with 115mm barrel and no buttstock. Broom handle type forestock
MP5K A1	As MP5K but with low-profile sights
MP5K A4	As MP5K with 3-round burst option
MP5K A5	As MP5K A1 but with 3-round burst option
Service	In service with British Special Forces and Police firearms teams. Used by similar forces worldwide.

Uzi

The Uzi sub-machine gun was developed in 1949 by Lieutenant Uziel Gal of the Israeli Army, and has since become one of the best-known SMGs in the world. It is still in widespread use, both with Israeli armed forces and elsewhere. It is instantly recognisable by the ribbed, box-shaped receiver, and the magazine housed in a vertical hand-grip.

The Uzi's mechanism uses a principle known as advanced primer ignition. The round is fired while the bolt is still travelling forward, allowing the bolt to be made lighter and giving a high rate of fire. The bolt is also overhung, which improves the weapon's balance and handling characteristics. The Uzi fires from an open bolt – the bolt is cocked and remains in the open position until the trigger is pulled. On firing, the bolt flies forward, collects a round from the magazine and pushes it into the chamber.

The friction of the round in the chamber is sufficient to push it back against the firing pin, igniting the primer and firing the round just before the bolt is fully closed. As the bolt reaches the closed position, the pressure is building up to drive it back again, drawing out the fired case with an extractor claw. An ejector lug knocks the fired case clear through the ejection slot, as the bolt continues rearwards against spring pressure. At the full extent of its travel, the bolt reverses direction and the cycle begins again – unless the trigger is released, in which case the sear engages and holds the bolt back in the cocked position ready to fire again.

The cocking handle travels in a slot on the top surface of the box-section receiver. A grip safety prevents the bolt moving unless the grip is held in the hand. A combined safety catch/fire selector is located at the top of the left grip. It is a sliding catch which can be operated with the thumb of the trigger hand – back for 'safe', forward one click for single shots and two clicks for fully automatic fire. The magazine catch is at the bottom of the left grip.

Specifications	
Manufacturer	Ta'as Israel Industries (formerly Israeli Military Industries), Israel
Model	Uzi
Calibre	9mm Parabellum
Action	Advanced primer ignition blowback, selective fully automatic
Feed	32-round box magazine
Rate of fire	950rpm
Sights	Post and aperture sights, with flip rearsight graduated for 100 and 200m
Weight	3.7kg
Length	470mm with folding buttstock folded; 650mm extended
Barrel	260mm
Service	Israeli armed forces, and others worldwide

Steyr AUG 9mm Para

The AUG Para is a 9mm version of the futuristic-looking Steyr AUG assault rifle, which was developed to fire the NATO 5.56mm x 45 round, and has been adopted by the armies of Australia, New Zealand, Ireland, Saudi Arabia, Oman and other countries.

The assault rifle can be converted to fire the 9mm Parabellum by means of a kit, which consists of a replacement barrel, bolt group, magazine adaptor and magazine. The conversion turns the AUG into a 9mm blowback weapon, with a one-piece bolt assembly. It has a separate firing pin, and fires from a closed bolt.

Controls are the same as on the standard assault rifle. There is a cross-bolt safety catch above the trigger. Fire selection is by trigger pressure: first pressure gives single shots; further pressure provides full automatic fire. The magazine catch is at the rear of the magazine adaptor/housing. The cocking handle is on the left side of the receiver.

<table>
<tr><td colspan="4">**Specifications**</td></tr>
<tr><td>Manufacturer</td><td>Steyr-Mannlicher, Austria</td><td>Feed</td><td>32-round magazine</td></tr>
<tr><td>Model</td><td>Steyr AUG Para</td><td>Rate of fire</td><td>700rpm</td></tr>
<tr><td>Calibre</td><td>9mm Parabellum</td><td>Sights</td><td>x1.5 optical sight</td></tr>
<tr><td>Action</td><td>Blowback, closed bolt, selective fully automatic</td><td>Weight
Length
Barrel</td><td>3.3kg
665mm
420mm</td></tr>
</table>

Beretta Model 12S

The Beretta Model 12 SMG was originally designed in the 1950s, and although it has been developed over the years the current Model 12S is largely the same in appearance and operation. It is the standard SMG of Italy's armed forces, and has been sold to a number of other countries, including Saudi Arabia, Nigeria, Libya and Brazil.

The weapon operates on the blowback principle: the chamber gases blow the bolt back on firing, ejecting the fired case and cocking the mechanism. The bolt returns, under spring pressure, collecting a new round from the magazine and loading it into the chamber. If the trigger is still pulled, the hammer falls and the cycle begins again.

The Model 12S uses a 'wrap around' bolt – much of its bulk is forward of the breech at the moment of firing. This improves the balance of the weapon, reduces vibrations and counters any tendency for the weapon to climb when fired on full automatic.

The cocking handle travels in a longitudinal slot on the left side of the receiver. To cock the weapon, it is pulled back and released. There is a grip safety which prevents the weapon firing unless the grip is firmly held in the hand. A safety catch above the left grip also provides fire selection – up for 'safe', middle position for single shots, and down for full automatic fire. The magazine catch is on the underside of the trigger guard, just behind the magazine itself.

<table>
<tr><td colspan="4">**Specifications**</td></tr>
<tr><td>Manufacturer</td><td>P. Beretta, Italy</td><td>Rate of fire</td><td>650rpm</td></tr>
<tr><td>Model</td><td>Model 12S</td><td>Sights</td><td>Blade and aperture open sights, with flip-up aperture rearsight</td></tr>
<tr><td>Calibre</td><td>9mm Parabellum</td><td></td><td></td></tr>
<tr><td>Action</td><td>Blowback, selective fully automatic</td><td>Weight</td><td>3.2kg</td></tr>
<tr><td>Feed</td><td>20- 32- or 40-round magazine</td><td>Length
Barrel</td><td>418mm
200mm</td></tr>
</table>

FN P90

The FN P90 was conceived as a cross between an assault rifle and a sub-machine gun – a personal weapon for support troops. It was designed to be compact enough to be carried by signals engineers, drivers, medics and similar personnel without getting in the way, yet provide enough firepower to be effective when needed. Being neither assault rifle nor sub-machine gun, it has been assigned to a special category of Personal Defence Weapon (PDW).

None of the available rounds fitted the PDW concept, so FN created a new round, the 5.7 x 28mm. This offers greater range, accuracy and stopping power than the 9mm Parabellum sub-machine gun round, yet is smaller than the standard NATO assault rifle round, the 5.56 x 45mm. The 5.7 x 28 uses a sharply pointed projectile known as a boat-tailed spire-point. This weighs 2.02g and achieves a very high muzzle velocity of 715m/sec. It has an effective range of 150m and gives outstanding penetration, passing through forty-eight layers of Kevlar at 150m.

The tip of the FMJ bullet has a steel penetrator followed by an aluminum core heavier than the forward tip. This causes the bullet to tumble in soft body tissue after 5cm of penetration, causing a larger wound cavity and much greater tissue damage than a 9mm Parabellum bullet.

The weapon itself looks and handles unlike any other weapon. Its bullpup design gives a squat shape, with fat, curved plastic grips and a very short barrel. It measures just 50cm long and weighs 3kg with a full magazine of 50 rounds. The combat sling allows it to be carried close to the body, where its shape and size mean that it can be

The FN P90 is neither a rifle nor a sub-machine gun; it is classified as a Personal Defence Weapon, and fires a specially developed 5.7mm round with outstanding penetration. Photo: Fabrique Nationale.

forgotten about while the user gets on with his primary task – yet be ready for firing almost instantly if an enemy appears.

The body casing of the P90 is a one-piece polymer shell which houses all the main parts, offering good protection from physical damage, moisture, dust and debris. The design incorporates a thumbhole semi-pistol grip, a forward grip which doubles as the trigger guard, and a hand protector that prevents the user letting his leading hand stray in front of the muzzle – potentially a problem with such a short weapon. The design and balance of the P90 means that it can be fired effectively with one hand, like a pistol, as well as held to the shoulder with two hands like a rifle.

The sights are mounted on a raised platform over the forward end of the barrel. Recent models have been fitted with a British-made x1 magnification Ring Sight colli-mating sight, with a day/night graticule. This may be used with one or both eyes open. A laser pointer can be fitted to the hand-protecting spur beneath the muzzle, with a switch in the hand grip.

The magazine is as unusual as the rest of the P90. It is located on top of the receiver, parallel to the barrel, and holds 50 rounds stacked at 90 degrees to the bore. The rounds are fed by spring pressure along a curved track that turns them through 90 degrees so that each round in turn is presented to the action in the correct align-ment. The magazine is made of semi-transparent polymer, enabling the user to see at a glance how much ammunition is left in the weapon.

The manufacturers also offer a pistol, the Five-seveN, which uses the same 5.7mm ammunition as the P90. The Five-seveN is an easily concealable double-action pistol with a 20-round magazine capacity. Maximum use has been made of composite materials in the frame and slide to result in an extremely lightweight pistol, weighing just 80g, with unusually good penetration and knock-down power.

Specifications			
Manufacturer	Fabrique Nationale, Belgium	Sights	Integral open sights and Ring Sight collimating optical sight with day/night graticules. Laser pointer optional
Model	P90		
Calibre	5.7 x 28mm		
Action	Blowback, selective fully automatic		
Feed	50-round box magazine	Weight	3kg
		Length	500mm
Rate of fire	900rpm	Barrel	250mm

ASSAULT RIFLES

The M16 A2 and variants

The ubiquitous M16 assault rifle has been the standard sidearm of US forces since the Vietnam War, and in its latest versions is still used by more than thirty countries

worldwide. It has been used in countless military engagements, and has proved popular with soldiers thanks to its reliability and ease of use in all environments, from Arctic conditions to jungles and deserts.

The original version of the M16 was designed by Eugene Stoner to fire the 5.56mm round. It was quickly adopted by US forces and went into service in time to be widely used in Vietnam. Combat experience in that war led to various improvements – notably the bolt return plunger known as 'forward assist'. Extended use of

The Diemaco C7 — a variant of the ubiquitous M16 assault rifle — fitted with the M203 grenade launcher, in use with troops fighting the Taleban in Afghanistan. Photo: Diemaco Canada.

The M16A2 can be field-stripped for cleaning without the need for special tools. Photo: © James Marchington.

The Diemaco C7 is the latest incarnation of the M16 assault rifle, the US infantryman's standard assault rifle since the Vietnam era. Photo: Diemaco.

The Diemaco C8FT. The C8 is a lighter weight, carbine version of the C7. The 'FT' refers to the 'flat top' rail on top of the receiver, allowing special sights to be fitted. Photo: Diemaco.

the original M16 in combat sometimes led to the bolt fouling and failing to close fully, preventing the weapon from firing. On the improved M16 A2, the infantryman can force the bolt home with a firm blow to the plunger.

The current version of the M16 A2 fires the standard NATO 5.56 x 45mm round, the military equivalent of the civilian .223. It has a detachable box magazine with a capacity of 30 rounds. It fires at a cyclic rate of between 700 and 950 rounds per minute, and has a nominal effective range of 400m.

Diemaco C7, C8 and SFW

Diemaco, of Ontario in Canada, produce a range of weapons derived from the M16 family. These are known by the designations C7, C8, etc. The C7 is a basic infantryman's weapon in 5.56 x 45mm calibre. It is gas-operated, offering single-shot, 3-round burst or full automatic fire. It is designed to be easily operated and maintained under severe military service conditions. All user maintenance is performed without tools, and all armourer maintenance can be carried out at unit level, with a minimum of special tools and gauges. The C7 is fully compatible with cold-weather clothing, NBC equipment, night-vision sights and training and simulation systems. It has a 50cm barrel and fixed buttstock, and measures 1m long overall. The stan-

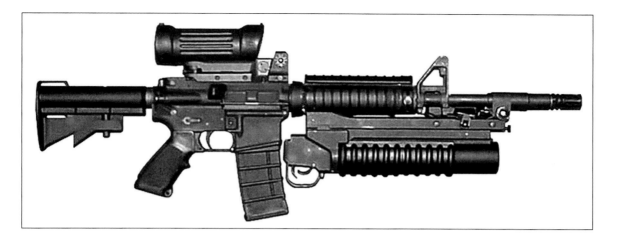

dard C7 has a carrying handle/rearsight. There is a 'flat top' version, the C7FT, with a standard Weaver sight rail that permits the use of a range of sights and tactical accessories.

The C8 Carbine is a lightweight, short version of the C7 family, and is intended for tank crews, drivers and other support troops who require a more compact weapon that retains the firepower of 5.56mm ammunition. The weapon is 24 per cent shorter and 20 per cent lighter than the C7, yet retains 90 per cent of the C7's striking energy and accuracy. It has a 36cm barrel and a telescoping stock, giving an overall length of 76cm with the stock retracted and 85cm extended. Most of the C8's parts are common to the C7 family, simplifying maintenance and spare parts inventory. There is also a 'flat top' version, the C8FT, with Weaver sight rail for mounting optical sights and the like.

Diemaco also produce a special version of the C7 designed for Special Forces use. This is designated the SFW (Special Forces Weapon), and is derived from the C7FT. It has a 41cm barrel to retain the performance of the 5.56 x 45mm round, and a telescoping buttstock similar to that on the C8. A modular handguard system makes it possible to fit a wide range of mission-specific accessories, such as an M203 grenade launcher (see below), bipod, laser target illuminator, etc. A special high endurance long-life barrel improves the weapon's ability to stay on target and withstand the heat of sustained semi-automatic and fully automatic fire. The weapon is available in a range of camouflage options, including Arctic white, desert tan and olive drab as well as standard black.

The Diemaco SFW is designed for Special Forces, and has a modular handguard to allow fitting of accessories such as the M203 grenade launcher. Photo: Diemaco.

Specifications

Manufacturer	Diemaco, Ontario, Canada
Model	SFW
Calibre	5.56 x 45mm
Action	Blowback, selective fully automatic
Feed	30-round box or 100-round drum magazine

Rate of fire	700–900rpm
Sights	Standard iron sights fitted. Rail-mount permits fitting of a variety of optical and electro-optical sighting systems, as required
Weight	3.6kg without sights, magazine empty
	4.4kg combat weight (optical sight, full magazine)
Length	80cm with stock retracted
	88cm with stock extended
Barrel	41cm (43cm with flash suppressor)

The M203 grenade launcher is designed to be fitted beneath the barrel of an M16 assault rifle, and is a powerful 'force multiplier' firing high-explosive, anti-tank and anti-personnel grenades up to 400 metres. Photo: Diemaco.

M203 Grenade Launcher

The M203 40mm Grenade Launcher was developed to be fitted to the M16 assault rifle, and adds considerable versatility and firepower at little cost in terms of the weapon's weight and handling – although the 40mm ammunition itself is somewhat

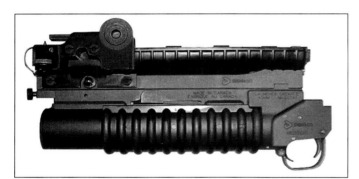

bulky and heavy to carry in any quantity. The combination of an M16 assault rifle and M203 grenade launcher has become popular with Special Forces – it was used, for instance, by SAS patrols in the Gulf War – and has influenced recent development work on future combat weapon systems.

There are a variety of 40mm grenades available for use with the M203, including high explosive (HE),

The trigger of the M203 is positioned directly in front of the rifle's magazine. The user can quickly shift his grip to fire the grenade launcher. Photo: © James Marchington.

anti-tank (AT), anti-personnel (AP), smoke and illuminating. These give a maximum effective range of 350m for area targets, and 150m for point targets. Depending on the nature of ammunition used, the muzzle velocity is around 70m/sec, with a maximum range (with the rifle aimed at 45 degrees) of around 400m.

The M203 is a single-shot, sliding-barrel, breech-loading weapon, weighing approximately 1.36kg unloaded and 1.63kg loaded. It is mounted under the forestock of the M16, with its trigger positioned directly forward of the M16's magazine. The user can quickly shift his grip on the weapon, using the M16 magazine as a pistol grip to fire the M203. A quadrant sight is fitted to the M16 to allow the user to aim the M203; this uses the M16's front post sight, but does not interfere with sighting the rifle itself. It is graduated in increments of 50m from 50 to 250m.

SA80

The standard service assault rifle of the British armed forces since the late 1980s, the SA80 – or L85A1 – has received much criticism. At the time of its introduction, it was hailed as a major advance over its predecessor, the L1A1. The bullpup design made it a compact weapon, and the 4x magnification SUSAT sighting system allowed the average infantryman to achieve a much higher level of accuracy at normal battlefield ranges.

It fires the standard NATO 5.56 x 45mm round, contained in a 30-round box magazine that is interchangeable with that of other NATO weapons such as the M16. The SA80 weighs approximately 5kg and measures 77cm long. The design makes extensive use of modern plastics and stamped metal parts. It is fitted with an adjustable sling that enables the user to wear the weapon close to his body, leaving his hands free to perform other tasks.

The weapon has a gas-operated mechanism. The bolt is carried on two guide rods, and rotates as it closes, engaging in two lugs behind the breech. On firing, the mechanism first rotates the bolt to unlock it, and the bolt then travels rearwards, driven by gas pressure, to eject the fired case and cock the mechanism. At the rear-most point of its travel, it reverses direction and is driven forwards by spring pressure to collect a fresh round and load it into the chamber.

A number of problems were reported with early models of the SA80. In particular, the plastic protectors around the barrel were inclined to fall off on firing, and there were reports of magazines dropping out. A higher than normal incidence of stoppages was also reported, particularly in harsh environments such as Arctic conditions, jungles and deserts.

Many of these criticisms were addressed in an improved version, known as the SA80-A2. The upgrade was launched in 2000. Heckler & Koch won the contract, and rebuilt components were retro-fitted to the British armed forces' 300,000 or so SA80s. The upgrade programme was completed in 2002, at a cost of around £92m. Live firing trials suggested that the main faults had been corrected, particularly the weapon's tendency to jam in adverse weather.

Experience in Afghanistan appears to confirm that the weapon is now considerably more reliable, but it is still unpopular with many soldiers. The Royal Marines are said to have experienced at least three stoppages in Afghanistan. The balance of the weapon is still unwieldy, and it cannot safely be fired left-handed. The SUSAT sight, for all its advantages, is still prone to misting up in cold, damp conditions, rendering it unusable.

At the time of writing, there is considerable pressure for the British armed forces to scrap the SA80 and adopt a new weapon, probably the Heckler & Koch G36, currently in use with the SAS.

Specifications	
Model	SA80-A2 (L85A1)
Calibre	5.56 x 45mm
Action	Gas-operated, selective fully automatic
Feed	30-round box magazine
Sights	SUSAT x4 optical sight, can be removed and weapon fitted with a variety of optical and electro-optical sights
Weight	3.9kg without sights, magazine empty
Length	77cm
Barrel	52cm
Muzzle velocity	900m/s

Heckler & Koch G36

The G36 is a relatively new assault rifle system from Heckler & Koch in 5.56mm x 45mm calibre. The weapon is constructed almost entirely of a tough, fibre-reinforced polymer material and uses a simple, self-regulating gas system. It is a high perform-ance, lightweight weapon that requires very little maintenance. The G36 has been adopted by the German Armed Forces (including the new NATO Rapid Reaction Force), and is also used by Britain's SAS.

Features of the G36 include a folding buttstock and a chrome-plated, cold hammer forged barrel. There is an ambidextrous cocking lever that doubles as a forward assist lever, and can be used to chamber a round silently. Empty cases are ejected down-wards, which reduces the weapon's visual signature. A removable magazine well makes it easier to clean the receiver and chamber areas. The polymer components can easily be cleaned with water-based cleaning solutions, or even water.

The G36 gas system is very resistant to fouling. In tests, it has remained reliable even after firing more than 15,000 rounds without cleaning.

The tough 30-round translucent polymer magazines lock together without a magazine clamp. They are 30 per cent lighter than metal magazines and are corro-sion proof. An optional 100-round drum magazine can also be used.

The Heckler & Koch G36 assault rifle has proved robust and reliable. It has been tipped as the natural successor to the British Army's SA80. Photo: © James Marchington.

The locations and functions of the G36's controls are similar to those on other Heckler & Koch weapons systems such as the MP5 series of sub-machine guns, HK53 and G3, reducing the need for training and making it easier for soldiers to switch from one weapon to another.

The standard G36 has a dual sighting system, comprising a x3 optical sight and an electronic red-dot sight. The G36E (Export) model has a x1.5 optical sight, with back-up open sights.

Specifications	
Manufacturer	Heckler & Koch, Germany
Model	G36
Calibre	5.56 x 45mm
Action	Gas-operated, selective fully automatic
Feed	30-round box magazine, optional 100-round drum magazine
Sights	Standard G36 has dual sighting system comprising x3 optical sight and electronic red-dot sight. Export 'E' model has x1.5 optical sight and back-up open sights
Weight	3.6kg without magazine
Length	76cm with buttstock folded, 1m with buttstock extended
Barrel	48cm
Rate of fire	750rpm

PISTOLS

SIG P226

The SIG-Sauer P226 is typical of the modern type of semi-automatic pistol, using the Colt/Browning short recoil mechanism. It was developed from earlier SIG-Sauer models to compete in the US Army's trials for a new combat pistol to replace the ageing Colt .45 1911 A1. It performed well in the trials, but eventually lost out on price to the Beretta 92F. Its performance, however, was not lost on some observers, and it has since been adopted by, among others, Britain's SAS and the FBI.

The SIG P226 has a double-action mechanism with a de-cocking lever allowing it to be fired either double- or single-action. When used in the double-action mode, the hammer can be safely dropped on to a loaded chamber by means of the de-cocking lever, so that the pistol may be carried in a safe condition but ready to fire simply by pulling the trigger. A firing pin safety mechanism locks the firing pin so that an accidental blow to the hammer will not fire the pistol – the firing pin is released only when the trigger is pulled back fully.

The mechanism is similar to the Colt/Browning short recoil action found in much older weapons such as the Colt 1911 A1 and the Browning GP35 High-Power. The locking mechanism is modified, however, so that the slide and barrel are locked by the squared-off chamber part of the barrel, which engages into the rectangular ejection port on top of the slide. The slide and barrel recoil a short distance together before a cam on the barrel engages in the frame, dropping the barrel out of engagement and arresting its travel. The slide continues rearwards to eject the spent case, re-cock the hammer mechanism and load the next round on the return stroke, collecting the barrel on the way and pushing it back into the engaged position.

The de-cocking lever is located at the top of the left grip, behind and above the trigger. Immediately behind this is the slide release, which is used to strip the

The SIG-Sauer P226 has been adopted by several units with a counter-terrorist role, including Britain's SAS and the US FBI. Photo: SIG-Sauer.

The Colt 1911 A1 remained a favourite sidearm of military and non-military users for decades, and its design still influences pistol manufacturers today. Photo: © James Marchington.

weapon. The ambidextrous magazine release catch is located in the grips behind the trigger guard, where it can be operated by the thumb of the firing hand, either left or right. The slide lock catch is on the left of the frame, above the trigger. There is no safety catch as such; the safety is automatic in that it locks the firing pin until the trigger is pulled fully rearwards.

The model P226 has a 15-round magazine and is 9mm Parabellum calibre. Other models in the series offer different magazine capacities and calibres.

Specifications

Manufacturer	SIG-Sauer, Switzerland/Germany
Model	P226
Calibre	9mm Parabellum
Action	Short-recoil double-action semi-automatic
Feed	15-round magazine
Sights	Blade and notch open sights. Various add-on sighting and target illumination systems available from third-party manufacturers
Weight	750g
Length	196mm
Barrel	112mm

Glock 17

The Glock 17 caused a stir when it was introduced in the early 1980s. It was produced by a company that had previously concentrated on knives and other edged tools, and could approach the business of designing a pistol from an objective angle. The result was a pistol that broke the mould. It made extensive use of polymers, had a squat, modern look with a squared-off slide and uncluttered lines. It did not appeal to everyone, but has proved itself to be a robust and dependable weapon and has been widely adopted by police forces and military users.

The Glock's basic operating system is nothing new – it uses the familiar Colt/Browning short-recoil dropping barrel design. It employs the elegant, SIG-style development of this principle, however, using a squared-off breech that locks into the ejection port.

The firing system is more radical, with no hammer as such but instead a self-cocking striker mechanism that is cocked and released as the trigger is pulled – in effect a double action only (DAO) mechanism without the external hammer. The trigger mechanism incorporates two safety systems. There is a safety spur that blocks the trigger until released by the pressure of the user's finger on the trigger blade. And the firing pin is locked until released by the movement of the trigger.

Controls on the Glock are deliberately kept to a minimum, in order to make the weapon simple and intuitive to use. There is no need for a manual safety catch, and no external hammer. Besides the trigger, there is a push-button magazine release catch on the left grip, behind the trigger guard. A small slide-release catch is located in the side of the frame, just above the trigger.

The Glock 17 has a relatively large magazine capacity of 17 rounds, using a double-stack magazine. Other models in the Glock family offer different calibres and barrel lengths; there is also a compact version, the 19, and a model offering full-automatic fire, the 18.

Specifications

Manufacturer	Glock, Austria
Model	17
Calibre	9mm Parabellum
Action	Double action only (DAO) semi-automatic
Feed	17-round double-stack magazine
Sights	Blade and notch open sights with white U and dot to aid aiming in poor lighting conditions. Various add-on sighting and target illumination systems available from third-party manufacturers
Weight	650g
Length	188mm
Barrel	114mm

Beretta Model 92FS

The Beretta Model 92FS was developed for the US Army's trials, and was adopted as their service pistol in 1985, with the designation M9. It is a robust and reliable weapon firing the 9mm Parabellum round with a double-action mechanism. It carries a 15-round magazine, and is recognisable by the distinctive cut-away slide design. The barrel is internally chromed to protect against corrosion and wear, and the outer

Beretta Model 92FS. Photo: US DoD

surfaces are coated with Bruniton, a Teflon-like material which protects against harsh environmental conditions.

Like so many modern pistols, the 92FS uses Browning's short-recoil principle. There is a wedge-shaped locking block which locks the barrel in place when the action is closed. When the gun is fired, the block is driven downwards, unlocking the barrel from the slide and stopping the barrel's rearward movement. The weapon has a double-action mechanism, and can be fired in single- or double-action mode.

The weapon's controls have been developed over many years to fall naturally to hand and operate smoothly and quickly when required. There is a combined safety/de-cocking lever on the rear of the slide. This also moves the trigger bar away from the sear and locks the firing pin. The magazine release is a push-button located at the rear of the trigger guard, where it can easily be operated by the thumb of the firing hand without releasing the grip.

A number of variants are available, including a compact version, a DAO version, alternative calibres, and a 93R fully automatic model with extended magazine and folding buttstock.

Specifications	
Manufacturer	P. Beretta, Italy
Model	92FS (US Army Pistol M9)
Calibre	9mm Parabellum
Action	Short-recoil double-action semi-automatic
Feed	15-round magazine
Sights	Blade and notch open sights, rearsight dovetailed to slide
Weight	960g
Length	217mm
Barrel	125mm

H&K USP

The Heckler & Koch USP (Universal Self-Loading Pistol) was conceived as a 'system' rather than a single weapon. There are laser sights, a silencer and other accessories designed specifically for the weapon. It is a modern type of pistol, making use of modern fibre-reinforced polymers as well as steel in its design, reducing its weight considerably. It incorporates an ingenious recoil-damping mechanism, making it particularly comfortable to shoot and allowing the user to fire a series of aimed shots more quickly; the recoil produces little more than a flick of the wrist, and the pistol is quickly brought back to the aim.

The USP was adopted by US Special Operations Command (SOCOM) as the Offensive Handgun Weapon System (OHWS) for US Navy Seals, US Army Special Forces and Delta Force. This is a departure from the normal approach to handguns, which are normally seen as a 'last resort' defensive weapon rather than an offensive weapon to be used in hostage rescue actions and the like, where it is difficult to achieve the necessary degree of accuracy with a pistol.

The USP's mechanism is based on the Browning system, but incorporates a special recoil-damping mechanism that buffers the barrel and slide in their rearward movement, preventing the recoil forces being transmitted directly to the frame and on to the user's hand.

On firing, the barrel and slide are initially locked together, and are forced back as one by the recoil. As they travel rearwards, the barrel tilts down and unlocks from the slide. At the same time, the barrel catches in a spring buffer which arrests its rearward movement and absorbs much of its recoil force. The slide continues rearwards, while the buffer pushes the barrel back into its forward position. At the end of its stroke, the slide hits the buffer, compressing the buffer spring which pushes it forward again, collecting and chambering the next round. The light weight of the slide, together with the recoil-damping effects of the mechanism, help to ensure long life for the various parts and reduce the need for maintenance.

The USP has a modular trigger and safety system, allowing the user to specify the configuration required. A weapon can be adapted by exchanging parts. The standard variant (V1) has a single/double-action trigger mechanism and a manual safety catch/de-cocking lever on the left side; this may be moved to the right side (V2) for a left-handed user. The single/double action mechanism can be replaced with a double-action only (DAO) mechanism (V5-8) which de-cocks automatically after every shot. Variants 9 and 10 have the single/double-action trigger but no de-cocking mechanism.

All the variants are equipped with automatic firing pin and hammer safeties, which disengage when the trigger is pulled. This prevents the pistol discharging accidentally if dropped.

The H&K USP has a recoil damping mechanism which makes it particularly comfortable to shoot, and enables rapid follow-up shots. Photo: © James Marchington.

Specifications

Manufacturer	Heckler & Koch, Germany
Model	USP (Universal Self-loading Pistol)
Calibre	9mm Parabellum, also available in .40 S&W and .45 ACP
Action	Recoil-operated semi-automatic, with redesigned Browning type action
Feed	15-round magazine (9mm) 13 rounds .40, 12 rounds .45
Sights	Square foresight and square U-notch rearsight, with white dots for rapid alignment in poor light. Laser targeting system optional
Weight	720g
Length	194mm
Barrel	136mm

SNIPER RIFLES

British Army L96A1/Accuracy International AW

A British sniper in Afghanistan, using the British Army's L96A1 sniper rifle. Note the sniper's 'drag-bag' which he has used to protect the rifle on the way to his hide. Photo: Edgar Brothers.

The British Army's current in-service sniper rifle is produced by Accuracy International in the UK. This is the Accuracy International AW, which has also been selected by thirty-five other countries worldwide, including Sweden and Belgium. It fires the 7.62 x 51mm NATO round, and is a single-shot bolt-action magazine-fed design. The barrel is made from stainless steel and is the floating type, being fitted to the receiver only at the threaded breech end. The stock consists of two halves bolted together, which allow access for maintenance and cleaning. The bolt has been specially designed to resist cold conditions (the 'AW' designation originally meant Arctic Warfare) and will operate at temperatures down to –40 degrees C.

The rifle is fitted with a detachable bipod, which is fully adjustable and can be used in conjunction with a spike at the toe of the butt to form a tripod if the sniper needs to maintain his position for long periods. The stock is adjustable for length by fitting or removing spacers.

A variety of telescopic and electro-optical sights may be fitted, depending on the operation, but typically the rifle will be used with a x6 or x10 telescopic sight with range-finding military graticule. For night-time operations and other specialist uses, the normal telescopic sight can be replaced with an imaging intensifying or thermal imaging sight.

Accuracy International have also produced versions of the AW in other

calibres, including .338 Super Magnum and .50. There is a suppressed (silenced) version of the 7.62mm model, with a reduced muzzle velocity to provide effective noise suppression.

Specifications

Manufacturer	Accuracy International, England
Model	AW (British Army designation L96A1)
Calibre	7.62 x 51mm NATO, also available in .338 Super Mag and .50
Action	Single-shot bolt-action
Feed	10-round magazine
Sights	Rail mounting system enables use of a variety of telescopic, optical and electro-optical sights
Weight	6.5kg
Muzzle velocity	2,756fps (840m/s)
Barrel	655mm, 4 grooves, RH twist, one turn in 305mm

USMC M40A3 (Remington 700 series)

The M40A3 is the latest military sniper incarnation of the Remington 700, a well proven action that has formed the basis of the US Army and USMC's sniper rifles – among others – for many years. Its predecessor, the M40A1, served the USMC well for years, and the M40A3 shows only relatively minor changes and improvements.

It is based on the Remington 700 Short Action, and built by USMC armourers at Quantico, Virginia. With a simple, rugged bolt action mechanism and composite stock, it is a tough, resilient and highly accurate rifle. It is fitted with a Harris bipod, Unertl x10 telescopic sight and McMillan Tactical A4 stock that is unaffected by moisture.

Specifications

Calibre	7.62 x 51mm NATO (.308 Win)
Barrel	Schneider Match Grade SS7, 610mm, 4 grooves, RH twist, one turn in 305mm
Action	Single-shot bolt action with 5-round box magazine
Muzzle velocity	2,540fps (775m/s)
Length	1,124mm
Weight	7.5kg
Trigger	Adjustable between 1.36kg and 2.27kg
Sight	Unertl x10 with Mil-Dots and BDC
Stock	McMillan Tactical A4
Max effective range	915m

There are many other variations of the Remington 700 action – one example is the Armalon PR series of rifles, produced by Armalon Ltd in the UK. The Armalon PR is a high-precision magazine-fed bolt-action rifle, available in 7.62 and 5.56mm calibres.

A US Marine Corps sniper and his spotter, here operating overtly from the top of an armoured vehicle, with a single-shot, bolt-action rifle based on the Remington 700 series action. Photo: US Marine Corps.

The Armalon PR sniper rifle is based on the proven Remington 700 action, fitted with an adjustable, composite stock and fluted barrel to reduce the mirage effect. Photo: Armalon.

The rifles are normally fitted with a HS Precision composite stock, which has an integral high strength 7075 alloy skeleton chassis and bedding block encapsulated within the carbon fibre, Kevlar and GRP outer shell structure of the stock. The PR series use a fluted barrel, and have an optional 'mirage band' to reduce the mirage effects of air passing over a hot barrel.

INDEX